REDEEMER

Redeemer

*Understanding the Meaning of the Life,
Death, and Resurrection of Jesus Christ*

Stephen B. Clark

Servant Publications
Ann Arbor, Michigan

Published by Servant Publications
P.O. Box 8617
Ann Arbor, Michigan 48107

Scripture texts used in this work are taken from *The Revised Standard Version* of the Bible, copyright © 1946, 1952, and 1971, by the Division of Christian Education of the National Council of Churches of Christ in the U.S.A., and are used by permission. Occasionally, the author has retranslated passages from the RSV. Where the author has retranslated the text, he has included the RSV translation in brackets.

Cover design by Gerald L. Gawronski

92 93 94 95 96 10 9 8 7 6 5 4 3 2 1
Printed in the United States of America
ISBN 0-89283-607-5

Library of Congress Cataloging-in-Publication Data

Clark, Stephen B.
  Redeemer : understanding the meaning of the life, death, and resurrection of Jesus Christ / Stephen B. Clark.
      p. cm.
Includes bibliographical references.
ISBN 0-89283-607-5
1. Redemption. 2. Jesus Christ—Person and offices. I. Title.
BT775.C53   1992
232'.3—dc20   92-3589

Contents

NOTE TO THE READER

THE QUOTATIONS FROM THE BIBLE are mainly drawn from the Revised Standard Version (RSV) and use the standard citations in the English-speaking world. I have chosen the RSV because it is the most widely accepted text that is ecumenically approved, and because it seems to be the most commonly used text at the moment in Christian theological discussions. Like most people who study the Scriptures in much depth on a subject, I have my own preferences for how the relevant texts should be translated, and they sometimes differ from the RSV. I have therefore retranslated the RSV at the points where I judged it to be especially helpful to do so. Where I have retranslated it, I have included the RSV translation in brackets.

Although I sometimes cite the Deuterocanonical/Apocryphal Books, I do not presuppose that all the Christian readers of the book will accept them as authoritative for establishing doctrine. Even for those who do not, they are helpful as witnesses to Jewish tradition and as background to the New Testament.

General Introduction

I believe in Jesus Christ, the only Son of the one God: who was crucified for us under Pontius Pilate, suffered, and was buried, who rose on the third day according to the Scriptures, who ascended into heaven and is seated at the right hand of the Father.   **The Nicene Creed**

TWO THOUSAND YEARS AGO, the human being who is the most famous person ever to walk on the earth lived and died—Jesus Christ. We divide the years of human history by his birth. Everything that has happened, happened before Christ (B.C.) or after Christ (A.D., "in the year of our Lord"). Christians would also say that his fame is based on his importance. The most important event for anyone happens when he or she enters into a relationship with Christ, whether early or late.

Christ lived in the land of Palestine. For a period of time, he preached, taught, healed, and delivered people from bondage due to evil spirits. Then he voluntarily chose to die, and die in a way that involved great suffering. His death was voluntary because he knew the governing authorities wanted to put him to death. Rather than avoid them he gave himself up to them. He also knew that the way they would put him to death would be crucifixion, a method that involved great suffering. That too he accepted.

9

Why would such a person choose to suffer and die? He had "so much to offer." Why did he not continue to work for the welfare of his people, but instead voluntarily undergo an early death? Even more, why did he voluntarily undergo a death of great and apparently senseless suffering? He did not seem to be a masochist. He did not show the signs of someone acting the part of a tragic hero. He never indicated that he was putting on a protest against the injustices of society. Rather, he seemed convinced that he was doing what God wanted and that such a death would produce a great good for others.

But why would a death involving great suffering help the human race? How can one person's voluntary suffering and death help people who live two millennia later?

The answer the followers of Christ have given to this question seems simple. He was the Redeemer of the human race, and his suffering and death saved us from our sins. But for modern people who have not been raised and instructed as Christians that is not much of an answer. It is not much of an answer for most Christians either. If they were candid, they would admit that the words are familiar to them, but not very enlightening. Even though they believe what is said, they too can make little sense of the connection between one person's voluntary suffering and death and a better life for a great number of human beings.

This book concerns that connection. It concerns what Christ did to free human beings from the bad effects of human sin. It therefore also concerns the difference that he made and can make in people's lives. In other words, this book concerns the reason why Christ's sufferings and death have been and can be of help to others.

The phrase that best captures the subject of this book is probably "the redeeming work of Christ." This is an old phrase used in Christian teaching. "The work of Christ" is often contrasted with "the person of Christ." Therefore, to say this book is about the work of Christ is to say that it concerns actions he performed, like the crucifixion and resurrection. It does not, on the other hand, concern who he is, especially who he is as the incarnate Son of God. That would come under the topic of his person.

The word "redeeming" is also important. Among Christian teachers, especially Western Christians, the word "redemption" is used to refer to what Christ did to deal with the problem of human sin. Much of what Christ said and did would be helpful for beings who have never sinned. But some of the things he said and did, especially his sufferings and crucifixion, were mainly aimed at handling human sin, and those things are commonly described as his redeeming work.

The chapters that follow are written for readers who have read the Scriptures and know the main outlines of the events of salvation history and Christian doctrine, but who have questions about why the sufferings, death, and resurrection of Christ occurred at all and occurred the way they did. They are written for those who wish to find answers to questions the modern mind raises about the central events of Christian teaching.

What follows could be seen as an introduction to the Christian teaching on the redemption. It provides an overview that explains the meanings of the basic terms, the issues past Christians have debated, and the significance of various traditional statements that are often misunderstood by modern people. All technical material used in the body of the text is explained. Discussion that is primarily academic is confined to the appendixes and select bibliography for those who wish to pursue further study.

This book, however, is also intended to be of help to those who have read a considerable amount on the redemption, but who cannot state for themselves how it all fits together and makes sense—or perhaps who would like to compare the view they have with someone else's. It therefore treats questions of theological synthesis somewhat more fully than some introductions do.

I wrote this book at the request of the publishers. They were looking for a book on the redemption that could be helpful to a wide range of Christians from various churches who believe the Nicene Creed in the way it was originally understood. In an age when Christians of diverse traditions are seeking common ground for a united witness and a defense of the gospel, a similar understanding of basic Christian truths is needed.

The subject of the redeeming work of Christ, in fact, has the good fortune of being relatively free of doctrinal differences between various churches and theological traditions. In this it contrasts with the application of the redeeming work of Christ to the lives of individuals which raises many ecumenical issues, the issues that have divided Christians since the Reformation. This book, therefore, has been able, for the most part, to avoid the necessity of discussing ecumenical differences and giving two sides of various issues.

The differences among Christians in the area of the redeeming work of Christ are not so much matters of doctrinal disagreements as they are matters of what could be called theological synthesis. When people read, for instance, a traditional Reformed presentation of the redeeming work of Christ and a traditional Eastern Orthodox presentation, they quickly notice that the approaches are quite different. The differences, however, are not rooted in contradictions between what is stated in the Reformed and Orthodox presentations. They rather stem from the way the facts of what Christ did and the understanding of these facts are put together into a whole. The different approaches have their strengths and weaknesses. One of the advantages of our age is that we can learn from the theological traditions of the various churches.

The synthesis in this book is my own attempt to present the truth about the redeeming work of Christ after having considered presentations made by the early Christian "Fathers of the Church," the most recognized Christian teachers through the centuries, and representative theologians from the main Christian theological traditions, including, of course, the Roman Catholic tradition which is my own. My hope is that there is nothing in the content being presented which is new or unacceptable to orthodox Christians of the various traditions. If there is any special usefulness to the presentation, it will be found in the way it puts together approaches from diverse theological traditions and the way it deals with contemporary thinking as it bears on the redemption.

This book is, in the words of the apostle Paul, a book about "Christ crucified" (1 Cor. 1:23). Paul goes on to say that the message of Christ crucified is folly to Gentiles. By that he means those who have had a non-Jewish education. In the modern world, that means the message of the cross is folly to those who have received an education of the sort almost all of us have received, whether we are Jews, Christians, or nonbelievers.

The truth about Christ the Redeemer, then, cannot be made completely understandable to the readers of this book. I find that encouraging rather than discouraging. If at the end of this book you find that the crucifixion of Christ does not make perfect sense to you, I will not have failed. It is an impossible task, and I do not attempt it. My goal is more modest—to shed enough light on the crucifixion that you can respond to it the way God desires. If you are looking down a well because you want a drink of water, you do not need to see the bottom of the well. All you need is to see far enough to find the bucket.

Part One

The Predicament
of the Race

Introduction to Part One

THE BEGINNING OF THE HUMAN STORY gives us an extraordinary picture of the omnipotent, omniscient, eternal sovereign of the universe, the Lord our God: "Then the Lord God formed man of dust from the ground, and breathed into his nostrils the breath of life; and man became a living being" (Gn 2:7). Genesis pictures the Lord of all in human form, on the earth he himself created, perhaps even kneeling. He is molding clay into a shape like his own and then breathing life into it. When he was finished, the first human was a living being who was like his Creator. God does not have two legs, two arms, lungs, and nostrils. The first chapter of Genesis makes clear that he himself existed before any such things. The rest of Scripture makes clear that God is the kind of being that transcends such limitations. Yet this passage and many others in Scripture describe him as if he were human.

And the picture it gives us of God is equally amazing: having put aside his royal robes, he labors in the dirt, his hands shaping a piece of clay. He has, so to speak, come down from his throne in heaven to give the creation of the first human his personal attention. Not even the most glorious angel in heaven was to perform this task. The Lord himself came down. He brought into existence a human son—the image of himself placed within his material creation, the bearer of something of his own spirit who could act on his behalf. In this picture of the Lord God kneeling on the ground, we see humility and personal love of a sort that we would never have expected. In his newly created son, we see a being awakening to discover himself to be the beneficiary of undeserved good fortune.

At the end of the next chapter of Genesis we are given a different picture. We see Adam, now with a wife, leaving the home his heavenly Father had made for him. We see the son of God in a wilderness of rocks and untended plants, separated from the one who had created him, on his own in an unfamiliar, inhospitable creation. Genesis tells us, "The Lord God sent him forth from the garden of Eden, to till the ground from which he was taken" (Gn 3:23).

God's son has been banished from his homeland—without the dignity given him by his Father, without the ability to determine his own future, and, as it turned out, without the ability to master himself. Adam finds himself laboring each day in a troublesome and often futile way. Created for a good life, he had come to know evil.

This book concerns the Redeemer of the human race, Jesus Christ, and his redeeming work. He did not come to a race for which everything was going well. He did not arrive with a further blessing to add to God's original creation, one that would simply enrich the human race as God had created it. Christ came to a human race separated from God, banished from the place it was made to live in, and in great need. He came to save a race caught in a predicament from which it could not free itself.

To describe people as in a "predicament" means they are trying to go someplace or reach some goal, but have gotten into a difficulty that keeps them from getting there. We drive past a car stuck in a ditch. We hear about a neighbor in bankruptcy. We find a lost child. We know a friend who cannot find a job. These are all predicaments—some major, some minor.

We only understand the nature of a predicament when we understand where some person is going and why the difficulty is keeping him or her from getting there. For example, we find a girl walking along a back road. We may assume that she is enjoying the country or on the way to visit a friend. Not until we learn that the girl wants to go home but does not know the way, do we find out that she is in a predicament. Perhaps only when she bursts into tears do we discover that the predicament is serious, and our help is very valuable.

We want to understand why Christ's redeeming work was worthwhile. To do so we have to understand the predicament of the human race which he came to resolve. We need to know the purpose or goal of human life and what has kept the human race from reaching it.

The main body of the book concerns the death and resurrection of Christ, his redeeming work. It includes an overview of the doctrine of the redemption with discussions of the interpretations of the passages on which it is based and of the arguments that might call it into question. This introductory part, however, presupposes a certain interpretation of the Scripture passages used and deals quickly with the issues that might point in a different direction. Its purpose is primarily to lay out the perspective from which the redemption itself can be understood.

In this introductory part, we will look at two questions which will help us to understand the predicament which Christ came to redeem us from:

1. What did God intend for the human race?
2. What is keeping the human race from the purpose for which God created it?

ONE

What God Wanted

A YOUNG WOMAN IN COLLEGE was heard to say, "But I have not yet decided what my life is going to be about." Such a sentiment is common these days. With that view of life, the young woman might find a Redeemer helpful only if she were not able to accomplish whatever she decided she wanted, provided the Redeemer offered to help, that is.

Some Christian preachers present the gospel message in much the same way: "What do you want? Turn to Christ, and he will give it to you." But Christ himself did not present the message in that framework. He knew the Creator of the human race and knew that human beings had been created for a purpose. And he knew they were in a predicament, whether they yet realized it or not.

But how do we discover the purpose of human existence? How do we find out what God intended when he created the human race? In Matthew, we find an account of an incident in the life of Christ which shows how he would have gone about answering such a question:

And Pharisees came up to him and tested him by asking, "Is it lawful to divorce one's wife for any cause?" He answered, "Have you not read that he who made them from the beginning made them male and female, and said, 'For this reason a man shall leave his father and mother and be

21

joined to his wife, and the two shall become one flesh'? So they are no longer two but one flesh. What therefore God has joined together, let not man put asunder." They said to him, "Why then did Moses command one to give a certificate of divorce, and to put her away?" He said to them, "For your hardness of heart Moses allowed you to divorce your wives, but from the beginning it was not so." **Mt 19:3-8**

Here we see Christ cornered by some opponents. They raise with him a current issue of considerable importance. In his day, some Jewish teachers held that a man could divorce his wife for almost any reason. Others held that there were only a small number of valid reasons. Jesus was being asked to choose between these views. Our concern here is not with the actual issue of divorce, but with the way Jesus approaches the question.

Jesus begins and ends his discussion by using a phrase "the beginning" which is drawn from Genesis 1:1: "In the beginning, God created the heavens and the earth." The phrase refers to the creation. Jesus is saying that if we want to understand how questions about marriage should be resolved, we have to go back to the beginning to understand God's original purposes for marriage. When we know how he intended it to function, difficulties can be repaired without making matters worse.

My cousin once came across a splintered piece of wood which appeared to be a remnant from some old piece of furniture. Being innovative, he cut off one end of the wood above the split and used it to prop open the door in his room. He was pleased with himself for having done something useful with it, until his father found it. His father recognized that the piece of wood was a leg for a table waiting to be repaired.

His father was angry because my cousin had made it impossible to glue the leg back together. Because he did not know what the piece of wood was for or how it was supposed to function, my cousin only made matters worse when he altered it and used it for a different purpose. His failure illustrates the reason Christ pointed people back to creation in order to know how to deal with the most fundamental human problems.

In this account in Matthew, Christ illustrates the way to find out God's original intentions for marriage. He cites a passage from the first chapter of Genesis, then another passage from the second chapter of Genesis, puts them together, and draws a conclusion from them about divorce, namely, that God never intended a marriage to end in divorce. When his opponents counter with a passage from a later book in Scripture (Dt 24:1-4) that seems based on the acceptability of divorce, Jesus replies that the Deuteronomy passage has to be understood in the light of the earlier account in Genesis. The later passage only teaches us a procedure for dealing with the situation once marriages have failed.

In explaining the redemption, Christian writers have traditionally taken this same approach. They have begun by looking at Genesis to understand God's purpose for the human race and the nature of its predicament. That not only gives them an understanding of the reason for the redemption but also an understanding of the later Old Testament writings, especially those that contain the old covenant law.

The means of redemption the old covenant law provides were only temporary measures for use until God was ready to restore the human race to its original purpose. In the next two chapters we will follow the traditional Christian approach.

The first eleven chapters of Genesis are the prologue to all of Scripture and tell us what happened "in the beginning." Modern commentaries often make these first chapters seem like an odd collection of Mesopotamian myths that somehow made their way into the Israelite Scriptures. Whatever their historical origin, these first chapters of Genesis are deliberately presented to teach us truths that hold the key to all that follows. They give us essential background to God's work of redeeming the human race that begins with the call of Abraham in chapter 12.

To understand what Genesis tells us about the purpose of the creation of the human race and why the race ended up unable to fulfill that purpose, we are going to use a typological interpretation. This involves a comparison of two events, one earlier and one later, that Scripture presents as being brought about by God and that correspond in some way. Looking at the events in relationship to one another helps us to understand more about one or the other or both in the plan and purpose of God.

We want to look at the creation and fall in relationship to Christ's redeeming work and see what Genesis can tell us about the purpose of that work. Some truths in Genesis cannot be seen simply by using a historical discussion of the text in its original setting but only appear as we look at it in light of what comes later. We will not raise the question of the historicity of the first chapters of Genesis: whether the people described in Genesis actually existed or the events described actually happened, and if so how they might relate to what secular historians tell us. Nor will we consider the various approaches to the interpretation of these chapters. For reasons of space, the approach adapted here will have to go unjustified. We will simply look at what these chapters teach about the predicament of the human race, especially as their teaching was understood by the New Testament and later Christian writers.

THE CREATION

The Son of God. The second chapter of Genesis gives us a picture of God's creation of the first human being. What the Lord creates is "the man"—perhaps better translated "the human" since the word in the text is used for all human beings, males and females alike. The name of the first creature is "Adam," an anglicized version of his Hebrew name which means "Human."

The creation of Human (Adam) as the first human being is the creation of the human race. In the beginning, therefore, what happened to him happened to the whole human race. Moreover, Scripture understands the call and significant features of the first father of any grouping to be passed on to his descendants. Therefore, what we read about Adam's life concerns not just himself personally but also the race that came from him, that inherited his nature and call.

Most modern readers can see clearly that in creating Adam God was creating the human race. Less clear is the fact that he created Adam to be his son. The genealogy of Christ in the Gospel of Luke ends the series of the ancestors of Christ with "...Seth, the son of Adam, the son of God" (Lk 3:38). The same truth is stated in Genesis 1:26 when it speaks about human beings as made in "the image and likeness" of God. The very phrase itself is used to indicate sonship, as we can see in Genesis 5:3 which speaks about Adam becoming "the father of a son in his own likeness and after his image." As Seth was in the image and likeness of Adam because he was the son of Adam, Adam was in the image and likeness of God (Gn 1:26) because he was the son of God.

God created a son for himself "from the earth" who would be like his heavenly father and represent him as the ruler of material creation, having dominion over all living things (Gn 1:26). In the course of time, Adam would give rise to a race that individually and corporately would be the son of God.

While modern readers often miss God's fatherly role in the first chapters of Genesis, Jewish readers in the time of Christ were less likely to do so. They knew that the responsibilities of a father towards a son were, in the words of the rabbis, to "circumcise him, redeem him, teach him torah, teach him a trade, and get him a wife." In other words, a father was to establish his son in life so that he could maintain and continue the family. Circumcision and redemption of the first-born did not come into existence until later, but Genesis shows God performing for Adam the other three responsibilities of a father.

God created a woman as a helper fit for Adam (Gn 2:18). The two were to be one flesh (2:24) and so to multiply and fill the earth (1:28). He created a place for Adam to live, the Garden of Eden (2:8-19), and gave him the work of keeping the garden in order to provide for himself and his family (2:15). Finally God instructed Adam in how to live, giving him a commandment (2:16-17). At the end of the process, Adam was to be established in life so he could live as God's son.

Paradise. The second chapter of Genesis also tells us about the place God created for Adam:

> And the Lord God planted a garden in Eden, in the east; and there he put the man whom he had formed. And out of the ground the Lord God made to grow every tree that is pleasant to the sight and good for food, the tree of life also in the midst of the garden, and the tree of the knowledge of good and evil. Gn 2:8-9

Adam's home was to be the Garden of Eden. English speakers often call it "paradise," the anglicized Greek word used to translate "garden." In paradise, God formed material creation in a special way for the human race.

A living being is closely connected to its environment in regard to the kind of life it lives. Polar bears are no more adapted to life in the tropics than elephants are to life in the arctic. The description of the dwelling place God created for the human race is intended to tell us something about the kind of life God created us to live. Here we can see what the world must be like to be a true home for the human race.

First, paradise is called "the garden of the Lord" or "of God" (Is 51:3; Ez 28:13; 31:8-9). It is the garden of God in the sense that God planted it himself. In an even more important sense, paradise is the place that belongs to God, the place where his presence may be found. Genesis 3:8 tells us that God "walked in the garden."

The meaning of Eden as the garden of God is presented more clearly in Ezekiel 28, a chapter that is commonly accepted as containing another description of paradise. This prophecy about the king of Tyre describes his downfall as being like the downfall of Adam from paradise. Here paradise is described as a mountain, the holy mountain of God (Ez 28:14). It was like Sinai (or Zion), the mountain where God dwelled, the earthly place filled with his personal presence. It is even described as a sanctuary that could be profaned (Ez 28:16). Paradise was a place where humans had access to God and where God and the human race could live together in friendship.

Second, paradise was named "Eden," which means "delight." Delight was the perpetual condition for which God created the human race, not pain or frustration or grief or depression. "Delight" is not simply "pleasure," although pleasure is often involved in it. The word "pleasure" is usually associated with sensual enjoyment of the sort involved in a good meal or sexual intercourse. Human beings delight in many things that do not primarily involve sensual pleasure. Delight comes from having a good conversation, achieving insight into a truth, building a high quality table, playing a game skillfully, hiking in beautiful scenery. Delight comes from human nature functioning in the way it should or bringing into existence a good result. Paradise was the garden of delight, because God intended human beings to live well all the time.

Third, paradise was a place in which Adam was to work. "The Lord God took the man and put him in the garden of Eden to till it and keep it" (Gn 2:15). The creation of work points us to what could be called the developmental aspect of creation. The material world was created good, but it did not come into its full potential by its bare creation. God intended it to be transformed into something better, and began the process himself by planting the garden.

When he created his human son, God gave him a share in the transformation of creation by means of his work. That son was to live in God's presence, learn wisdom from him, and so be able to carry on the work of developing creation according to the mind of his heavenly Father. As he "increased and multiplied," the whole earth would gradually become paradise, a temple to God's glory, filled with sons and daughters of God, who would also work to shape and tend creation. Through the human race, material creation would itself achieve the purpose for which it was created.

Unfallen Humanity. I recently visited a friend whose little son was unsuccessfully trying to walk. Other human beings, even pretty small ones, could do it, so why could not he? His mother seemed to know why. She confidently informed me that he would not be able to walk for another month or two because he was not yet old enough. Unlike the family puppy, someday her son would be able to walk erect. To live a human life, her son not only needed the right environment but also a nature that equipped him to do it, and that he had.

The beginning chapters of Genesis speak about the nature of human beings as created by God, and thus something about the kind of life for which God created them. First, we find that the human race was created in God's image and likeness (Gn 1:26-28). As we have seen, this indicates they were to be like God in the way Seth was like Adam.

They could not, however, have been of exactly the same nature. God is not made from the earth since he created the earth along with everything else. Yet there had to be an important sameness. In the account in Genesis 2, this sameness shows up in the fact that God speaks with Adam and Adam can reply to God. Also God allows Adam to name the animals, an indication that Adam would rule over them.

Many Christian teachers have used the word "rationality" to describe the most important aspect of the similarity in nature between God and the human race. In this context it means that human beings can recognize what things are, know what is true and right, and consequently direct their actions in accord with what they see to be worthwhile. They are not blindly directed by their own tendencies, instincts, and responses to internal and external stimuli. They are not simply animals. They are at least "rational" animals.

As a result of their rationality, human beings can know God's mind and therefore shape their lives and material creation in accord with God's wisdom. "Like father, like son," they can act like him and on his behalf, the way a son should. Human beings are fitted to know God and the things of God, and to be given responsibility for parts of his creation.

All of us share that rationality. We can understand that some things are worth doing and others are to be avoided, and direct our actions accordingly. But we also are aware that we and other human beings do not always do what we believe would be good to do, or even what we want to do. Perhaps we just ate too much once again. Perhaps we just lost our temper without a good reason. More seriously, we may have on our conscience some sexual misdeeds, some acts of cruelty, some theft or embezzlement, some negligence leading to a car accident that seriously injured someone else.

Even if our conscience is clean, we know that we are surrounded by others who do such things. We are part of a race that may be "rational" but does much evil. And most of us have the conviction that it will not stop. We can predict with certainty similar to that by which we know the sun will rise that the morning paper will bring more news of human evil. The human beings we know seem to be like the little boy on the verge of walking. He could get up and totter a bit, but something had not yet developed so that he could get all the way across the room on his own two legs.

Scripture's description of the first human beings indicates

an important difference from us, however. Adam and Eve did not seem to do such evil things. Even more, they must have had some inner strength or orientation that enabled them to be free from doing evil and to live in a way that was fitting for sons and daughters of God.

This ability to "walk" in a morally successful way is expressed in Scripture in different ways. We can see it symbolically portrayed in the description of the unfallen king of Tyre in Ezekiel 28. This passage implies that the first human being in paradise had a covering, like the garment that the high priest wore in the temple (Ex 28:17-20). By implication Adam is understood as having worn priestly robes, the clothing which allowed a priest to come into the presence of God in an acceptable way. This probably indicates that Adam was created in a morally good, holy way and that he lived and acted in a way pleasing to God.

In teaching about the restoration of the human race in Christ, the New Testament uses the kind of language we find in Genesis, and interprets it in a way that gives us a similar insight into the state of human beings as they were created. Life in Christ is described as a re-creation and as a renewal of the image of God in the human race (Col 3:9-14; Eph 4:22-24). The same passages also speak about putting on the new human being as if it were a kind of garment. Re-created human beings are likewise described in phrases used to describe priests like "holy and blameless before him" (Eph 1:4).

When such passages go on to describe the qualities of the restored image and the new clothing, they make clear that the newness involves living a righteous, godly, loving life and leaving behind pagan immorality or unrighteousness. It involves what we might call "good character" or consistently living a moral life. Since humanity restored after the image of God has good character, the first human being created after the image of God must have had good character as well.

Some of the early Christian writers, the Church Fathers,

based on certain Scripture passages like Second Corinthians 3-4, expressed these same truths in a different way. They said that as a result of their good relationship with God, Adam and Eve were covered or filled with a "glory" that we lack. Because we tend to understand "glory" as meaning only "radiance" or "brilliance," we can easily miss the meaning of what they are saying. It does have such a meaning in Scripture and Christian writings, but even more it carries the meaning of power and greatness.

A king is glorious by the splendor of his court, but more so in achieving victory. Lightning is glorious by illuminating the countryside, but more so by cutting down the great trees in its path. The glory of God himself is his "shining out" in majesty, but is most commonly shown in the greatness of his power in creation or redemption. The outward splendor, in fact, comes from the inward power.

The word "glory" can be used to speak about actions that show power and greatness, but also the inner strength and mastery that produces such actions. It can even be a synonym for "nature" (cf. 1 Cor 15:40-43). God's glory is his nature, especially as manifested to us in his actions. "Glory" can therefore be used to refer to something inside human beings that gives them the capacity to act in certain desirable ways.

John Chrysostom describes the glory of Adam and Eve at their creation by saying that they "did not know, after all, that they were naked, clad as they were in ineffable glory, which adorned them better than any clothing" (*Homilies on Genesis, 16,14*). When he speaks of the covering of Adam and Eve in such a way, he probably does not mean that they were simply covered with an exterior splendor, although that is included. By "glory" Chrysostom probably also meant the internal power given to human beings that enabled them to live in a more godlike way, or perhaps he meant the ongoing presence within them of the grace or operations of God that produced such an ability.

This glory was manifested outwardly in their human

bodies, as it was in Christ's body when he was transfigured. It therefore was visible and acted as a kind of covering. The glory that Chrysostom describes was the same thing as the priestly garments in the description in Ezekiel—a covering and also an inner state.

In traditional Christian understanding, this glory gave Adam and Eve the power to live in a morally good way. It also resulted in freedom from physical sickness and weakness. Such human glory, glory that is true and not empty, was recognized as a reflection of the glory of God who gives human beings whatever strength of character and moral greatness they have (2 Cor 3:18).

There has been much discussion by Christian teachers about the state of human nature as God originally created it. For our purposes, we only need to see that Adam and Eve were created to be different from us in having an inner capacity that would allow them to actually live the way God wanted the human race to live. The various ways of speaking about Adam and Eve all point to this conclusion. They were in the image and likeness of God. They had priestly garments. They were filled and covered with glory.

This does not mean that Adam and Eve had reached the full perfection human beings could attain. As we will see, the presence of the two trees in the garden probably indicates that God intended to develop their nature. But the first human beings had some clear advantages over us. They were able to live free from the futility and frustration which is common in our lives, and which seems to be rooted in an interior weakness.

The Two Trees. Ephesians 5:32 tells us that one of the passages in the first chapters of Genesis contains "a great mystery." Its meaning is at least partly hidden, only to be revealed in the light of further revelation. The passage referred to is Genesis 2:24, but that is by no means the only section that contains great mysteries. Tacked onto the description of paradise, seemingly as an afterthought, is a statement that also contains a great mystery: "the tree of life [was] also in the midst of the garden, and the tree of the knowledge of good and evil" (Gn 2:9).

The two trees are only mentioned. The various aspects of the account have so far told us truths about human life as it was created. The two trees, on the other hand, point to the future. Adam and Eve do not eat their fruit. One, the tree of the knowledge of good and evil, was put off limits by God. Only at the end of the story do we find that the other had never been touched (Gn 3:22). Yet the two trees are important because they were put there by God to make changes in the human race.

Let us begin with the tree of the knowledge of good and evil. The name itself provides the first clue to its significance: it has something to do with providing knowledge of good and evil, as the tree of life has something to do with providing life. The dialogue between the serpent and Eve reveals another truth about the knowledge of good and evil that modern readers sometimes miss: such knowledge makes people wise (Gn 3:6). This tree could even be renamed the tree of wisdom to bring out more of its significance.

According to the Scriptures, "wisdom" is one of the greatest goods that the human race can possess. Wisdom is not the same as intelligence or cleverness. A human being can have a very high intelligence quotient and still not be wise at all. Wisdom is manifested in knowing how to act. It is the possession of moral truth, knowledge of the difference between what is truly good and what is not. Wisdom is therefore knowledge of how to live in a good way. It is in short, the same as the knowledge of good and evil.

All human beings who have reached a level of maturity are supposed to possess some degree of such wisdom or knowledge. In Isaiah 7:15, the ability to "refuse the evil and choose the good" indicates that a child has grown up to a certain degree, perhaps has reached what we would call "the age of reason." In Second Samuel 14:17 and First Kings 3:9, the king's ability to act as a good judge is described as the ability to "discern good and evil." In Hebrews 5:14, the "mature" are described as "those who have their faculties trained by practice to distinguish good from evil." If such passages indicate the meaning of "the knowledge of good and evil", then the tree conferred some level of maturity in wisdom, perhaps an increasing level the more someone ate of it.

Wisdom or the knowledge of good and evil is one of the keys to human blessedness. If human beings do not live morally but instead do evil things, they can only destroy their own happiness and that of others. Jesus summed up the wisdom God seeks to teach the human race in the two great commandments: love of God and love of neighbor. Human beings need to honor God as the Lord of the universe and live in a way pleasing to him. They also need to care for their neighbor as themselves, consistently seeking the welfare of others. If they instead kill and steal and lie to one another, or worship demons and follow demonic teachings, they will make society a place of misery. Or if they let themselves be ruled by their desires instead of by what God has taught about what is good and evil, they will at least make their own lives miserable.

This all raises the question of why God forbade the first human beings to eat fruit that imparted something as good as wisdom. We will return to that question in the next chapter. Here it is enough to see that the tree of the knowledge of good and evil, like everything else God created, was good or at least potentially good (Gn 1:31). It was created to provide wisdom, and that points to God's intention for the human race to develop beyond what he originally created.

Along with the tree of the knowledge of good and evil was the tree of life. It was a tree that gives life, but what sort of life? Adam and Eve were already alive and since they never ate the fruit of the tree, they did not need it to stay alive. The passage at the end of Genesis provides more information: if

Adam were to eat of the tree of life, he would live forever. The fruit would impart some kind of immortality, enabling human beings to overcome a limitation they had as a result of the way they were created. Sooner or later they would die, at least physically, unless they ate of the tree of life.

Some human beings seem to desire life indefinitely, almost at any cost. Most of us, especially as we grow older, do not show great enthusiasm for prolonging this same sort of existence century after century. We might be interested in a different sort of life, but not this kind drawn out to infinity. The tree, therefore, probably did not just offer more of the same.

Here again the New Testament provides us with additional understanding. As we will see in later chapters, it presents the life God has in mind for human beings as something higher, more "spiritualized," than the kind we know. A more spiritual life does not mean that we will cease to be material. But it means that we will be capable of more, especially in relating to God and spiritual things. A more spiritual life also seems to mean that we will pass eternity in a better way than we could now, without tiring of life or growing bored.

If God's intention is to give the human race a higher and better kind of life, then there is a very good chance that the tree of life was the original means to such a change. Many Christian teachers have taken such a view and held that eating of the tree of life would not only prevent death but would raise human beings to a new kind of life. Perhaps this change would have occurred instantaneously, perhaps gradually. Perhaps God's plan was for the future of the race to be one of unending growth to a fuller and fuller participation in God's glory by regularly eating the fruit of the tree.

The tree of the knowledge of good and evil and the tree of life are mentioned together. That probably indicates that they are connected. The Book of Proverbs says that wisdom "is a tree of life to those who lay hold of her" (Prv 3:18), and it has wisdom say "he who finds me finds life" (Prv 8:35). This perhaps indicates that the tree of the knowledge of good and evil was the way to the tree of life. The book of Sirach seems to teach as much when it says, "The knowledge of the Lord's commandments is life-giving discipline; and those who do what is pleasing to him enjoy the fruit of the tree of immortality" (Sir 19:19).

In an early Christian writing that is almost contemporary to the New Testament, the *Epistle of Diogenes*, we read, "Indeed, there is a deep meaning in the passage of Scripture which tells how God in the beginning planted a tree of knowledge and a tree of life in the midst of paradise, to show that life is attained through knowledge.... And so the two trees were planted close together" (Sec. 12). As knowledge of the gospel and Christian teaching leads to spiritual life, so the tree of knowledge of good and evil may have been intended to lead to the better life the tree of life would provide. However the connection between them is to be understood, the two trees standing together in the middle of the garden indicate that God intended something better for the human race than they had by their original creation.

THE PURPOSE OF REDEMPTION

I once had the experience of getting lost in an unfamilar city. When I asked a stranger how to get back to the place where I first had lost my way, he asked me where I wanted to go. After I told him, the man said, "Well, I could tell you how to get back to the place where you got lost, but I can do something better than that. If you go around that corner, you will find a throughway that will take you directly where you want to go."

This incident illustrates two ways of viewing human redemption. Many of us see redemption as primarily a repair job, simply the removal of a problem caused by sin, usually by taking care of the guilt of sin. But it is more helpful to see redemption as the way of getting us onto a road that brings us to the purpose for which the human race was created.

The first chapters of Genesis present a series of pictures: a garden, a life without pain, two trees, the naming of animals, and more. As we understand the meaning of the story, especially as we see it in the way the early Christians did, one important truth stands out. The first human beings were created for a life different than we live now. They were created to be sons and daughters of God with natures filled with glory, priests who stand in God's presence and serve him, inhabitants of a delightful, life-fostering material creation. They were created to be in harmony with God and nature and inwardly capable of helping to bring creation to the full excellence God intended.

Most peoples on earth have stories about a lost paradise and a happier past. The human race seems to be haunted by a truth that it cannot avoid: this life is not the life God made us for. Human life was meant to be different at the beginning. It is still meant to be different. The Redeemer of the human race, Jesus Christ, did not come simply to remove the difficulties human beings experience. He came to put the human race back on the road to fulfilling God's original purpose.

TWO

The Great Downfall

G OD CREATED THE HUMAN RACE with great care and established it in a way that gave high hopes for the future. Adam was like a young person of good family, a favored son who received the best education available, who was betrothed or married to a woman of equal background. The son of God should have had a good prospect for his life.

But as we know from experience, not all such young people do well. Adam did not. Along with Eve, he ended up driven out of paradise by God with no chance of return. Facing a life of poverty and hard work, Adam turned out something of a failure. Having undergone what Christians have called "the fall," Adam and Eve were in a predicament of great magnitude.

One time when I was hiking in the mountains, I turned the bend and saw a man sitting, half lying, by the side of the trail. At first I thought he was just resting. But when I reached him, I found that he could hardly move. This man had twisted his ankle and fallen. He was waiting for a friend to come back with help. Ironically, he was young and strong and an experienced hiker. It never should have happened, but there he was. It did not occur to me at the time, but he made a good image of the human race as we see it at the end of the third chapter of Genesis—fallen, unable to help itself.

Some image like that of the hiker at the side of the trail is behind the use of the word "fall." The Scriptures use this word to speak about many human setbacks or disasters. When David heard of the defeat and death of King Saul and his son Jonathan, the refrain of his lament was, "How are the mighty fallen in the midst of the battle!" (2 Sm 1:25). Here "fall" refers to defeat and destruction. In a similar way, in view of the siege of Babylon by the army of Medes and its sudden capitulation, a prophecy in Jeremiah proclaims: "Suddenly Babylon has fallen and been broken; wail for her!" (Jer 51:8). Her domination, her future prospects of wealth and prosperity, are all gone.

The word "fall" is used more broadly than for defeats in war. A proverb says, "A righteous man falls seven times, and rises again…" (Prv 24:16). It is speaking about various failures a righteous man has to endure, and perhaps has moral failures in mind. Because they are a kind of defeat, "falls" can certainly refer to moral failures. We are warned by the Apostle Paul, "Let anyone who thinks that he stands, take heed lest he fall" (1 Cor 10:12). In view of all the possible kinds of falls, we are instructed by Ecclesiastes, "Two are better than one, because… if they fall, one will lift up his fellow; but woe to him who is alone when he falls and has not another to lift him up" (Eccl 4:9-10).

We do not speak about the fall of a snake, and do not think much about the fall of a four-legged animal like a dog or a cow. But because normal human posture is erect, a fall is very important for human beings. If they fall and cannot rise, they become unable to walk or run. A fall is a kind of predicament, at least when it is not complete ruin.

The phrase "the fall of the human race" or "the downfall of the human race" as it might better be translated, sums up the great failure that produced the predicament we are now in. The human race had been created in the image and likeness of God, filled with glory, established as the ruler of material creation, with an even better future in store. Yet it ended up in exile, banished by God, having suffered a great loss. How had such a great defeat happened?

The downfall of the human race was not an accident. Nor did it happen because God changed his mind. It was not even the result of a great enemy overpowering Adam and Eve and destroying paradise. It happened because of something human beings did. "The man" had "put forth his hand" (Gn 3:22) to take the one thing his Father had commanded him not to take. He had, to use a familiar word, "sinned."

"Sin" is one of many words used in the Bible to speak about moral failures or wrongdoing. Through a lengthy historical process, it became the main word used in Christian teaching to refer to the failures of people to live the way they should. "Sin" especially refers to those failures as offenses against God. When we say that someone has sinned, we usually mean that they have done something that God has forbidden.

We also use the word "sin" in other ways. When we speak about human beings who live in a way not pleasing to God, we say they are living in sin. "Sin" here refers to the state of sin, the state of someone who lacks a good relationship with God. In addition, when we speak about tendencies inside human beings that cause them to commit sins, we also use the word "sin." We say their bad actions were caused by their sin or their "sinfulness." As we go on, we will be more concerned with the state of sin and with sinfulness. At the outset, we have to look primarily at sinful actions.

According to Christian teaching, sins are the main cause of the human predicament. They are the reason the human race cannot reach its intended purpose. That teaching stems from Genesis chapter 3 which describes the first sin and presents it as the one which caused the downfall of the human race. The first sin, however, was more than just the cause of the fallen state of the race. It was also the prototype or "model" of all subsequent sin. Genesis, in other words, describes the first sin in a way that allows us to understand the nature of all sin.

THE "MODEL" SIN

The Test. The next section of Genesis 2 contains the only words that God said to unfallen human beings that are recorded in Scripture: "The Lord God took the man and put him in the garden of Eden to till it and keep it. And the Lord God commanded the man, saying, 'You may freely eat of every tree of the garden; but of the tree of the knowledge of good and evil you shall not eat, for in the day that you eat of it you shall die'" (Gn 2:15-17).

Here we come to a controversial section. Why did God command Adam (and Eve probably through him) to avoid the fruit of the tree of knowledge of good and evil? The view of the serpent as presented in Genesis 3:1-15 was that God wanted to keep the human race in a state of inferiority. This view has been expressed in other ways by modern people who claim that Christianity retards the advance of the human race or acts as the opiate of the people. The serpent's view is certainly plausible. After all, why should God forbid the first human beings to eat fruit that gave something as good as wisdom?

One of the best answers given by Christian commentators is that the prohibition was intended to be only temporary. The knowledge of good and evil was something good that the tree conferred, something God wanted the human race to have, but something that should only come in a certain way. Adam first needed to acquire age and experience before he could eat of the tree safely. He needed to be taught the "fear of the Lord" (Ps 34:11).

The "fear of the Lord" is the respect for God that leads to obedience to him. "The fear of the Lord is the beginning of wisdom" (Prv 9:10). True wisdom comes through knowing that only what God holds to be good is truly good and that what God commands is good to follow—even when we do not understand why he commands it. It is based on a commitment to God's teaching over any rival forms of teaching, on a trust in its goodness, and on a willingness to accept the limits he imposes to protect us when our own wisdom is inadequate.

Without fear of the Lord and personal maturity, knowledge, especially when manifested in increasing power and mastery of the world, can lead to destruction. We have only to consider modern warfare, where human beings have the knowledge that can cause tremendous destruction without the wisdom that ensures its use for good rather than evil purposes.

Knowledge without fear of God can also lead to evil effects in a person. It can lead to pride, the belief that one can determine what is good and evil for oneself, or to seeking wisdom for self-glorification at the expense of greater goods (Ez 28:1-10). To many can it be said, "You corrupted your wisdom for the sake of your splendor" (Ez 28:17).

To protect his newly created son, God commanded Adam not to eat from the tree of the knowledge of good and evil. Adam first needed to learn obedience. Like a good father, God probably intended to lay the foundation of Adam's wisdom—to "teach him torah"—so that Adam might then eat of the tree and acquire more wisdom on his own. Such an understanding of the need to acquire knowledge of good and evil in the right way probably lies behind Paul's instruction in Romans 16:19. Alluding to the tree of knowledge, he exhorts Christians to be wise as to what is good and blameless [RSV: guileless] as to what is evil. They should not, in other words, acquire knowledge of good and evil by doing evil.

In such an understanding, eating of the tree of the knowledge of good and evil would eventually have been part of the process by which God formed his son, and with him the human race, to govern his creation, making of it something good, completely free from evil. Adam would then have been able to act like his Father, the Lord God. He would have been in his Father's image and likeness not just because of his natural capability, but even more because of his formation and character.

The account in Genesis implies that Adam had received

enough instruction to know how to conduct himself, at least how to conduct himself in regard to the tree of knowledge. If, however, Adam's instruction was to be complete, it had to involve undergoing a test. Genesis 3 is the account of the great test that came to the human race. In line with the interpretation of the Genesis narrative we have been following, that test was probably part of God's plan.

The Hebrew and Greek words which are normally translated "test" are sometimes also translated "temptation." The account in Genesis 3, in fact, is commonly described as the temptation of Adam and Eve. In English, we use the word "temptation" when a test involves an inducement to do wrong and when it is clear which choice we ought to make. The focus in the English word on the presence of possible wrongdoing, however, can obscure the fact that someone who has fallen to temptation is someone who has failed a test.

The word "test," however, can also be misleading. If we say that Adam had to pass a test in the course of being educated by his Father, what comes to mind most readily is a test in the modern school or university. Such a test provides a way for a teacher to find out whether the pupils have acquired the necessary information or not. They respond to questions or do exercises that show what is in their mind.

Such a view of a test is misleading as an understanding of the events in Genesis 3. It is misleading, first of all, because Genesis 3 describes a test of wisdom. Wisdom, in the scriptural sense, is not primarily theoretical information about what is right and wrong. Wisdom involves the ability to live and act well, to make choices that are good and just. Wisdom is not proved through the ability to answer questions, but through the ability to handle concrete situations in which there is an issue about good and evil. Any test of Adam's wisdom and his fear of the Lord would have to involve a practical situation in which a choice was needed.

There is a further way in which the test Adam underwent was different from tests in modern schools. In the ancient world, tests were not used simply to determine whether pupils had completed the educational process adequately. Rather, they were seen as an actual part of the educational process, as a way to learn, because wisdom, or any practical knowledge, cannot be acquired apart from action.

Young people can go through instructions, but until they play real games, they have not learned a sport, and until they fight real battles they are not warriors. When James says, "when you meet various temptations [RSV: trials] ... you know that the testing of your faith produces steadfastness" (Jas 1:2-3), he is reflecting the scriptural view that character, the ability to live a good life, is only produced by testing. When the discourse of Moses in the book of Deuteronomy tells us that God tested the children of Israel "to know what was in your heart, whether you would keep his commandments, or not" (Dt 8:2), he probably was taking the view that only in choosing to obey, especially in situations of difficulty, was obedience actually established.

If we accept such a view of testing, we cannot be said to be fully moral or faithful until we have come successfully through temptation. We could even say that it is not clear what is in our hearts until we make real life choices and adopt and hold to certain courses of action. If God wanted a son who could rule over creation, that son would have to undergo a real test. He would have to handle a situation on his own, but handle it rightfully, in the way his Father taught him. By choosing well and following God's commandments, Adam and Eve would become the people they were meant to be. But of course, a choice is no choice at all unless there is a real alternative, nor is a test a real test unless there is the possibility of failure. In other words, to be what God intended them to be, Adam and Eve had to decide not to sin.

The External Source. The account of the first sin is found in the third chapter of Genesis:

Now the serpent was more subtle than any other wild creature that the Lord God had made. He said to the woman, "Did God say, 'You shall not eat of any tree of the garden'?" And the woman said to the serpent, "We may eat of the fruit of the trees of the garden; but God said, 'You shall not eat of the fruit of the tree which is in the midst of the garden, neither shall you touch it, lest you die.'" But the serpent said to the woman, "You will not die. For God knows that when you eat of it your eyes will be opened, and you will be like God, knowing good and evil." **Gn 3:1-5**

Here we see the dynamics of the first sin, the archetypal sin, portrayed in narrative form. At the outset of the chapter, we see the serpent, the one who originates the idea of sinning. The incitement to sin, in other words, came from outside Adam and Eve.

The serpent is a strange figure, a talking reptile who convinces Eve to take a sinful course of action. In the Book of Revelation, we find the serpent identified as "Satan" (Rv 12:9). A being of angelic nature, Satan appears from time to time in the Old Testament as someone who seeks to bring harm to human beings because of their guilt or possible guilt. He is the "accuser," the attorney for the prosecution, the opponent of human beings in the great trial which is the earthly life. He seeks to get human beings condemned and so ruined. In identifying Satan with the serpent, Revelation is following a tradition probably also found in the Book of Wisdom, written in the first century B.C., where it says: "Through the devil's envy, death entered the world" (Wis 2:24).

Satan's role in the downfall of the human race raises many questions. How did he become the sort of being who would want to cause the downfall of the human race? How did he himself fall? Revelation 12 seems to tell us that the history behind Satan's appearance happened in heaven and not in this material creation. It also indicates that Satan was not alone, but the leader of angels who were in rebellion against God. Here we need to limit ourselves to a simple consideration of Genesis 2 and 3, but the fact that Satan was a rebel against God is important for the Christian understanding of what follows.

To rebel against his Creator and rightful Lord, a mighty angelic prince like Satan had to be filled with pride. In other words, he had to be filled with the desire to be God's equal and not subject to him. When manifested in rebellion, pride regularly expresses itself in hostility toward the target of rebellion. Throughout human history, then, Satan is a rebel and an enemy of God.

As an enemy of God, Satan is also an enemy of God's son, Adam, and of the human race. The Book of Wisdom says he acted in the temptation "out of envy." Perhaps his envy stemmed from resentment at seeing another being favored the way he himself had been. Satan may have expected Adam to take the place from which he himself had fallen. Perhaps his envy was just the expression of hate for a rival or potential rival. Whatever his motivation, Satan wanted the human race to disobey God and so be subject to the stated punishment for disobeying the command of God—death. As Jesus put it, Satan's actions were those of a murderer (Jn 8:44) because he sought to kill the as yet innocent human race.

The conversation between Satan and Eve reveals something further about Satan's influence on the first sin. We discover that his words do not seem hostile to the human race. Satan presents himself as a friend, a knowledgeable friend, one who knows more about the human condition than Eve. Even more, he presents himself as someone who knows that God has spoken falsely to Adam and Eve.

Eating of the fruit of the tree of the knowledge of good and evil will not produce death, but just what the name of the tree seems to indicate: greater knowledge or wisdom, and hence equality with God. God does not hold his position by an intrinsic excellence no creature can attain, but by knowledge that can be had for the asking, or better, for the eating. Knowledge is power. Enough power is equality. Eve can have all that by reaching out and eating of the fruit.

Eve believed Satan, but later, confronted by God as the judge, she is quite clear that she has not become equal to the Lord of all. She then confesses, "The serpent beguiled me"

(Gn 3:13). Her words are sometimes translated "he tricked me" or "he deceived me." Eve had learned an important truth through the results of her conversation with Satan: sin is a result of deception which originates in the influence of Satan.

Very few human beings, of course, have experienced Satan or any other demonic being appearing to them and trying to persuade them to sin. The New Testament, however, tells us that Satan is the ruler of "this world," that is, of fallen human society that has not yet been redeemed. It also tells us that his "rule" is manifested in various doctrines, religions, and theories which lead human beings to sin. We will consider Satan more fully further on. At this point, we simply need to see his influence as coming to us from the various voices in society that lead human beings to sin.

Satan did not use force to overpower Adam and Eve, and he does not use force to overcome other human beings. He seeks a choice on the part of human beings—the choice of disobedience to God expressed in disobedience to his instructions. To attain his goal Satan makes false statements about God and the consequences of disobeying God. Sin, in other words, involves choosing falsehood rather than accepting what God has said. It is based, at least implicitly, on disbelief, rejection of God's Word.

The Inner Source. The account in Genesis then turns to Eve's response to the influence of the serpent. "So when the woman saw that the tree was good for food, and that it was a delight to the eyes, and that the tree was to be desired to make one wise, she took of its fruit and ate; and she also gave some to her husband, and he ate" (Gn 3:6).

This passage portrays the way sin originates inside a human being. The external agent succeeded only because he was an effective motivator who knew how to arouse something inside Eve to get her to do what he wanted. When she heard the words of Satan, Eve looked up to the tree to see its fruit. She could tell it would be nourishing. She saw it was attractive, enticing to look at. And she understood that it would produce a beneficial change in her, wisdom.

Something awoke inside of Eve. The first letter of John, probably referring to this passage, describes what was happening inside of Eve as "the lust of the flesh and the lust of the eyes and the pride of life" (1 Jn 2:16). "Pride of life" seems to mean the desire to be something great or to live at a higher station.

The cause of sin inside of Eve, then, was desires of various sorts. But is desire bad? After all, the contents of paradise were all very good (Gn 1:31) and all the trees in it were "pleasant to the sight and good for food" (Gn 2:9), probably including the tree of knowledge. The fruit of the tree that was now tempting Eve is purposely described in Genesis with many of the same words used to describe the original creation. The tempting fruit, in other words, had been made good and fulfilling by God.

Just as importantly, the desires Eve experienced were also created in her by God. The desire to eat what may have been the world's most luscious and nourishing fruit was a good desire. Even the desire to be wise, to be as great and noble as possible, can be good. To push it further, even the desire to be "like God" could be good, since God wants humans to imitate him (Eph 5:1) and be partners with him in ruling his creation (Gn 1:26).

Eve's desires were starting to move her to a wrong choice, but they were not, in themselves, bad desires. She was not even experiencing her sinful human nature at work, because she did not have a sinful human nature. Eve had not yet fallen. She was a human being the way God created human beings to be, responding to something that God had made good and desirable. Yet in so doing, Eve sinned and Adam sinned with her.

Sometimes we hear about people who seem to take great pleasure in torturing and killing other human beings, often innocent children or animals, or who take pleasure in wanton destruction of nature. We might consider these actions the paradigm case of sin, sheer evil or desire for what is in no way good. But these are expressions of a nature far gone in the corrupting results of sin—either the sin of those who do such deeds, or the sin of their parents or others who have made them to be what they are, Satan not the least. Such actions are not the disease as first caught but the disease in its last stages, morally destroying the being in whom it lives. The paradigm case of sin is rather the first sin, the sin that caused the downfall of the human race.

Here we have arrived at an important truth about the nature of sin. Sin is a parasite that grows on God's good creation. In the first sin, a good person with healthy desires responded to something good created by God, but made the fatal mistake of approaching it in a way that violated the right kind of relationship with God.

Eve sought something God wanted for her—to be wise and to be more like him—but in a way that violated the truth of her creaturehood. We cannot relate to God well except on the basis of the reality of who he is and who we are. We need to acknowledge that we are not the source of our own being or of the good things that come to us. We have to accept the limits involved in being a creature. We therefore need to respond in gratitude to the one who has created us out of his goodness and to live in a way that is pleasing to the one who is willing to keep us in existence. Wisdom requires the acceptance of reality as it is. Only on such a basis can human beings grow in wisdom and become like God.

Sinful actions, then, do not have to be evil through and through to be seriously sinful. They simply need to violate the relationship with God by doing something he has made clear he cannot accept. Consequently, of their very nature they break the relationship with him. Normally, a human action does need to be seriously evil in itself to break the relationship with God, an action like murder, adultery, or idolatry. Such was not the case with the transgression of Adam and Eve. Eating the fruit of a tree is not intrinsically evil. Under other circumstances, such an action would have been good.

An action that was not intrinsically evil was probably chosen because of its fitness to stand for the essence of all sin: disobedience, disordered choice, failure to live in unity with the one who created us and who made a certain kind of life good for his human creatures to live. To choose to do something that could be good, but to do it when it has been forbidden by God, is to choose to do evil.

This leads us back once again to the central truth about sin. Sin comes from the outside, external influences. Sin also comes from the inside, the internal desires of human nature which are capable of embracing good and evil. But sin is ultimately the choice or decision of the sinner to act in a way that destructively damages the purpose for which every human being is created: the love of God. Sin is a failure of the sinner.

THE CONSEQUENCES

A recent newspaper article told of a little girl who had disregarded her mother's warning to stay away from the street. She had been hit by a car and ended up in the hospital with an injury that would affect her for the rest of her life. Simply crossing the street seems trivial. Yet that step involved rejecting the instructions given by her mother in order to protect her. Despite the warning, it also involved much greater consequences than the little girl ever imagined before she stepped off the curb or than we would have expected if we had only been told that a little girl crossed the street against her mother's orders.

In the previous section, we looked at the first human sin as the pattern or prototype of that problematic interaction with God which is at the root of human misfortune. Now we will look at the way Genesis presents the first sin as affecting the subsequent state of the human race. The significance of sin begins to appear immediately after the first sinful act, but much of what happened in the fall becomes clear only in the light of the later course of the human race.

The Judgment. No sooner had Adam and Eve eaten the fruit of the tree of the knowledge of good and evil, than the consequences began to unfold.

> The eyes of both were opened, and they knew that they were naked; and they sewed fig leaves together and made themselves aprons. And they heard the sound of the Lord God walking in the garden in the cool of the day, and the man and his wife hid themselves from the presence of the Lord God among the trees of the garden. But the Lord God called to the man and said to him, "Where are you?" And he said, "I heard the sound of thee in the garden, and I was afraid, because I was naked; and I hid myself."
>
> **Gn 3:7-10**

Once Adam and Eve had eaten of the fruit they immediately realized that something was wrong. Even more significantly, they realized that something was wrong with them. They experienced themselves as naked and ashamed. They were conscious that their actions had affected their relationship with God, and they began to be afraid of him.

John Chrysostom described the result of the transgression of the first human beings by saying, "Through their guilt they consequently divested themselves of the glory surrounding them" (*Homilies on Genesis 16,14*). He first speaks of the guilt that came from having disobeyed God's commandment. In doing so, he sums up a truth that Genesis presents in narrative form: sin led to a change in the state of the human race.

Seriously evil actions result in a sinful state for the human race, as well as for individual human beings. Christian teachers have described this change of state in a variety of ways. Sometimes they say Adam and Eve lost their "innocence." We tend to understand that word to mean the kind of innocence children have, unaware of good and evil and in a certain way incapable of sin (or, for that matter, virtue). As applied to the human race before the fall, however, "innocence" means rather that Adam and Eve were free of guilt, blameless in their conduct, able to be in God's presence without profaning his holiness. Now they had lost that innocence.

Sometimes Christian teachers say that Adam and Eve lost their "original righteousness" or "original justice." That phrase means that they lost the good or right relationship with God given them by their origin, that is, by the very way God made them. Along with this, they lost their habitual goodness of conduct. As a consequence of the fall, Adam and Eve were left in a bad relationship with God which could be described as a state of alienation or separation. As Isaiah puts it, "Your iniquities have made a separation between you and your God, and your sins have hid his face from you so that he does not hear" (Is 59:2).

Chrysostom also indicates that their guilt resulted in the loss of their glory, by which he meant an exterior radiance that clothed them in a personal splendor. Their external glory, as we have seen, came from an inner glory or power which enabled Adam and Eve to rule themselves, to control their actions, to be people of good character. No longer in good relationship with God and no longer subject to him, they were no longer able to keep themselves in subjection and to direct their actions in consistently good ways. They had lost that interior excellence and moral greatness that comes from being in the image and likeness of God in an unmarred way. With it, they had lost a mastery of themselves and became subject to their own desires, prone to sin.

God did not need to especially intervene to punish Adam and Eve. Punishment had already begun in the form of the evil consequences of their transgression. They experienced the change in their own persons. As a result their eyes were opened in a new way to the significance of moral matters in human life. Conscious of the shamefulness of their new state, they experienced for the first time the fear of God that arises from sinfulness.

Adam and Eve had previously feared God with the awe and respect due him as their Creator and Lord, their Father.

Now they feared even to come into his presence. They knew they were unworthy to stand before God's awesome holiness, his absolute moral perfection. Their sinfulness made them unseemly. To use the words of later Scriptures, they had become impure or unclean. Their sinfulness also made them afraid of what God would do with them.

God then summoned Adam and Eve and the serpent before him. He sat before them as judge, judge because he was ruler of the universe, but also judge because he was their Father. God began, as a good judge should, by questioning Adam and then Eve, probably giving them a chance to accept responsibility for their actions and to repent. There is, however, no indication of repentance in their responses, only a desire to avoid the unfortunate consequences of their actions.

The rest of Scripture tells us that repentance is a way to repair wrongdoing. By the way it describes the response of Adam and Eve, Genesis 3 probably indicates that it was not just the first sin that caused the fall of the human race, but also the unwillingness to take advantage of the opportunity for repentance. Had they repented, their sin may not have changed the course of human history the way it did.

The sentences God pronounced contain a curse on the serpent and a curse on the ground from which the human race was taken. Since humans needed to work the ground to grow food, the curse on the ground was also a curse on the relationship of the human race to nature, the source of the materials human beings need to live. It was consequently a curse on human labor. Although the word "curse" is not used, there was probably a curse on childbirth as well. The natural function that should have been simple delight for the woman became one of pain mixed with joy. God's pronouncements indicate the way in which the sin of the human race negatively affects the natural functions of human life. As a result of sin, ordinary human actions lose much of their delightfulness and become difficult and onerous.

The last evil consequence of their sinful action that directly affected Adam and Eve is described at the end of Genesis 3:

> Then the Lord God said, "Behold, the man has become like one of us, knowing good and evil; and now, lest he put forth his hand and take also of the tree of life, and eat, and live for ever"—therefore the Lord God sent him forth from the garden of Eden, to till the ground from which he was taken. He drove out the man; and at the east of the garden of Eden he placed the cherubim, and a flaming sword which turned every way, to guard the way to the tree of life. **Gn 3:22-24**

Adam and Eve were banished or exiled from paradise, and thus deprived of the tree of life and so of their expected immortality. Yet there was more to their exile than this loss. In an age of great mobility and modern communications, modern people have forgotten much of the significance of exile. Exile deprived people of their home, of their family and friends, and of the way of life they were raised to live. In short, exile deprived them of much of what made their life worth living. As a result, exile often was used as a punishment for wrongdoing.

The exile of Adam and Eve from paradise was itself one of the worst consequences of their sin. They had lost the garden of God: the place of God's presence and human blessedness, the place filled with delight, the place for human life to be lived the way it was supposed to be lived.

Yet there is even more to the loss of paradise than clearly appears in Genesis. Paradise was described as an earthly place and the tree of life as bearing fruit that would prolong earthly life. Teaching in later Scriptures makes clear that God created the human race for an even greater nearness to him than Adam and Eve seemed to have before the fall. With that nearness would come fuller blessedness. Christians have come to use the word "heaven" for the place where that state could be experienced, because "heaven" is the scriptural word for the place of God's dwelling or presence.

There are differing views on the relationship of paradise and heaven. God may have intended the earthly paradise to develop to the point where by living in paradise human beings would be living "in heaven." God may have intended at some point to change the mode of human existence more radically so that paradise would have been "swallowed up" in heaven (2 Cor 5:4). Either way, the loss of paradise turns out to be more than just the loss of a good and prolonged earthly life. In Christian terms, it was the loss of heaven as well. It was the loss of the full, blessed life which God had intended for the human race—which they had begun to experience in paradise, which would be completely given to them in heaven, and which they would be able to enjoy eternally.

There is also more to the sentence of death than appears in Genesis. Death is the loss of life. But as Scripture uses "life" to mean a good, blessed life and not just physical existence, so it uses "death" to mean a loss of good, blessed life. It can refer, in other words, to what Christians have called "spiritual death" (Eph 2:1-2), a state in which human beings live without the presence of God, without spiritual blessedness, unable to live as they were created to live. Genesis shows us that sin can produce spiritual death even before physical death occurs.

Furthermore, the Scriptures indicate that physical death does not mean that human beings simply go out of existence, but that they go down to the place of the dead, Sheol or Hades. Those who have not been rescued from the consequences of the fall live there without the presence of God and the blessedness that comes from being united to him. For those who "die in their sins," the state of death involves unfortunate consequences resulting from their sinful actions.

Many questions surround the afterlife and the place or places of those who do not end up in heaven. For our purposes here, it is enough to note that the punishment of death referred to in Genesis involved more than a simple termination of earthly existence. It involved, first, a change in Adam and Eve so that earthly life itself became a type of living death. Second, even after the termination of earthly life, death did not produce annihilation but a continued existence deprived of much of what makes human life worthwhile.

The Aftermath. The consequences of sin as described by Genesis were not restricted to the lives of Adam and Eve but extended to their descendants, whose lives are portrayed in Genesis 4-11. The sin of Adam and Eve was disobedience to God, motivated by pride and based on disbelief. It was a sin directly against God himself. This sin against God also seems to characterize Cain, their first-born son. But he adds a further sin—murder, brother killing brother.

In the story of Cain's murder of his brother Abel, we see how the state of sin produces hatred and envy between human beings. The subsequent narrative of the lives of his descendants shows an intensification of evil. By the time of the flood the earth was "filled with violence" (Gn 6:11). Human beings, in short, inflict many of the most serious consequences of sin upon one another. The greatest danger to the human race is not what external forces will do, but what the race will do to itself. The first chapters of Genesis show us that disruption and disorder in the relationship with God leads to disruption and disorder in our relationships with one another.

But the story of the human race is not one of unmitigated evil. Adam and Eve themselves do not seem to have turned completely away from God after the fall. The Book of Wisdom seems to preserve the tradition that Adam repented because of the good influence of God's instruction (Wis 10:1). Most Christian teachers have taken that same view.

Moreover, from Adam and Eve sprang two sons, the murderer Cain and the righteous Abel (Heb 11:4). With them came two ways of life—that of the sons of Cain and that of the sons of Seth, who replaced Abel (Gn 4:25). The sons of Seth called upon the name of the Lord (Gn 4:26), gave rise to Enoch who walked with God (Gn 5:23), and gave rise to righteous Noah (Gn 6:9). Noah in turn gave rise to Abraham. Sin clearly predominates in human life, but there is also goodness and hope, something worth saving.

This goodness is related to another truth presented in Genesis: God did not abandon the human race. Punishment does not mean total rejection. No sooner had he finished passing sentence, than with fatherly kindness he clothed Adam and Eve himself, because they did not know how to provide for themselves very well in their new circumstances. He continued the human race through Adam and Eve by blessing them with children.

God also cared for the descendants of Adam and Eve. He accepted Abel's offering, allowing human beings to maintain a relationship with him. He then replaced the line of Abel after Abel's murder. He even protected Cain from the worst consequences of his sin. When God judged the race as a whole worthy of destruction as a result of human evil, he preserved it by Noah, and renewed his original commission. Moreover, he added a special pledge of protection that no matter how evil the human race would become, he would never let it be completely destroyed. The fall, in short, did not cut the human race off from God completely. He was constantly at work to preserve it and lead it to the point where it could once again fulfill its purpose.

Some Christian teachers, primarily in the Western tradition, have called the state of sin that resulted from the first act of disobedience "original sin." "Original" means the sin comes from the origin of the human race. "Sin" means sinful state rather than sinful actions. Original sin, then, is the sinful state which has resulted from the origins of the human race, the state of human estrangement from God with a related internal condition of sinfulness. As distinguished from the sinful actions human beings themselves perform, this sinful state comes to all human beings through their membership in the race. It is the state of the race as a whole, but therefore a state that affects individual human beings as well.

Many questions have been raised about original sin through the centuries. Some of these center around the guilt that might be due to individuals because of it. Others center around how corrupt or depraved human nature has become as a result of the fall. Because of what could be called the "stronger" views of original sin, many Christians even avoid the term because it seems to imply more than they can accept.

Nonetheless, a consensus exists among orthodox Christians that something is wrong with the human race. It is not in the relationship with God it was created for. Apart from the grace of God, the state of the race inevitably leads to sinful actions by most, if not all, who reach the age of being able to perform such actions. Moreover, on their own human beings seem unable to radically change the way they live. For the purposes of this book, such a consensus is enough.

Many people believe the scriptural teaching on original sin can be found in Genesis 3, but this chapter only tells of the first sin. Genesis 4-11 narrates the fact that the first sin was not an isolated event, soon reversed by the repentance of Adam and Eve or by a fresh start with the birth of righteous Abel. Rather, the first sin led to a pattern which illustrates the truth that the fall of the human race has made human beings prone to sinful actions.

PUNISHMENT AND JUSTICE

The Penalty of Sin. Most people do not find it difficult to accept the fact of human sinfulness. After all, the spontaneous conviction of the great majority of human beings is that the human race does evil. This evil can then be described as sin, once we recognize the existence of a personal God and moral obligations to him. Genesis, however, as well as later Scriptures and Christian teachers, seems to add an important perspective to that commonly accepted fact. It seems to say that the state of sin, along with mortality and the pain and labor of life, is in some way penal. These things originate in punishment by God. The meaning and truth of such a view need consideration.

God's punishment of sin can happen in some different ways. The first is through the bad consequences that follow from sin. These are in large part natural, built into the way human life works. For instance, if murder is allowed, conflict will follow, life will become insecure, and sooner or later social life will become less viable for its members. Murder has bad consequences beyond those for the victim—usually for the murderer, but also for society. Sin, in other words, does not produce bad consequences only when it provokes external judgment, but sinful actions are themselves intrinsically destructive.

Some would not use the word "punishment" for the bad consequences of sin, but would reserve that word for something deliberately inflicted by an authority that has the responsibility to punish wrongdoing. Parents, however, at times punish their children by allowing them to suffer the consequences of some disobedience. They may give their children an allowance with instructions for its use. If the children choose not to follow them, the parents may let them live through the bad results of their own actions by not helping them when they run out of money.

Sometimes parents follow such a course of action simply for instructional reasons. Sometimes they do so specifically as a way of punishing disobedience. When we remember that God created the universe, his approach to sin can be seen as similar to such parental punishment. God set up human life in such a way that unfortunate consequences are connected to sinful actions. In this sense, the bad consequences of sin are in fact punishments which operate as deterrents for future sin.

Genesis seems to present a second way that God punishes sin. He seems to have inflicted pain or difficulty through the "curses" as a special response to the sin of Adam and Eve. Some people have held that the curses simply stated the bad consequences that would come as a result of sin. In this view, when God proclaimed the curses to Adam and Eve, he was not by that fact imposing them but merely predicting what would happen to them. This was intended to help them realize that their own actions were responsible for what was befalling them. Sinfulness would simply produce its normal consequences in daily living. Pain and difficulty would come upon the two main areas of human life: family life and work. Some would even understand the sentence of death and banishment from paradise in the same way.

More commonly, however, the "curses" are viewed as an added difficulty that God inflicted upon the human race—above and beyond the automatic bad consequences of sin. For us the word "curse" usually implies hostility and malice. The biblical words translated for "curse," especially when used of God, do not imply either hostility or malice, but are the actions of a judge imposing a penalty that is deserved. The term "curse" is probably too misleading to be a good translation now, but its use cannot always be avoided.

In this second view of "curses," they are added as a special disciplinary measure designed to lead human beings to repentance. In such an understanding, God intended the very difficulty of natural human life as a reminder that something is wrong, that the human race is in a different state than when it was originally created. He intended it to lead to a salutary change of attitude, or at least a readiness to receive help when he offered it.

There is yet a further way God punishes sin. He punishes sin without any remedial goal in view and simply condemns those who have gone too far, at least when he has no hope for their improvement. In a similar way, human beings with governmental authority at times execute or banish other human beings. Execution simply ends human life and is reserved for the greatest of criminals, at least the ones who are deemed hopeless. Banishment eliminates people from a given society and is used in a similar way. Lifelong imprisonment in our society is a type of banishment. These penalties have a certain inevitability about them. Some people behave, or, given the chance, will behave in a way that is so harmful of others or of the common good that they cannot be left part of the common life without penalizing others.

The flood by which God "determined to make an end of all flesh" (Gn 6:13) has been traditionally understood as such a condemnation. It has therefore been taken as a "type" of damnation or condemnation to hell which Christian teachers have seen as simply penal, with no remedial role. Hell is the place for those who cannot be part of heaven and have heaven still be a place of blessedness for the others who would live in it. Full blessedness and closeness to God can only happen in a society or community where people freely love God and one another. Those who will not, or will not without having their freedom destroyed, can only be excluded from heaven.

The main punishment for the first sin, however, seems to be neither the evil consequences of what happened nor any added punishments that were specifically inflicted. Rather, it is the loss of the relationship with God that was given to Adam and Eve at their creation, a loss expressed in the banishment from paradise. That is the loss of the greatest good that the human race can ever have and the source of the worst evils that have ensued.

A loss is difficult to comprehend for someone who has never experienced what is missing. Those born blind do not seem as unhappy about their handicap as those who have become blind. The Scriptures teach that "seeing God" is itself a great good. Those who have come into such an experiential knowledge of God testify to its being a source of deep joy.

Heaven itself is often described in terms of the beatific vision. The glory of God is such that just to be able to see him is the cause of overflowing happiness. Even though many human beings do not realize what they are missing, the worst consequence of the fall is the loss of their original closeness to God.

The loss of the relationship with God is also serious because it leads to the further loss of a good human life. God is necessary for human beings to fully achieve even a natural happiness. Without a good relationship to him involving submission to his instructions, human beings are unable to live with the kind of moral goodness and character that allows them to achieve a good life and avoid much misfortune.

Furthermore, the failure to submit to God and follow his ways cuts the human race off from the wisdom and blessing and help which alone could protect it from demonic influences and guard it from its own weakness. Sin, in short, is partly as important as it is because human beings need God to live well, and because serious sin cuts us off from God. The state of sin is the absence of that blessed relationship with God which allows us to have true life.

Sin, then, has many ways of producing bad consequences, and in origin God is the source of all of them. He has created the universe and governs it in such a way that when human beings sin, they are deprived of much of what makes human life as worthwhile and blessed as God intended it to be. We can, therefore, describe the current state of the human race and many of the circumstances of human life as "penal."

By describing sin as penal, we do not necessarily mean that all the results of human sin are punishments directly inflicted by God as a result of human wrongdoing, although most Christian teachers think that some of them are. We simply mean that the unfortunate state of the human race is due to the deserved consequences of sin, whether directly inflicted or simply the result of human actions and the disruption of the relationship with God which those actions produced. We also are saying that in ensuring that the universe was governed in such a way that wrongdoing produced negative consequences, God has acted as a father and judge should.

Justice and Hope. If sin is punished by God, then we are concerned with the question of God's penal justice, both his penal justice as manifested in the way he handled the first sin and the way he currently relates to the fallen human race.

"Justice" traditionally has been defined in Western thought as "giving others their due." To be just, therefore, certain actions need to have a good reason, a justifiable reason, otherwise they should not be done.

Punishments are in such a category since they involve depriving people of what normally would be considered as "due" to them. People in prison no longer have that freedom of action which is their due or, to put it in another way, their ordinary right. Penal justice is the justice which governs such matters. A just ruler would not inflict punishments without good reason.

But is God a just ruler? Does he even have to be just? Some thinkers, including some Christian theologians, have held that God is above justice. As a Creator, God is free to act as he will, so that what he does cannot be unjust. Most have held that if God is to be considered morally good at all and so distinguishable from Satan, he must act in a way that we can somehow recognize as justice—even if it does not correspond exactly to what we would call just in an earthly ruler. Since the Scriptures call God "just" with the same word that they use for good earthly rulers, he must at least intend to be just in much the same way.

Then was God just in allowing the descendants of Adam and Eve to suffer as a result of the sins of their parents? The first chapters of Genesis give us a preliminary perspective.

First, we are dealing with creation. God could create the human race the way he wished. Whatever benefits he gave human beings were more than they deserved. That the descendants of Adam ended up with less than they might have if Adam had responded differently is not a reflection on God.

Second, Genesis seems to indicate that from God's point of view, human beings can at any time return to a better state by turning away from sin and toward God. Sin is still the problem, not God. Sin leads to bad consequences. Sin deserves punishment. The human race does not always live in perfect evil, and as a result, does not always live in perfect misery either. Human history is a play of light and shadow, and the freer from sin human beings live, the better their lives become.

True as these observations are, and perhaps the best we can draw from Genesis, they are not complete answers for the predicament of the human race once we see it in the light of God's full revelation. The truth about "heaven and hell" gives us a different perspective. Once we know about the existence of a life of eternal gladness in the presence of God and of eternal loss in separation from God, the predicament looks different, grimmer. The truth about the human condition adds to that different perspective. Once we see the weakness of the human race, its proneness to sin, and its consequent inability to please God in a way that could deserve the gift of heaven, the predicament looks different, still grimmer.

If we look at the predicament of the human race just within the framework of this life, improvement does not so clearly seem beyond human effort, bad as the record may have been to date. Once, however, we see the glory of what God intended for his sons and daughters, the loss seems irreparable.

Genesis provides further help for us in a seemingly obscure but significant passage in the curse on the serpent: "I will put enmity between you and the woman, and between your seed and her seed; he shall bruise your head, and you shall bruise his heel" (Gn 3:15). Some Christian writers, based on the New Testament (Rom 16:19-20), have seen this as the first proclamation of the gospel. If so, it is a prophetic one, and like most prophecy it is somewhat obscure before its fulfillment.

The words of this passage promise hostility between the serpent (Satan) and the woman, here representing the human race. There will be lasting conflict, but the conflict will involve the human race having the upper hand. The picture behind the prophecy is of a barefoot man being bitten as he crushes and destroys that snake.

According to many Christian teachers, that image has been fulfilled in the sufferings and death of Christ. The enemy of the human race, the one who caused its downfall, will himself be defeated by a future representative of the human race. That representative, Christ, will be wounded in the process (have his heel bruised), but will not be destroyed and will prove victorious in crushing Satan. In other words, the first "curse" is actually a promise of blessing for the human race. God's words of punishment begin with a promise of deliverance for his sons and daughters. God's justice can only be understood in the light of his future plan.

RESCUING A LOST RACE

There is a fairy tale about a baby found in the woods and raised by simple peasants. One day a knight comes to the family's hut and sees the child. He looks and acts like a peasant child, uneducated, unable to speak his native language in a proper way, with simple, somewhat rude manners. But when the knight looks at him, he is struck by the child's appearance. Despite his peasant-like and unpromising manner and behavior, the child looks like the king. The knight has discovered the son of the king who years before had been kidnapped by an enemy and left in the forest to die.

The human race is much like that child. As we consider human affairs, we see much evil—wars, murders, robberies, violence, and cruelty. We see senseless brutalities—sadism, torture, genocide. We even see human beings destroying themselves, giving themselves over to enslaving addictions, or letting themselves deteriorate to satiate some lust. We see noble empires fall into ruin; great endeavors wither. Futility, insecurity, and failure seem the constant accompaniment of human life.

Yet we also see a race that is capable of great kindness, heroic deeds, high successes, and vast accomplishments. We see individuals whose character we can admire, whose wisdom we can learn from. Even more, we see a race that seems capable of recognizing that much that it does is evil, that knows a great deal about how to distinguish good from evil, and that seems to want a society of peace and justice. We, in short, see a race that was made in the image of the King—the Lord of the universe, who made all things good—but a race that has fallen into great evil. The state of the human race as the Scripture teaches us does not have to be proven. It is all around us to see.

How can the son of the king be restored to his Father and his royal state? How can the image of the great King be recreated so that the likeness is recognizable in every respect?

The answer of a Christian reflection on Genesis is that sin has to be taken away, removed from the human race. Not only does the human race have to cease doing those things which cause evil and further ruin and which deserve punishment, but the sinful state of the human race which causes those actions has to be changed. The disease which leads to death has to be healed. Sinfulness has to be eradicated; true health, true life, has to be given. The human race needs a Redeemer, someone who can rescue it from the misfortune into which it has fallen and restore it to true life. The rest of this book will concern that Redeemer, Jesus Christ, and what he did to rescue the human race from the predicament in which it found itself.

Part Two

The Death of
the Redeemer

Introduction to Part Two

THE NEW TESTAMENT TELLS US MANY TIMES that Christ died for us.[1] Similar passages say that he gave himself up or was given up for us.[2] The death of Christ on the cross—an event which scandalized the Jews and seemed foolishness to the pagans (1 Cor 1:23)—was "for us." The crucifixion was not just an accident or a setback or an unexplained tragedy, but something Christ deliberately underwent for our sake.

Paul says, "God has... destined us... to obtain salvation through our Lord Jesus Christ, who died for us" (1 Thes 5:9). Christ's death made it possible for us to obtain salvation. This same truth is expressed in different words in many of the other passages about Christ dying for us or giving himself for us. They tell us that Christ died to bring us to God (1 Pt 3:18), to redeem us (Ti 2:14), to deliver us (Gal 1:4), to give us life (1 Thes 5:10). His death produced something that was immensely beneficial for us.

As we have seen, such statements about Christ's death pose a question. Granted that his death produced such great benefits as salvation, redemption, deliverance, life, and relationship with God, why did it do that? Why was Christ's death so different that it could be "for us," people who live almost two thousand years after he died?

A simple answer is because it took care of our sin problem.

---

1. For passages which say Christ died for us, see page 301.
2. For passages which say Christ gave himself up or was given up for us, see page 301.

As Paul states the truth of the gospel, "Christ died for our sins." "Our sins" were the obstacle to receiving the benefits, the new life, that God wanted to give us. Christ's death provided a way to take care of that obstacle. His death was the way out of the human predicament.

Saying that Christ's death took care of our sins, however, simply rephrases the same questions in a different form. Instead of saying that Christ's death had good results for us, it says that his death took away the obstacle to our receiving those good results. Such an answer still does not tell us *how* his death came to be so useful.

If, for instance, we say that a woman took care of her debts, we know the result of what she did. We might still wonder how she did it. Did she work and pay them off, or use her savings, or receive an inheritance? In a similar way, we want to know how Christ took care of the sin problem. What was it about his sufferings and death that enabled them to produce the kind of results they did?

The New Testament gives us various descriptions of Christ's sufferings and death that allow us to see how it was special and how it could be helpful to us.

The three main descriptions are:

1. He paid for our redemption.
2 He underwent a punishment instead of us.
3. He gave himself as a sacrifice for our sins.

These statements do not describe three different steps Jesus took or three different events in his life. They are simply three different ways of looking at the same action and seeing how it accomplished something beneficial for us. Together they help us to understand how Christ's death was effective in dealing with human sin and, therefore, in making possible a change in the state of the human race.

In each of the chapters of Part Two, we will focus on the meaning of one of these statements and why it can be applied to the death of Christ. We will then, be able to answer why such a death was, in fact, successful in taking care of the sin problem.

When we focus on Christ's death in this way, we are looking at one event in a process. That process includes further events that involved Christ himself: he was raised from the dead; he ascended to the right hand of the Father; and he poured out the Holy Spirit on his disciples. These complete what he did to redeem us. That process also includes events like our conversion or baptism. These allow us to receive the benefits of what Christ did.

While we cannot separate the death of Christ from those other events and completely understand it, they will not be central to our concern in this part. We will focus as much as possible on understanding his death in itself. In the subsequent parts, we will look more at the whole process.

THREE

The Cost of Redemption

T HE SCRIPTURAL ACCOUNT OF THE ESTABLISHMENT of the old covenant begins with the Israelites in a very difficult situation. They had come to Egypt as refugees from a famine when one of their number, Joseph, was second in power to the Pharaoh. Centuries later, the Hebrews lived under a Pharaoh who had no respect for the memory of Joseph. Even worse, he feared this large and powerful people, because they were not Egyptians and perhaps because they did not worship the gods of Egypt.

Pharaoh adopted a simple expedient to solve "the Hebrew question." He put them into bondage and set them to hard labor with the intention of gradually causing them to die out. When that plan seemed to be failing, Pharaoh made their slavery still more oppressive, their labor more rigorous, and their lives more bitter. He finally even attempted to put all their male children to death.

In answer to their cries, the God of the people of Israel, the Lord of heaven and earth, acted. He called Moses, an Israelite who had been raised in the Egyptian royal family, and established him as a deliverer for his people. By signs and wonders which led to plagues on the Egyptians, he induced Pharaoh to let his people go so that they might serve him freely. To protect them from the death inflicted upon the Egyptians' first-born, God instructed the Israelites to offer the sacrifice of the Passover lamb. He parted the Red Sea, led them through on dry land, and then let the waters return, destroying Pharaoh's army.

When the Israelites safely reached the far shore of the Red Sea and beheld the destruction of Pharaoh's army, they held a great celebration. They had been redeemed by the Lord (Ex 15:13). Their deliverance from Egypt was not enough to make their lives go well. The Israelites had to be led across the desert, a place where a large group of people could not easily survive. They needed to be taught how to live in the right way and given a land in which to live. But nonetheless, the Israelites had been redeemed, and simply being free was a great blessing.

People these days rarely use the word "redemption," and then most commonly in connection with the work of Christ. With no other use, it has no other meaning than to refer to whatever it was Christ may have done for us. It has ended up in the category of vague, religious words that describe something good. The word is commonly used in the English Bible, however, even to describe many happenings that were not specifically religious. The most important use of the word is the one that gave rise to describing the Exodus from Egypt as a redemption: the buying of a slave.

Even when slavery was common in English speaking countries, the word "redeem" was rarely used for buying slaves. We would usually say that someone "bought" or "purchased" a slave. We would say someone "freed" or "emancipated" a slave, if the slave was released afterwards. We talk about "ransoming" captives or people who have been kidnapped, so we might even speak about ransoming such slaves. Yet in English biblical translations "redeem" and "redemption" are the most common translations for certain Hebrew and Greek words that are used to describe buying slaves.

When we speak about Christ's death as making our redemption possible, we are therefore using a "Bible word" that means freedom from slavery through purchase. The New Testament applies the word to the results of what Christ did, especially the results of his death. In this chapter, then, we will consider the meaning of Christ's death as "redeeming" and as a "payment." In so doing we will look at his death as the means for freeing human beings from the problematic situation created by human sin.

THE MEANING OF REDEMPTION

The Slavery of Sin. The New Testament speaks about Christ as having redeemed us from slavery. Paul makes such a statement in the course of giving directions to the Corinthians about how to deal with new converts who are slaves: "For he who was called in the Lord as a slave is a freedman of the Lord. Likewise, he who was freed when called is a slave of Christ. You were bought with a price; do not become slaves of men" (1 Cor 7:23).

His statement is somewhat paradoxical. All Christians are both freed people and slaves at the same time—freed people because they were bought from slavery by Christ, slaves because Christ is their new master. Nonetheless, Paul is clearly describing what Christ did as freeing us from a slavery. Moreover, many other New Testament passages speak about Christ's death as either redeeming us from slavery, or they simply speak about redeeming us, but in a way that might have in mind freedom from slavery.[1]

Slavery is unfamiliar to most modern people. Our most accessible historical memories are of the New World slavery which ended in the nineteenth century with Wilberforce's anti-slavery campaign and the American Civil War. Such slavery, however, can be misleading for understanding how New Testament passages apply the idea of slavery to the redemptive work of Christ. Slavery as known by Old and New Testa-

---

1. For passages which speak about Christ's death as redemptive, see page 301.

ment people had some features unfamiliar to us.

First, redemption was not usually the same as emancipation. When someone "redeemed" a slave, that person became the slave's new master. Thus, the words "buy" and "purchase" are often used as synonyms for "redeem." If an Israelite redeemed a family member from slavery under the old covenant law, he could have the redeemed relative work as a slave for as many as seven years. When God redeemed Israel, he became the "owner" of Israel and Israel served him. In the passage quoted above, Christ is clearly understood to have become the owner of new Christians, even though he has redeemed them.

Although redemption was not normally emancipation, it could still be a deliverance. Leaving a cruel master who subjects you to hard labor and oppressive conditions and coming into the household of a good master who gives you honorable work and kind treatment is a great benefit. The better the master, the greater the benefit.

Some people, in fact, freely chose to be slaves because they loved their master or mistress and wanted to serve him or her. They found that their lives went much better as part of the master's household than on their own (see Ex 21:5). The story of Joseph is the most famous illustration of the fact that purchase by the right master could be much better than emancipation.

Second, slavery in the ancient world did not always originate in some act of injustice or oppression. Modern World slavery existed for economic reasons. It was often based on the kidnapping of innocent victims who could rarely get free as long as they lived. The Scripture does offer some examples of slavery that functioned in such a way. In fact, the condition of the Israelite slaves in Egypt was not so different from that of African slaves in the New World.

Most forms of slavery in the ancient world, however, were not like that of the Israelites. Most common was slavery for debt. If people could not pay their debts, or could not find someone else to do so on their behalf, they became slaves to their creditors and worked off the debt. They were supposed to be treated well and released after a certain period of time. Prisoners of war were also commonly made slaves, often on the view that they deserved to make up for their unjust actions that gave rise to the war. In some cultures, slavery functioned as an alternative to a prison system to punish someone for a crime. In short, slavery was not necessarily an unjust oppression but could be a condition deserved by certain actions. Redemption, therefore, often involved paying something to make up for what was owed in justice.

"Redemption" is used in Scripture to refer to more than redemption from slavery. Someone could "redeem" property by buying it back and returning it to the ownership of the family. Offerings could be redeemed. Someone might offer a house to God and then, in order to keep the house and yet still make the offering, substitute something else of value instead. Redemption, in short, simply meant buying something back, usually from a situation which was in some way unfortunate. Frequently it was done because of a claim based on relationship or previous ownership.

The word "redemption" could also be applied to God's action in freeing people from a variety of other difficulties such as enemy attack, human oppression, and danger of death. The psalmist even prays, "Redeem Israel, O God, out of all his troubles" (Ps 25:22). In these cases, God's action does not involve any actual purchase. In other words, "redemption" was used in an extended sense for freeing people from oppressive or problematic circumstances which kept them from living a normal life and from which they could not free themselves.

As we have seen, however, many New Testament texts about redemption do concern purchase from slavery. But in the ordinary sense of the words, becoming a Christian does not involve freedom from slavery or from some previous slave master. Most people are not slaves when they become Christians. Nor were most converts in the first century. Even more significantly, the slaves who became Christians in the first century were not freed as soon as they became Christians (1 Cor 7:20-24).

What then is the slavery from which Christians are redeemed? The first letter of Peter gives us an answer. Christians are "ransomed from the futile ways inherited from your fathers" (1 Pt 1:18). "Futile ways" here means more than activities that are a waste of time or that do not get us anywhere, like trying to maintain our youthful looks as we grow old. "Futile" means reaching no good end or failing to reach the purpose for which something was intended. "Ways" means a way of life or how we live. We were, then, liberated from a way of life that did not reach the purpose for which we were made, from a bad way to live.

Titus 2:14 gives us another answer. Christ "gave himself for us to redeem us from all iniquity." We were liberated from iniquity or wrongdoing or sin. Since sin is what makes our way of life bad and makes it fail to reach the purpose for which we were created, the two passages are saying much the same thing. Christ redeemed or ransomed us from a futile way of living, a sinful way of life.

The New Testament states in more than one passage that we were slaves to sin before the redemption (Rom 6:17; Jn 8:34). In seeing sin as a slavery, the New Testament writings are saying that our sinful state or sinful actions are more than a misfortune in which we need some help. Rather, sin is an oppressive condition we cannot get out of by ourselves. We need to be redeemed, because we are in the power of something we are helpless to change.

If the slavery we were in is sin, how are we redeemed or freed from sin? Ephesians 1:7 gives us a perspective on the process of redemption by saying, "In him we have redemption through his blood, the forgiveness of our trespasses...." This passage seems to equate redemption by the death of Christ with forgiveness of trespasses or sinful actions. Colossians 1:14 says the same (see also Heb 9:15; Rom 3:24; Gal 3:13).

In other words, our redemption or liberation from a sinful way of life involves forgiveness of our sins. We are not delivered from our futile way of life if we are not forgiven for our sin. Understanding forgiveness of sin, then, is central to understanding the process of redemption.

Redemption and Forgiveness. According to the Gospel of Luke, Jesus explained early in his public ministry what he was about (Lk 4:16-21). He read a passage from Isaiah (61:1-2) and announced to those in the synagogue that he would fulfill it: "The Spirit of the Lord is upon me, because he has anointed me to preach good news to the poor. He has sent me to proclaim release to the captives and the recovering of sight to the blind, to release [RSV: set at liberty] those who are oppressed, to proclaim the acceptable year of the Lord".

The passage in Isaiah refers to the jubilee year, or the "year of release" as it was translated into Greek. This was a year in which slaves were released from their bondage, and debtors were released from their debts and received their land back. It was "a year of liberty"—a year of release from past failures, a year in which everyone could make a fresh start. (For background, see Lv 25.)

Despite attempts to identify Christian liberation with social improvement, we have no record of Jesus actually trying to get a release to occur in the literal Old Testament sense. He led no movement to free slaves or reclaim debtors' property. Rather, he proclaimed the jubilee year in a "fulfilled" sense as the prophecy in Isaiah itself seems to intend.

The good news he proclaimed to "the poor" was the good news of the kingdom of God (Mk 1:15; Mt 4:17). With that good news, he called for repentance, that is, change of attitude and change of life. Repentance in turn would lead to forgiveness of sins. In the Greek of the Gospel text, the word for "forgiveness" is the same as the word "release" in the Isaiah passage. When Jesus offered forgiveness of sins, then, he was proclaiming a release, the true release.

"Forgiveness" is the most common English word for the blessing that Isaiah and other prophets foretold and that Jesus offered. The New Testament word is also translated "remission," "pardon," or "taking away." It is a word that can be used to speak about a variety of ways of freeing people from the undesirable consequences of their actions.

The English word "forgiveness" probably most readily brings to mind a relationship difficulty in which one person offends another. When we forgive someone's offense, we agree to no longer let that offense affect the relationship adversely or affect how we treat the offending party. The same word is used for cancelling debts. When we forgive someone else's debt, we no longer require the debt to be repaid. The Scripture often understands our sins as a kind of debt, because committing sins puts us under an obligation of reparation. Finally, "forgiveness" is a synonym of "pardon," the word we use for letting off prisoners or criminals who are sentenced to some kind of penalty for their misdeeds. When we pardon others, they are released without having to pay the whole penalty or any penalty at all.

"Forgiveness" (or its close synonym "pardon"), therefore, is used in contexts where there is some obligation to undergo unfortunate consequences of our actions. Unrepaired offenses, unpaid debts, and criminal sentences all suggest that we ought to do something to "make up for" what we have done. Such an obligation puts us in or keeps us in an unfortunate condition. In speaking of sin, Christian teachers have often used the terms "debt of sin" or "debt of punishment" to refer to such an obligation in regard to sin. Forgiveness conveys the idea of release from such an obligation granted by somebody in a position to do so. For these reasons, it is a good translation of the Greek word in the phrase "forgiveness of sins."

Yet the word "forgiveness" is, in the final analysis, not strong enough because Jesus came to actually take our sins away. There are many scriptural images or phrases that express such a view. Our sins are supposed to be blotted out or erased. "Deleted" might be a better word in a computer age. They are supposed to be washed out of our garments like so many stains, lifted off us like burdens we were carrying, carried away as the scapegoat carried the sins of Israel into the wilderness. What was once on our wagon (or in the trunk of our car) was put into God's wagon, and he hauled the load off to the dump. Our sins were forgotten by God, and whatever the all-knowing God forgets just ceases to exist. All these images and phrases convey something more than just cancelling of debts or pardoning of sentences. They convey the elimination of sins from our life.

To be freed from the slavery of sin, we actually need to be freed from sin itself, so that we cease sinning and so that sinfulness no longer determines our actions and the way our life goes. Pardon or cancellation of debt—essential as it may be—is not enough. Without pardon, our life could not be made better. We would still have to endure the evil consequences of past sin. But if we are pardoned and then soon after relapse into sin, we have gained little. The stories of so many criminals—released from prison only to be sent back after a few weeks or months because of another crime—illustrates the futility of mere pardon. The salvation Jesus came to bring is not meant to be a short reprieve in a life of prison or slavery.

Even more, our sins themselves are our slavery, because they keep us from fulfilling the purpose for which we were made. They produce futility. They result in a life that no one of true wisdom should want. As Paul put it, they are themselves a "due penalty" in "their own persons" for wrongdoing (Rom 1:27). The release that Jesus came to offer in the jubilee year he proclaimed involved the release from the debt of sin, but also the release from sin itself. It involved deliverance from the necessity of living a sinful way of life. He was therefore offering a transformation of the human person, a new life.

The meanings of the words "redemption" and "forgiveness" are primarily negative. Cancellation of debt, discharge from prison, and escape from captivity mainly point to being freed from an unfortunate state. Even forgiveness of an offense does not automatically have to result in the restoration of a positive relationship. Moreover, a merely emancipated slave could be released into a life of poverty and new forms of oppression. Redemption, in order to fully free us from sin, has to include, or at least lead to, the bestowing of a positive life that replaces sin.

The positive side of redemption comes through the new relationship that redemption leads to. As we discussed earlier, redemption from slavery was not simply emancipation but a purchase. In redeeming the children of Israel from bondage, God purchased a people for himself. In freeing us from sin, Christ acquired us to be his. Redemption is a relationship with a new master which promises a much better life. The new fulfilled jubilee year proclaimed by Jesus was more than just one solar year. It was the age of the new covenant (Mt 26:28; 1 Cor 11:25). Release from all our sins, not only our real debt but also our real slavery, is to be had by entering into that covenantal relationship which is open to those with faith in Christ. This is the true redemption

THE PAYMENT FOR REDEMPTION

The Actual Payment. Since they were a valuable commodity, slaves were rarely just given away. The passages from First Corinthians 7 about redemption from slavery end with the phrase "You were bought with a price." A more idiomatic way of saying this would be "a big payment was made to get you." Christ made a payment for all Christians to buy them from their slavery. The nature of the payment is not described here, but it cannot be a money payment. Christ does not write out checks or pay cash for all new Christians.

Very similar statements are in the Book of Revelation. The heavenly hymn to Christ the Lamb says, "For thou wast slain, and by thy blood did buy [RSV: ransom] men for God" (Rv 5:9). Here the payment is more clearly indicated. The payment was Christ's blood, the blood shed when he died on the cross.

The same connection between our freedom and the death of Christ is presented in First Peter: "You know that you were redeemed [RSV: ransomed] from the futile ways inherited from your fathers, not with perishable things such as silver or gold, but with the precious blood of Christ, like that of a lamb without blemish or spot" (1 Pt 1:18-19). The image is much the same as the one in First Corinthians and Revelation. We were freed or redeemed by the payment of something more valuable than silver or gold—the blood of Christ. The same idea was probably present in the passage in Ephesians 1:7 which spoke of "redemption through [Christ's] blood."

The word "redemption" could be used more broadly than for a "buying back." In the Exodus, God acted through Moses to free his people from the control of Pharaoh and lead them into the wilderness where they could serve him. God was described as redeeming his people, yet he did not pay for them in any ordinary sense of the word. He did not give Pharaoh and the Egyptians a compensation for the loss of their Israelite slaves.

The return of the Jews from Babylonia was also described as a redemption. After having been given by God into captivity and exile because of their sins, the Jewish people were released in an extraordinary set of events. They came to understand by the prophets that they had been freed by God and described their rescue as God's redeeming them. In this case as well, no obvious purchase was made. The word "redemption," in other words, could be used for any time

God freed his people from misfortune, even though there was nothing done that could be described as making a payment.

Yet in some New Testament passages, as we have seen, Christ's death is explicitly understood as a kind of a payment. Moreover, in other New Testament passages that speak about Christ having redeemed us, it might be understood the same way, although the aspect of payment is not specifically expressed. This raises the question of what way Christ's death (or anyone's death for that matter) can be a payment to buy someone out of slavery.

The same question is raised by the nature of the slavery involved. If the slavery is sin, not even a normal payment for a slave will work. "Silver or gold" (1 Pt 1:18), some monetary or material compensation, might pay for our release from the obligation to work for an earthly debt. There are, however, no grounds to believe it can pay for our release from sin. The only payment that will accomplish the task is something which deals with the debt involved in sin—that debt which keeps us under the control of Satan, our slave master, and the sentence of hard labor. The death of Christ has to provide this "payment" to make our redemption possible.

Jesus himself described his approaching death as a kind of payment. He said, "... the Son of man also came not to be served but to serve, and give his life as a ransom for many" (Mk 10:45; Mt 20:28). That saying is restated in First Timothy 2:6 where it says Christ Jesus "gave himself as a ransom for all." By understanding the word "ransom" that is used in these passages, we can better understand the way Christ's death was a payment.

The word "ransom" used in the RSV has deficiencies as a translation. We only speak of ransoming captives or hostages, whereas the Greek word translated by "ransom" was used more broadly. It is used in the Greek translation of the Old Testament (the Septuagint) for a few Hebrew words that are used for compensations of various kinds. It could be used to speak about compensations for slaves or for property to be redeemed. It could also be used for compensations that involved penalties before the law.

For instance, if someone's ox gored a man or woman to death, and if the owner knew the ox often went after people, according to the law the owner was responsible for the death of another human being and had to be put to death himself. However, the owner had an alternative to dying: "If a ransom is laid on him, then he shall give for the redemption of his life, whatever is laid upon him" (Ex 21:30). In other words, he could make a compensatory payment and be redeemed from death—freed from the necessity of having to die for his wrongdoing or culpable negligence. We might say, "He could pay a fine instead."

The same word with the same meaning is found in Numbers 35:31-32. Speaking of a murderer who kills someone deliberately, rather than by irresponsible neglect as the owner of the ox, the passage says, "Moreover, you shall accept no ransom for the life of a murderer,... but he shall be put to death." In such cases, the law allowed no compensatory payment, no way of gaining redemption or liberation. The murderer had to die.

We see the same word used again in Proverbs 6:35 which discusses the case of a man who commits adultery. The proverb says about the wronged husband, "He will accept no ransom [RSV: compensation], nor be appeased when you multiply gifts." In other words, stay away from adultery because the wronged husband will not stop until he sees the legal penalty for adultery (death) inflicted upon you.

We can see from these passages that a "ransom" can be a compensation for a wrongdoing, and at times could even keep someone from being put to death. Moreover, since under the old covenant law people were usually in slavery because of wrongdoing or failure to repay debts, payment to redeem someone from slavery was in fact normally also the commutation of a penalty. What to us would have only a commercial or humanitarian purpose, in Scripture normally included the aspect of meeting the requirement due to some penalty or legal action.

The Greek word in Mark 10:45, then, was commonly used for the payment given when someone was subject to an unfortunate situation, usually penal, as a result of their own actions. They could be released from slavery or death upon the payment of the "ransom," the compensatory payment. These considerations provide likely background to the sayings in Mark 10:45 and First Timothy 2:6. With his own death imminent, Christ said that he came to give his life as a "ransom." This ransom would be given for the release "of many" or "of all"—that is, all those due to die for their sins, the whole human race, Gentiles as well as Jews.

In the next chapter, we will more fully consider this statement, especially the way Jesus understood the giving of his life to be a ransom for all. Here we simply want to notice that when he described his death, the word he used was the one often used in the Greek Old Testament for the compensatory payment that might allow release from the juridical consequences of wrongdoing. This could include not only slavery but even the penalty of death. Therefore, "ransom" can fittingly be used for a payment which makes possible redemption from the slavery of sin, a slavery which is penal in origin and leads to death. Christ was saying to his disciples that he would make such a compensatory payment or give such a "ransom" by dying. He would pay for our redemption by his own life, by his blood. It was for this, in fact, that he came.

A Limited Description. The teaching about the death of Christ as a payment for redemption is common in the New Testament. We find it in the synoptic Gospels, in Acts, in the Pauline writings, in First and Second Peter, and in Revelation. We find it not so much as a central theme developed at great length, but as a constant background understanding. It emerges in a variety of circumstances, usually when a New

Testament author is trying to emphasize how obligated we are to Christ for what he has done for us or how confident we should be because of how committed Christ is to us.

Christ's death as a payment for our redemption is a New Testament way of speaking about Christ's work of releasing us from the sinful state of the human race. It expresses the fact that Christ's death released us from something very bad, something that had an oppressive hold on us—namely, our sinful way of life and the bad consequences of our sinful actions. It also expresses the fact that we needed to be freed from an obligation, a penal obligation or debt, in order to be freed from the slavery of sin. Finally, it indicates that our redemption cost something. It cost the life of the Redeemer.

At the same time, this description has some significant limitations as an understanding of what Christ did. First of all, he did not pay his death to anyone in order to buy us. His death was not given to Satan, or at least the Scripture never says it was. Moreover, Christ's death was not exactly a payment or resource Satan could make use of for other purposes.

Nor do we pay God. Although he might be considered our "jailer" as the just ruler whom we have offended by our sins, the Scriptures never see our sin as slavery that God keeps us in, nor does it see him as a master who gives us sin as work to do. Our sinful actions bring no benefit to God the way a slave's work would to a master. Nor would God find the death of his beloved Son in any way a payment he might make good use of and be glad to receive. When we try to follow out what seem to be logical extensions of the idea of Christ's death as a payment, we draw a blank. We cannot ask the question about the identity of the recipient of the payment, as we can with normal purchase from slavery, and come up with a clear answer that is free of incongruities.

The description of Christ's death as a compensatory payment also contains some gaps when we try to approach it as a comprehensive understanding. Most especially, it gives us no help in seeing the connection between a death and a release from sin. Why can someone's death be a useful payment? Why might God want it or be willing to have it? Nor does it help much in questions like why the death of one human being could release a whole race from the death that was its lot because of the sin of Adam, or why Christ's death could pay for all sin when the old covenant law clearly states that no release payment is allowed for some crimes.

Understanding Christ's death as a payment for our redemption gives us some light, light we could not get as easily without it. But it does not give us a full understanding of why Christ's death was effective in redeeming the human race. The next chapter will provide more light by considering Christ's death as a punishment undergone for our sins.

THE BLESSING OF REDEMPTION

When the Lord delivered the people of Israel from their slavery in Egypt, they rejoiced in the great victory God had won. Immediately after the destruction of Pharaoh's army in the waters of the Red Sea, Moses and the people of Israel sang this song to the Lord:

> I will sing to the Lord, for he has triumphed gloriously;
>   the horse and his rider he has thrown into the sea.
> The Lord is my strength and my song,
>   and he has become my salvation;...
> Who is like thee, O Lord, among the gods?
>   Who is like thee, majestic in holiness, terrible in glorious
>   deeds, doing wonders?
> Thou didst stretch out thy right hand, the earth swallowed
>   them. Ex 15:1-2,11-12

Moses and the people of Israel sang a victory song to give thanks for God's work of deliverance. Then they sang about the completion of this work when they would be brought to the promised land, where God would live among them in his temple:

> Thou hast led in thy steadfast love the people whom thou
>   has redeemed,
>> thou hast guided them by thy strength to thy holy
>>   abode....
> Terror and dread [will] fall upon them [the inhabitants of
>   Canaan]; because of the greatness of thy arm, they are
>   as still as a stone,
> till thy people, O Lord, pass by,
>> till the people pass by whom thou hast purchased.
> Thou wilt bring them in, and plant them on thy own
>   mountain,
> the place, O Lord, which thou hast made for thy abode,
> the sanctuary, O Lord, which thy hands have established.
> The Lord will reign for ever and ever. Ex 15:13-18

God had won a great victory and the people of Israel knew it. Even more, the result of that victory was the great benefit of freedom from slavery. No longer would they have to spend their days in hard labor, benefitting only someone who hated them and wanted to see them die. No longer would they live in poverty, subsisting on meager rations of food that barely kept them alive. No longer would they belong to a cruel master who wanted only what was bitter to them. They had been redeemed, freed from all that. That redemption was a source of great joy.

The early Christians often taught about our redemption in terms of the Exodus as a type or foreshadowing of the true redemption in Christ. Egypt, "the house of bondage," stands for the world or unredeemed human society. The hard labor of the Israelites stands for the sins of the human race, a servitude that is evil not only because of its consequences but also because of the very nature of sin. Pharaoh stands for Satan, the ruler of this world and the one who seeks to keep the human race in sin and under his control. The promised land stands for heaven, the age to come in which we find a blessed life. It also stands for that good life we receive through Christ now, freed from the slavery of sin and the oppression of Satan. The Exodus shows us a picture of redemption, and therefore a picture of the redemption Christ offers from our sinful state.

Christ brings freedom (Gal 5:1). Many modern people seek freedom through democratic government. Others seek freedom through economic development, leading to a higher standard of living. Others seek it through the acquisition of knowledge or technical expertise. All hope to find some condition that will allow them to do what they want.

Christ brings a different message. The greatest slavery is to want the wrong things and to be in bondage to destructive desires. The greatest slavery is sin, because it makes our life futile. Only when we are free to live the life we were meant to live are we truly free. That great freedom was purchased for us by Christ the Redeemer.

FOUR

Punished
Instead of Us

IN THE GOSPEL ACCORDING TO JOHN, we find the Jewish high priest and the Sanhedrin, the governing council of the Jewish people, faced with a dilemma. Jesus had just raised Lazarus from the dead. Many of the people had come to believe that he was the Messiah. As a result, an insurrection seemed to be brewing—one in which the rulers saw only prospects for defeat at the hands of the Roman army. The vengeance of the Roman governors would be terrible. The conclusion was, "If we let him go on thus, everyone will believe in him, and the Romans will come and destroy both our holy place and our nation" (Jn 11:48).

Some action was clearly needed. The high priest for that year, Caiaphas, then spoke up: "You know nothing at all; you do not understand that it is expedient for you that one man should die for the people, and that the whole nation should not perish" (Jn 11:49-50). He pointed to the obvious remedy. If Jesus died, the whole nation would not have to be destroyed. One man for the nation would be a fair trade and an effective solution. At this point, the question of whether Jesus had done anything deserving death was not the issue.

Caiaphas seemed to be taking a limited view of the desirability of Christ's death, seeing it in terms of the political requirements of the situation. Yet there was more to Caiaphas' answer than he himself realized. As John goes on to comment, "He did not say this of his own accord, but being high priest that year he prophesied that Jesus should die for the nation, and not for the nation only, but to gather into one the children of God who are scattered abroad" (Jn 11:51-52).

God was speaking through Caiaphas, saying something that "the prophet" himself and those around him could not comprehend. His very words were capable of being understood in two quite different ways. In the plan of Caiaphas, Jesus could be substituted for the nation in the sense that his death would put an end to the threat of insurrection and satisfy the Romans. In the plan of God likewise, Jesus could likewise be substituted for the nation. So far God and Caiaphas agreed that if Christ died the nation would not have to.

However, Caiaphas' words understood as a prophecy and therefore as God's view did not concern the immediate political problem presented by the Romans. Rather, they referred to the more serious problem that threatened those who belonged to the nation because of their sin—especially the sin of rejecting God's messenger and therefore the one who sent the messenger. Eternal destruction threatened them. Compared to that, the worst the Roman army could do would be mild.

However, one person could die so that the nation would not have to. In fact, one person could die, God's only Son, and save not only the Jewish nation, but the Gentiles as well, including the oppressive Romans. Christ underwent the suffering and death that meant the whole human race could be spared the punishment of final destruction. As Augustine put it, "He loved us so much that, sinless himself, he suffered for us sinners the punishment we deserved for our sins" (*Sermo Guelferbytanus 3*). In other words, Christ underwent punishment instead of us.

This view is sometimes described by theologians as a "penal substitution." Christ's death substituted for ours, but not out of expediency the way Caiaphas planned. Rather, his death took care of the penalty for our sins. In this chapter, we will consider the teaching of the Scriptures on how Christ could substitute for other human beings so that they would not have to perish. Understanding Christ's death as a penal substitution or punishment he underwent instead of us will show us something more about the nature of the payment that made our redemption possible.

PENALTY AND SUBSTITUTION

In one respect, to say that Christ "underwent a punishment instead of us" is easy. Christ was clearly executed as a criminal. He was punished. Yet in another respect, it is a very difficult statement to make. What is the connection between the unjust punishment of Jesus of Nazareth and freedom for others from the necessity of undergoing a punishment they deserve?

We can pick out three important elements in saying that Christ underwent a punishment instead of us. First, his death was a substitution for us. It happened to him. It would have happened to us if it had not happened to him. It did not happen to us as a result of the fact that it did happen to him.

To say Christ's death was a substitution is similar to saying his death was a payment, but also different in an important way. If we give money for a slave, we would not normally refer to the money as a substitute for the slave. We would be more likely to use the word "compensation" or perhaps "equivalent." We would save the word "substitute" for a time when we could find someone to take the slave's place and be a slave instead of him. We are concerned here with a personal replacement.

Second, Christ's sufferings and death were penal. They involved a punishment or retribution for some sort of wrong. Not all suffering, of course, is due to a punishment. People who die of cancer or are accidentally wounded are having a misfortune befall them. They are not usually undergoing a punishment.

Even inflicted suffering can be disciplinary or remedial rather than penal. A mother may spank a child who runs across the street. She is mainly interested in training the child not to do that. Her purpose is disciplinary. But a judge who gives a convicted murderer the death penalty is not attempting to train him to act differently. The judge is giving him the appropriate penalty for his action. Therefore, the purpose is penal.

There is another way of saying that Christ's death was penal. Often Christian teachers will say that Christ made satisfaction for our sins. The word "satisfaction" was originally derived from Roman law. When people were punished for a crime, they were said to have satisfied the sentence of the law or satisfied justice. They "did enough" to meet the requirements of penal justice. When Christian teachers say Christ made satisfaction for our sins, then, they are saying that he did something which met the requirements of divine penal justice so we did not have to. Moreover, the commonly used theological term "vicarious satisfaction" is a close equivalent of "penal substitution," because the word "vicarious" means "done instead of or in the place of another."

The third element involved in saying that Christ underwent a punishment instead of us is the way desert or merit enter in. Christ did not himself deserve the suffering he underwent. He endured them for others. Christ's sufferings are penal, then, in the sense that they take care of a penalty due to others. Apart from that, it would be more appropriate to see Christ as a martyr, because martyrs undergo punishments for the sake of supposed crimes that are in fact virtues.

Paul, basing himself on Psalm 32, describes the connection between Christ's death and the penalty due to others by saying that Christ's death counted for or was reckoned to others (Rom 4:3-8). To use another word derived from Latin that has become common in theological discussions, Christ's death was "imputed" to others with the result that their own sins were no longer counted or reckoned or imputed against them (2 Cor 5:19). Perhaps the image was drawn from accounting. Christ's sufferings and death were of a certain value in regard to the debt of punishment. After he died, the result was credited to the account of others rather than to his own.

Behind the imputation to others of what Christ did is the decision of God to "account" Christ's sufferings and death in a certain way. God saw that Christ actually underwent a punishment, but that punishment was not required for Christ himself because he was sinless. He therefore agreed to take the satisfaction that came from undergoing a punishment and apply it to the account of others.

There are two different views of the way Christ underwent a punishment for us. Some Christian teachers have held that God the Father actually punished Christ instead of us and accepted that punishment as counting for ours. A more common view is that Christ was punished by Caiaphas and the other Jewish leaders along with Herod and the Roman army. Although God was not responsible for inflicting the punishment on Christ, he accepted it as adequate and a fitting satisfaction for human sin.

In this chapter we will consider the statement that Christ underwent a punishment instead of us with the understanding that God accepted what Christ did as counting for us. We will not attempt to discuss whether God could be said to have punished Christ. We will consider God the Father's role in Christ's death in the second part of the book.

THE SCRIPTURAL PRESENTATION

Isaiah 53. The first letter of Peter contains a passage exhorting Christian slaves to behave in a good way towards their masters, even those who do not treat them well. As an encouragement, it gives the example of Christ, who related well towards the Roman and Jewish authorities even though they treated him unjustly and put him to death. First Peter says:

> He committed no sin; no guile was found on his lips. When he was reviled, he did not revile in return; when he suffered, he did not threaten; but he trusted to him who judges justly. He himself bore our sins in his body on the tree, that we might die to sin and live to righteousness. By his wounds, you have been healed. For you were straying like sheep, but have now returned to the Shepherd and Guardian of your souls. 1 Pt 2:22-25

The point of this example is that Christ endured unjust treatment which was able to save human beings (including the Christian slaves who might be listening to the exhortation). Those slaves should in turn bear unjust treatment in a way that might allow their masters to be won without a word to Christ .

The example of Christ does not apply to the Christian slaves in every respect. They do not bear their master's sins in their bodies, since the phrase "to bear sins" is a Hebraic idiom that indicates Christ's death was a punishment for the sins of others. The example applies to slaves only insofar as they can imitate Christ's willingness to suffer unjustly and to trust God.

The exhortation to the Christian slaves is not our concern here. Rather, the passage is chiefly helpful to us because it applies several quotes from Isaiah 53 to the death of Christ. This is a very important Old Testament prophecy which speaks about a servant of God, one who undergoes punishment for wrongdoing yet is innocent. His punishment, however, frees others from the penalty due to their own sins. The key section for our purposes is found in Isaiah 53:4-12:

> Surely he has borne our griefs
>   and carried our sorrows;
> yet we esteemed him stricken,

smitten by God, and afflicted.
But he was wounded for our transgressions,
    he was bruised for our iniquities;
upon him was the chastisement that made us whole,
    and with his stripes we are healed.
All we like sheep have gone astray;
    we have turned everyone to his own way;
and the Lord has laid on him the iniquity of us all.

He was oppressed, and he was afflicted,
    yet he opened not his mouth;
like a lamb that is led to the slaughter,
    and like a sheep that before its shearers is dumb,
    so he opened not his mouth.
By oppression and judgment he was taken away;
    and as for his generation, who considered
that he was cut off out of the land of the living,
    stricken for the transgression of my people?
And they made his grave with the wicked
    and with a rich man in his death,
although he had done no violence,
    and there was no deceit in his mouth.

Yet it was the will of the Lord to bruise him;
    he has put him to grief;
when he makes himself an offering for sin,
    he shall see his offspring, he shall prolong his days;
the will of the Lord shall prosper in his hand;
    he shall see the fruit of the travail of his soul and be
        satisfied;
by his knowledge shall the righteous one, my servant,
    make many to be accounted righteous;
    and he shall bear their iniquities.
Therefore I will divide him a portion with the great,
    and he shall divide the spoil with the strong;
because he poured out his soul to death,
    and was numbered with the transgressors.

The passage from First Peter sees this prophecy as fulfilled in Christ. It uses phrases from the Greek translation of the prophecy to describe what happened to Christ: "He committed no sin; no guile was found on his lips"; "he bore our sins"; "by his wounds you have been healed"; "you were straying like sheep." It also alludes to Isaiah 53 by describing Christ as unwilling to revile or threaten. It clearly states that this righteous man who patiently endured mistreatment was the innocent one who bore our sins, the one punished (wounded) who brings us salvation (healing).

In the next chapter of First Peter the teaching is developed further: "For Christ also died for sins once for all, the righteous for the unrighteous, that he might bring us to God" (1 Pt 3:18). This addition tells us that Christ's death was a punishment unmerited by the one punished. Moreover, the punishment resulted in a benefit for those who were unrighteous and therefore did deserve to be punished. Instead of punishment, they received a restored relationship with God because their sins were taken care of. In the context of the quote from Isaiah, we can reasonably understand "the righteous for the unrighteous" as meaning the innocent one *substituting for* the guilty ones.

The prophecy in Isaiah 53 is the Scripture passage that speaks most clearly about an innocent servant of God dying instead of others and thereby freeing them from needing to undergo the penalty of their own guilt. As can be seen in First Peter, the early Christians used it to explain the significance of the death of Christ. The account of Philip and the Ethiopian eunuch in Acts 8:32-36 shows the same thing. There are many other New Testament references to it as well (ten literal quotations and thirty-two allusions by one count).

According to the Gospels, Christ was the one who first applied this passage to himself. One of the more significant references to Isaiah 53 is in the saying we have already discussed where Christ speaks about his role as a servant: "The Son of Man came not to be served but to serve and to give his life as a ransom for [the] many" (Mk 10:45). "Many" or, as some would translate it, "the many" is quite likely an allusion to Isaiah 53:11 and 12. These are the ones whose sins the Suffering Servant bears. "The many" in the original prophecy and in Jesus' understanding of it, probably refers to Gentiles as well as Jews (see Is 42:1, 4, 6 and 49:6 for some background).

The same phrase is found in the statement of Christ at the Last Supper: "This is my blood of the covenant, which is poured out for many for the forgiveness of sins" (Mt 26:28). If "many," and possibly also "poured out for," are allusions to Isaiah 53, then Christ is speaking of his upcoming death in terms of that prophecy here as well. Both New Testament passages, then, probably indicate that Christ saw his death as a fulfillment of Isaiah's prophecy, and as a punishment that he was undergoing that would be a remedy for the sins of many others. Moreover, by using this phrase from the prophecy, Christ is stressing that his death will be for Gentiles as well as Jews, that is, for the whole human race.

When we combine what we saw in the last chapter about the meaning of "ransom" as a compensatory penal payment with "[the] many" understood as an allusion to Isaiah 53, we have a very striking result. Christ seems to be saying that he has come as a servant. Even more, his service is to give his life for others. He came to provide a compensatory payment (a ransom) so that they will not have to undergo the penalty of death.

As we saw, in the case where a "ransom" could replace the death penalty, there was a limit set by the Old Testament law to what one could give a payment for. Intentional murder, for instance, required the life of the murderer. "Life for life" (Dt 19:21) or "blood for blood" (Gn 9:6) was required. Christ then seems to be saying that since the normal money payment will not do, he will give a different sort of ransom. He will give his own life in exchange for theirs, life for life, blood for blood. He will fulfill the prophecy in Isaiah 53 by "pouring out his life [RSV: soul] to death" (v. 12), so "making many to be accounted righteous" (v. 11).

In alluding to Isaiah 53, then, Christ is saying that he will take care of the sin problem and redeem the human race by substituting his life for the lives of the many who otherwise would be condemned to death. Why his life would be acceptable in their place is a further question. Here we simply need to see the important fact that Christ understood that the Servant of the Lord spoken about in Isaiah 53 could do such a thing, that he was that servant, and that he would therefore willingly undertake such a task.

Becoming a Curse. Another set of passages in the New Testament present Christ's death as a punishment for our sins. They speak of Christ bearing the curse of the law "on the tree." The fullest example is in Paul's letter to the Galatians where he treats the death of Christ in relation to the curse of the law:

> For all who rely on works of the law are under a curse; for it is written, "Cursed be every one who does not abide by all things written in the book of the law, and do them." Now it is evident that no man is justified before God by the law; for... "He who does them shall live by them." Christ purchased [RSV: redeemed] us from the curse of the law, having become a curse for us—for it is written, "Cursed be every one who hangs on a tree"—that in Christ Jesus the blessing of Abraham might come upon the Gentiles, that we might receive the promise of the Spirit through faith.
>
> **Gal 3:10-14**

This passage teaches about the death of Christ as his undergoing a punishment instead of us and connects that with his purchasing or redeeming us. To see its meaning, we need to consider some background. In Galatians Paul is arguing against the necessity for Gentile converts to Christianity to be circumcised and thereby become subject to the law of Moses.

His position rests on the fact that the blessing of the new life in the Spirit does not come through keeping the law. Rather, it comes only through belief in the gospel message and in the promises of God contained in the Old Testament and fulfilled by Christ. In the passage quoted above, Paul states one important reason why the law is inadequate to bring the new life: the law cannot bring life because it brings a "curse."

As discussed earlier, the word "curse," when God is the agent, describes God's action in punishing wrongdoing. Paul is referring to one of the curses of the covenant. They are God's promises to stand behind his covenant and back it up by punishing serious violations. This does not mean that God bears personal hostility toward those who violate the covenant. Rather, as the just ruler of his people, God will enforce the law contained in the covenant.

Paul quotes a verse from Deuteronomy from a list of specific curses for actions which are forbidden by the law of the old covenant. The curse Paul quotes is the last one, "Cursed be he who does not confirm the words of this law by doing them..." (Dt 27:26). This is a concluding summary curse which highlights the fact that God stands behind the law as a whole. Even more, it asserts that the law as a whole must be kept or it brings the judgment of God. Paul seems to refer to this curse to affirm that keeping the law is in part a way of avoiding final punishment. As long as we keep the law, we do not fall under the curse, and therefore we can stay alive.

The law itself, however, does not bring life. This is true partly because it does not provide the source of life, the Holy Spirit who brings the blessing promised to Abraham. More importantly for our purpose here, it is also true because the law does not provide an adequate means of forgiveness for the breaking of the law. It therefore does not provide a way to be righteous or justified before God for those who have not kept the law, and so does not give them a way to stay alive once they have committed wrongdoing.

What the law does not provide, Christ does. The key line for our purposes is "Christ purchased [RSV: redeemed] us

from the curse of the law, having become a curse for us..."
(Gal 3:13). "Having become a curse for us" could be re-
phrased more idiomatically by saying "having become accursed for us." Christ, in other words, took upon himself the
curse that should fall on law-breakers. This means that Christ
underwent the punishment stipulated by the curse in the
law. As a result, we do not have to be subject to the curse by
undergoing that punishment ourselves. In personally undergoing a punishment, Christ made the payment that redeemed us from the necessity of undergoing the penalty
proclaimed by the curse in the law.

In support of this view, Paul quotes another passage from
the law, "A hanged man is accursed by God" (Dt 21:23). This
does not refer to death by hanging but to the practice of
hanging up the bodies of criminals of the worst sort after
they had been executed to show that the criminals had
undergone the severest of penalties. The law required that
no one be left hanging overnight, because such a person was
under a curse and so the body would have been defiling to
the Lord.

In the time of Jesus, crucifixion was seen as "hanging on a
tree," and so involving the sort of curse referred to in Deuteronomy. In crucifixion the executed person was hung
upon a tree to put him to death. However, this procedure
was also appropriately understood to be an equivalent to the
earlier Israelite custom, because public crucifixion was
intended to make an example of those crucified as the worst
sort of criminals.

Many think that the Jewish leaders wanted Christ crucified
precisely because such a death would disprove his claims to
be the Messiah. They believed no true messiah would die
accursed. The Christians, however, and perhaps Christ himself, acknowledged that Christ's death involved undergoing a
curse. But they asserted that he underwent that curse "for
us," and therefore by the plan of God.

Paradoxically, the old covenant law itself which led to

condemnation also contained a provision that led to an escape from condemnation—by the surprising action of God. The death of Christ "on a tree" meant that he vicariously underwent the penalty established by the curse in the law for those who break the law. But he did that for us rather than for himself. As First Peter 2:24 puts it, "He himself bore *our* sins in his body on the tree, that *we* might die to sin and live to righteousness."

In using the phrase "on the tree," the passage in First Peter is taking the view of Christ's death found in Galatians 3:13. Acts 5:30 and Acts 10:39 also use that phrase to express the same truth. Moreover, Christ's resurrection is mentioned at the same time to stress the fact that his death as one accursed did not indicate that Christ himself was under God's displeasure. The resurrection was a sign of God's approval and vindication of the innocent sufferer who bore the sins of others.

Other New Testament Passages. The actual phrase "underwent a punishment instead of us" cannot be found in the New Testament (RSV). As we have seen, the equivalent phrase "bore our sins" from Isaiah 53:11 is used in First Peter 2:24 and Hebrews 9:28. "Christ... [became] a curse for us" (Gal 3:13) is also an equivalent. The Old Testament contains a more obvious equivalent in "upon him was the chastisement that made us whole" (Is 53:5). Many other passages, however, either allude to or presuppose the view that Christ underwent a punishment instead of us.

One large group are the ones that emphasize that Christ suffered when he died, and especially the ones that say it was the Messiah that suffered.[1] As we have seen, for the Jews of the first century, one of the most scandalous features of Christ's life was the way he died. A righteous man should not die in such a way since that would normally indicate that God saw him as guilty of serious sin. Most especially, the Messiah

---

1. For passages which stress that Christ suffered when he died, or which indicate that it was the Messiah who suffered, see pages 301-302.

should not die that way. He should show his identity by being victorious and successful. When early Christians stressed the sufferings of Christ, they were probably implicitly emphasizing the way his death was foreordained by God and prophesied as a way for the Messiah to provide liberation from the penalty due to our sins.

Probably for a similar reason, certain passages stress that Christ died although he was innocent (Acts 3:13-14; 1 Pt 3:18; 1 Cor 15:21). They are reminding the hearers that Christ's death did not occur because of what he deserved but was undergone for the sins of others. They are therefore also confessions of the Christian belief that this was the main task for which the Messiah came.

One fact, however, described at length in Scripture, is even more convincing than any list of references that Christ's death was a punishment he underwent for others. His death on the cross actually was a punishment. He was handed over by the highest Jewish authorities to be executed for blasphemy against God. He was condemned by the Roman governor as an insurrectionist, a rebel. He was killed by the most painful and humiliating death available at the time, reserved for the worst criminals. And yet he was innocent, condemned unjustly.

In the most literal sense, Christ's death was not a payment to bring people out of slavery since a death is not payment. Nor was it literally an old covenant sacrifice for sins, since he was not brought to the temple and ritually slaughtered and given over to God. Rather, Christ was literally condemned as a criminal and penally executed with great suffering.

If the facts of the crucifixion have any significance, if they impress upon us a truth about its meaning, then Jesus' death was a punishment he underwent so others did not have to. It is not accidental that a penal substitution view seems to come most naturally to Christians on days like Good Friday or at times of meditating on the crucifixion. They are then most readily led to the view as stated in the vesper hymn for the

Byzantine Feast of the Exaltation of the Cross, "The curse of a just condemnation is loosed by the unjust punishment inflicted on the one who was just."

A SPECIAL PENAL SUBSTITUTION

As we have seen, many New Testament passages seem to teach clearly that Christ underwent the punishment for our sins instead of us. If we think of such a statement in its normal meaning, however, we run into two main types of difficulties. The first bears on the nature of the punishment from which Christ's death frees us. The second bears upon the way Christ's suffering and death was a substitute for our punishment. These difficulties show us that Christ's death only relieves us from a certain type of punishment and that he could substitute for our sins only in a certain way.

A Heavenly Corporate Penalty. The first type of difficulty begins to appear when we consider the disproportion between Christ's one life and the number of lives he saved. When we read the sort of Christian devotional literature that instructs us to meditate on Christ's death on the cross as substituting for us personally and are encouraged to realize that he would have done it if we were the only sinners in the world, the difficulties are not so severe. The main awkwardness comes for those who are not yet conscious of having committed any serious sin which merits the death penalty. Most readers of devotional literature, however, are not bold enough to let themselves off so easily. Apart from that question, one human being for one human being seems reasonable.

Once we step out of the individual perspective, however, the substitution does not seem so reasonable. The death of one man does not seem to adequately compensate for all the individuals in the human race. Even if we took the number

144,000 in the Book of Revelation to be a literal number for all the redeemed, we would be inclined to say that whoever accepted the death penalty inflicted upon one man as a fair price for all the crimes committed by so many human beings was either giving a tremendous bargain or was a bad "businessman." As some have put it, as a compensation it was "underkill."

A further difficulty arises when we think of Christ's punishment as something needed by all human beings to be saved. The punishment he underwent was death in the harshest form. But only certain crimes required the death penalty. According to the old covenant law, these would include idolatry, sorcery, cursing God, cursing the ruler, cursing parents, working on the sabbath, disobeying parents, disobeying judges, intentional murder, adultery, incest, homosexuality, bestiality, some forms of fornication, kidnapping, and false witness leading to the death of the person unjustly accused. We can add to that some crimes for which God promises to execute people himself without the action of human judges: a set of ritual violations which dishonor God and serious violations of justice by judges who can escape from human punishment because no human authority is able to police them.

This is significant because Christians have traditionally taught that Christ's death was needed for the sins of all human beings or at least of the elect. He was a "ransom for all" (1 Tm 2:6). Yet it is not true that all human beings, much less the elect, are penally guilty of breaking an old covenant law that requires the death penalty. Even if we add all the capital crimes in the American penal code or the Chinese penal code that are not covered by old covenant law, many of the human beings in those countries would still not qualify for the death penalty. In terms of law, then, the death of Christ meets the need of a set of human beings but not of all. For many human beings, as a penal remedy it is "overkill."

These difficulties require a consideration of the nature of

the penalty that Christ's death frees us from. First of all, he did not substitute as a punishment for our sins in the sense of one human being dying to satisfy any earthly law, including the law of the old covenant, and so procuring a release for others. In fact, Christians have never understood Christ's death as an earthly penal substitution. Neither the New Testament nor traditional Christian understanding suggests that anyone should escape criminal penalties because of the death of Christ. In fact, judges in periods when whole nations considered themselves Christian never took the death of Christ as an acceptable plea to secure release for a murderer, nor did criminals ever make such a plea.

Perhaps still more significantly, if earthly death is the penalty from which we are freed, no one who has become a Christian seems to have been preserved from it. All Christians who were born more than one hundred and twenty years ago have died an earthly death. The earthly death of Christ has not yet substituted for the earthly personal death of others. Moreover, no amount of faith seems to hold the promise of letting Christians escape the necessity of dying.

Nor does undergoing an earthly penalty by itself handle a heavenly one. Criminals electrocuted for murder have done all that is necessary to satisfy the earthly penal requirements. They are now dead. But they may face an even more serious situation because of the way in which their earthly actions were not just earthly crimes but sin—a rebellion against the Creator and a violation of his law. In this context, the law of the old covenant is not of significance because it tells us about the earthly consequences of our sinful actions, but because it instructs us about the seriousness with which those actions are taken before the throne of God.

These considerations simply tell us that the punishment from which Christ freed us has to be seen in a different way. Although he died literally and historically upon earth, the significance of his death was not primarily earthly. Rather, its special significance comes because of the way it is received by

God. The death of Christ is an earthly event that releases us from eternal consequences, the kind not handled by undergoing earthly penalties.

The fact that Christ satisfied heavenly justice rather than earthly justice is not to deny that our sinful actions or sinful state have penal consequences within this world. Nor is it to deny that the release Christ procures for us makes possible a better earthly life in this world. It is most certainly not to deny that the result of his death leads to new spiritual life in this world. It is simply to say that the penal aspect of what Christ did cannot be understood primarily in terms of this life. Whatever consequences we enjoy in this life come to pass because Christ's death on the cross is accepted before the throne of God in heaven as making a difference for us.

Another set of difficulties raises the question of the nature of the sin his death takes care of. When we think of penal substitution, what comes to mind is an image used in much preaching and devotional literature. We stand before a court charged with a violation of a law, perhaps multiple violations. We hear a death sentence pronounced upon us and are about to be hauled off to the gallows, guillotine, or electric chair. We then hear Christ speak up and say, "Let that one go, I will go instead."

This image conveys the truth of Christ's substitution in a powerful way. It has, however, the unfortunate side effect of narrowing our view of the way Christ deals with the sin problem. It leads us to primarily see him as substituting for a serious violation of the law. Many people, however, do not fit in such a picture and so would be excluded from the benefits of Christ's death. Infants who die too early to sin seriously would be the clearest example.

This view of the sin taken care of by Christ's death is first of all inadequate because there is more to sin than major violations of the law. Much of what makes our lives futile or at least largely unsatisfactory from the point of view of the purpose for which we were made, are the smaller sins, imperfections, and general sinfulness that marks human life. They are not adequately heinous for a full-dress judicial condemnation. They are, nonetheless, a major part of the problem.

More significantly, Christ's death cannot just deal with the actual sins of individuals. It has to deal with the state of the race as a whole. He cannot free the human race from the penal consequences of sin without freeing it from its whole sinful state and condition. The sentence of death, "the curse of Adam," stands against the human race as a whole, which is in a bad relationship with its Creator. In addition, as a result of the state of the human race, individuals are born into a condition which means that even if they have not yet gotten to the point of deserving the death penalty by their actions, they are not good candidates for the blessed, eternal life in God's presence that the human race was created for.

Christ came to deal with all the penal consequences of human sin, not just the part due to actual serious violations of the moral law. Seeing Christ's death as a penal substitution can be misleading if it leads us to take the "penalty" in too limited a way. Christ was "the Lamb of God who takes away the sin of the world," that is, all the sin of the human race.

A Sacrificial Substitution. The second type of difficulty bears on the way Christ's suffering and death was a substitute for our punishment. We need to raise the question of what it means to say that Christ was punished. In answering such a question, we will see that we are speaking in a special way when we call his sufferings and death a punishment.

This difficulty is raised most acutely by the fact that killing the innocent instead of the guilty is a questionable procedure. The Old Testament law clearly admonishes judges: "Do not slay the innocent and righteous, for I will not acquit the wicked" (Ex 23:7). The role of the judge is described as "acquitting the innocent and condemning the guilty" (Dt 25:1). The law also says that "the fathers shall not be put to death for the children, nor shall the children be put to death for the fathers; every man shall be put to death for his own sin" (Dt 24:16). Such passages raise a question about undergoing punishment as a substitute for others—right in the area where it is supposed to be most helpful. A penal substitution is supposed to satisfy the requirements of the law, and yet it seems to violate those requirements at the same time.

A just penalty punishes the wrongdoer. Even where a compensatory payment or ransom is allowed, the law presumes that either the guilty person would make the compensatory payment, or that the guilty person would compensate someone else who did by working for him as a slave. The payment itself would be quite costly, depending on how large the damages were (Ex 21:23-24; Lv 24:18-20; Dt 19:21). Even so, the old covenant law did not allow individuals to take on a personal punishment like death as a way of making a compensation for someone else.

Christ could not have been legally put to death for a Jewish murderer and gotten that person released. Nor could he as a citizen of a modern nation volunteer to be electrocuted for someone condemned to death and have that person released. Even if he managed to get himself put to death, no judge would release a criminal on such a basis. The famous example of Maximilian Kolbe, the Polish priest who volunteered to die instead of another prisoner in a Nazi concentration camp, occurred in a *lawless* situation.

There is a further difficulty. When we ask what judge condemned Christ instead of others, we cannot give a convincing answer. No earthly judge put him to death as a penal substitute. Neither did Satan. Even if he could be said to have acted as a "spiritual" judge, Satan certainly had no intention of accepting Christ's death as a substitute for the human race. At most he was tricked into cooperating with the process by putting Christ to death, and only afterward discovering the consequences.

Nor did God the Father do so. Unlike Satan, he was a legitimate judge. God was, in fact, the just judge into whose hands Christ surrendered himself (1 Pt 2:24). However, the New Testament does not say that God acted as a judge to *condemn* his son. He is rather referred to as the judge who saw the innocence of the condemned one and vindicated him through the resurrection (see 1 Tm 3:16; Acts 13:28-37; Is 50:7-9).

We will consider the Father's role in his Son's death more fully later on. For our purposes here, it is enough to see that we cannot clearly identify a judge who had jurisdiction over Jesus and condemned him to death as a penal substitution. Consequently we cannot use such a view to give a comprehensive view of the redemption based on what Scripture tells us.

All of these considerations indicate that viewing Christ's death as a penal substitution for our sins is a limited way of understanding how his death was effective. Just as we saw that Christ's death viewed as a payment for release from slavery got us only so far, we find the same thing happening with a penal understanding of his death. At a certain point we need to move to a sacrificial understanding. It is not an accident that the passage which most clearly provides the penal substitutionary view, Isaiah 53, links the bearing of sins with the suffering servant making himself an offering for sin. This understanding is restated by Hebrews 9:28, which says, "Christ (was) offered once to bear the sins of many."

In the old covenant law, sacrifices can release human beings from the deserved consequences of sin. Sacrifices can be offered for human beings who have done wrong and make possible forgiveness of their sins. Sacrificial offering fills a gap in the penal substitution view by providing the basis for a "just imputation," which a penal condemnation cannot provide. In order to understand that more fully, we have to consider the atoning nature of sacrifice in the next chapter. Only when we see the way Christ's death was *at the same time* a release payment, a punishment undergone for others, and an atoning sacrifice, do we have a complete understanding of how his death could have the effect it did.

While penal substitution makes sense only in combination with other descriptions of Christ's death, understanding the death of Christ as a punishment undergone instead of others allows us to see some important truths nonetheless. First, it tells us that Christ dealt with the state of the human race as it is due to the penal consequences of sin. Seeing Christ's death as redemption from slavery could indicate that the slavery we were in was penal in origin, but it does not have to, because slavery can be due to other causes. When we add to it the understanding of penal substitution, we state the cause of the condition more clearly and also indicate that some satisfaction of penal justice is due.

Second, such an understanding tells us that Christ's painful, degrading sufferings were not an accidental feature of what happened, nor were they chosen just to provide a good example, much less to show his heroism. They were part of what Christ endured because he was freeing us from what might come our way as a result of sin. It may not have been strictly necessary for Christ to have been penally executed as a criminal in order to have adequately satisfied divine justice for a race and individuals condemned to die because of sin. On the other hand, such a death fulfills the job description admirably.

Finally, understanding the death of Christ as his undergoing the punishment for our sins also tells us something about the way his death could be a payment for our redemption. No payment of money or possessions would do, but only a "payment" which involved satisfying the penal requirements of justice. It would not have been enough for Christ to have found something of value other than himself. Because punishment is personal, it was only appropriate for Christ in his own person to do what needed to be done. A penal substitution description forcefully expresses to us the fact that Christ himself redeemed us by dealing with the penal requirements of justice—personally doing for us what we could not do for ourselves.

ANALOGICAL DESCRIPTIONS

We have considered in these last two chapters two descriptions of the death of Christ: he paid for our redemption and he underwent a punishment instead of us. Both of them indicate why Christ's death was effective in helping us. One states that it acted the way a payment does for the release of a slave. The other states that it acted the way undergoing a punishment does for satisfying penal justice.

We also saw that both of those descriptions were not simple literal descriptions. Christ's death was not a compensation that was useful to anyone, nor did any actual slave get released. Likewise, no one inflicted death on Christ as a substitute for others, nor did any criminal escape an earthly legal penalty as a result. At this point, we might want to say that payment for redemption and penal substitution are just metaphors or images. The Scripture uses them to speak about the death of Christ in order to vividly present it as something that helps us.

Such a response, however, would be misleading. Metaphors and images are, in the most proper sense of the words, figures of speech designed to adorn or enliven literary works. While not simply literal descriptions, these ways of seeing the death of Christ are more than figures of speech. They actually teach us important truths about the death of Christ; they do not just let us see it in a more striking way.

Alternatively, we might say that these descriptions are analogies or comparisons, but that too would be misleading. They are not just examples skillfully chosen to make a point a bit clearer or easier to grasp. Rather, they are ways the Scripture writers make their primary statements about the significance of the death of Christ.

Another feature of these descriptions also indicates how they function. As we considered Christ's death as a payment for redemption and as a penal substitution, we noticed something peculiar about each description. Each one told us something about the death of Christ that the other did not, but neither could be pushed too far without resulting in unanswerable or even meaningless questions or incongruous answers.

Speaking about Christ's death as a payment for our redemption is a way of saying that his death freed us from an oppressive condition from which we could not escape: our pattern of sinful behavior. It likewise is a way of saying that our release cost something: had Christ not died, we would not be freed. On the other hand, it fails to tell us why a death is a useful payment. It also runs into the question of to whom the payment was made, which only has answers that contain incongruities with other Christian truths.

Penal substitution is a way of saying that Christ's death happened in the way it did because it was dealing with the penalty for sin. Christ handled that penalty instead of us, so that we have escaped the deserved consequences of our state. Such a statement answers the question of how a death like Christ's could be a payment for sins. If slavery is penal, undergoing a fitting punishment should be a way of release from the necessity of being in that state. On the other hand, it fails to tell us how one person could in fact justly substitute for another. It also leaves the unanswerable question of which just judge condemned the innocent victim in order to release others.

There is a better way to see these two descriptions than as figures of speech or simple comparisons. An illustration from physical science might help. In discussing the nature of light, scientists have used two different models at the same time: a wave model and a particle model. In normal experience, either something is a wave, or a particle, or neither. Yet light is in some ways like a wave and in some ways like a particle.

Taken as limited models, they can be used in combination to describe the way light works. Each describes something about light that the other does not. Neither can give a complete description of light. Moreover, each has limitations that need to be respected. Pushed too far, each would lead us to see light in ways that are not congruous with our other knowledge or even meaningful. But each gives us formulas as well as a concrete image that allow us to deal with light, and, in an important sense, to understand its nature better.

The descriptions of Christ's death are not, however, scientific theories. Since the death of Christ is a unique event which could only happen once, there cannot be any theories of redemptive deaths that will allow us to predict how such deaths "behave." A better way of understanding payment for redemption and penal substitution is to see them as analogical descriptions. When we see a slave redeemed or freed on the payment of some money, and then say that the death of Christ was the payment for our redemption, we are using an analogical description.

"Analogical" here does not mean the description is a simple comparison. It is a technical term meaning that the description applies in some respects but not in others. For instance, when we speak about Christ's death as redemptive, we are saying that it truly frees human beings from an oppressive state they could not escape otherwise. Yet we are not saying that there was a transaction in which something of value was given to their owner or oppressor. The statement applies in a limited but true way.

The death of Christ has to be described in a special way. We normally understand human events by seeing them as a type of event that is familiar to us. If we go into a building and come out with shorter hair, we can say we got a haircut, and that statement makes something strange comprehensible. The death of Christ, however, is like no other event. No other human being ever died and freed the human race from its most serious predicament. No one else ever will. Therefore, when we want to describe how his death worked, we are forced to look around for another event more familiar to us. We say it is the same as that but not in all respects.

In human experience, what Christ did was most like

paying to free a slave, or like being punished instead of someone else, or like offering himself as a sacrifice. Christ's death
was "most like" such things, but not fully the same as any one
of them. Our normal life experience only helps us make
some sense of this unique, unprecedented, unrepeatable
event. They give us enough light to understand how to relate
to it well and receive salvation from the Redeemer—once we
believe the good news that he died for our sins.

FIVE

Given as a Sacrifice

I T IS A SPRING DAY IN A.D. 30 OR 33 IN JERUSALEM. The feast of Passover is just about to begin. A Judaean farmer joins thousands of other Jewish men in the court of the temple before the holy place itself, the earthly throne room of God. He brings and ritually slaughters a lamb. While psalms of praise and thanksgiving are sung by the choir of Levites, a priest takes the blood of the lamb in a basin and pours it out at the altar as a way of offering the lamb to the almighty Lord of the universe. The body of this lamb will become the center of the family meal at the feast which celebrates the Exodus, the redemption of the people of Israel from the bondage of Egypt.

At the very moment the Judaean farmer is offering his lamb, the Messiah dies on the cross and the veil of the temple is torn in two. His death fulfills the ceremony of the Passover lamb and begins the true redemption of the human race. Without realizing it, the Judaean farmer is standing in front of the earthly image of the throne room of God with its veil torn in two and the way inside now open—a sign of a new access to God's throne for all.

About five months later on the Day of Atonement, the same Judaean farmer, fasting, again visits the temple. The choir of Levites is again singing psalms, but more somberly. The farmer is without a lamb or any sacrifice of his own. What needs to be done can only be done by the high priest, the specially chosen representative of the nation as a whole. The sins of the whole nation are to be atoned for all at once. Compared to the offering of so many lambs at Passover, the high priest's offering of a bull for himself and two goats for the people seems quite little. But this is the offering appointed by God, the one that he will accept for the sins of all the people.

This, the most effective offering for sin, will be presented to God in a special way. The high priest is allowed this one time each year to take sacrificial blood and to sprinkle it on the holiest place on earth. Once he would sprinkle it on the mercy seat, the covering of the ark of the covenant which is the earthly footstool to the throne of God. Now, since the loss of the ark at the time of exile, he will sprinkle it where the ark once stood. Only the high priest, only the holiest place, only the blood of the appointed sacrifice is of any use.

But this year even this great ceremony has been fulfilled. The great high priest after the order of Melchizedek has come. He has entered into the holiest place in the universe, the heavenly throne room of God. He has brought his own blood as an offering for the sins not just of the Jewish nation, but of the whole human race.

Christ's death on the cross replaced these sacrifices of the old covenant. It did not cancel them or destroy their significance, but it replaced them by fulfilling them. What the ceremonies of the old covenant sought—the forgiveness of sins and restoration of relationship with God—was achieved by Christ's death and resurrection. Since the one sacrifice of Christ truly accomplished all that the many sacrifices of the old covenant sought and only partially reached, his sacrifice "fulfilled" those old covenant sacrifices. They in turn "foreshadowed" his.

In this chapter, we will consider the way Christ's death was a sacrifice as well as a payment and a punishment. Understanding its sacrificial nature will show us another aspect of Christ's death. At the same time it will allow us to see more about why his death was able to have the effect it did.

CHRIST'S DEATH AS A SACRIFICE

A Gift Offered to God. The death of Christ is spoken about as a sacrifice in the New Testament more often than as a payment or a punishment. In First Corinthians 5:7 we read, "... Christ, our paschal lamb, has been sacrificed." In Ephesians 5:2 we read, "Christ loved us and gave himself up for us, a fragrant offering and a sacrifice to God."

The clearest and most extended presentation of Christ's death as a sacrifice is in the Letter to the Hebrews, chapters 8-10. This truth is stated simply, "[Christ] appeared... at the end of the age to put away sin by the sacrifice of himself" (Heb 9:26). Or more fully:

> When Christ appeared as a high priest of the good things that have come... he entered once for all into the Holy Place, taking not the blood of goats and calves but his own blood, thus securing an eternal redemption. For if the sprinkling of defiled persons with the blood of goats and bulls and with the ashes of a heifer sanctifies for the purification of the flesh, how much more shall the blood of Christ who... offered himself without blemish to God, purify your conscience from dead works to serve the living God. **Heb 9:11-14**

Many other New Testament passages clearly refer to Christ's death as sacrificial. However, many more references are hidden by sacrificial terms that are now unfamiliar to us. "Blood," for instance, often means "sacrificial death," or more precisely, life taken away by ritual slaughter. When Ephesians 1:7 states, "In him we have redemption through his blood, the forgiveness of our sins [RSV:trespasses]," it is saying that we are freed from the bad consequences due to our sins because Christ's sacrificial death—his life offered in sacrifice—obtains forgiveness or release for us.[1]

To "give" or "give up" is another term that often has a

---

1. For further passages which use the word "blood" this way, see page 302.

sacrificial meaning. In stating in Mark 10:45 that he came to "give his life" as a ransom for many, Christ is probably saying that he came to offer his life as the atoning sacrifice that would be the release payment or ransom for many.[2] If that is the case, he is probably restating the phrase in the prophecy about the suffering servant in Isaiah 53: "When he makes himself an offering for sin" (Is 53:10).

There are still other terms that contain either direct or indirect sacrificial references. When all the sacrifical passages are put together, the sacrificial understanding of the death of Christ can be seen as the most pervasive of all.[3] As a result, even though Christ's death replaced the sacrifices of the old covenant, understanding the meaning of sacrifice as we find it in the Old Testament is crucial for understanding the death of Christ.

Modern Christians can tend to limit their understanding of sacrifice to death, usually painful death, and to view the purpose of sacrifice solely as an offering for sin. This is possibly because the main example of sacrifice with which modern Christians are familiar is Christ's. Looking at what we might call "secular sacrifices" in the Old Testament is a helpful way to gain a more complete understanding of sacrifice. This term refers to actions which are described with the same language as sacrifices, and therefore are similar to sacrifices, but are not directed to God and so are not really sacrifices.

The first "secular sacrifice" can be found where the messianic Psalm 72 describes a great king who will rule over the whole earth:

> May he have dominion from sea to sea,
>   and from the River to the ends of the earth!
> May his foes bow down before him,
>   and his enemies lick the dust!
> May the kings of Tarshish and of the isles
>   render him tribute,

---

2. For further passages which use the word "give" or "give up" this way, see page 302.
3. For further passages on Christ's death as a sacrifice, see page 302.

may the kings of Sheba and Seba bring gifts!
May all kings fall down before him,
   all nations serve him! Ps 72:8-11

This passage is talking about foreign kings who accept the rule of the great King of Israel. In order to acknowledge their new relationship of friendship and subjection they pay him homage by rendering tribute and bringing gifts. The gift expresses honor, just as it does for us at a graduation or retirement. In this case, the tribute and gifts are intended to give honor to the king of Israel as an overlord.

The Hebrew word for "tribute" in this psalm is used to describe certain kinds of offerings in the Old Testament, the kind described most fully in Leviticus 2. The word for "bring gifts" is likewise used with a sacrificial meaning for the offering of all sorts of sacrificial gifts. The use of the same terms for the sacrifices offered to God as were used for gifts to acknowledge the sovereignty of kings indicates that the two actions were seen in similar ways. A sacrifice, then, is the offering of some gift to God acknowledging him as our sovereign Lord and Creator.

The very way the sacrifice was performed in the old covenant expressed its meaning as an acknowledgment of God's sovereignty. The making of offerings occurred in the context of a special ceremony (2 Chr 29:25-30; see also Sir 50:5-21). Psalms and hymns were sung expressing the worship of God. Petitions were made to him as the ruler of the universe. The priest imparted a blessing on God's behalf at the conclusion of the offering. The people often shared a meal of celebration in which they partook of the sacrificial offerings that God ordained should be returned to them to celebrate his goodness. All of this was connected to the sacrificial action and expressed more fully the fact that the sacrifice was an interchange between the people and their God, one in which they offered gifts to pay him homage.

There were other ways of making an offering to God. Cloth, metal, or other items of value could be given for use in the worship services and were commonly stored in the temple treasury. What we call sacrifice, however, was the main way of making an offering. Sacrificial offerings were foods—animals or grain, wine and oil—the main items in an Israelite banquet. These gifts were presented to God by the worshiper and used for no other purpose than the sacrificial ceremony itself.

For sacrifices to be gift-giving to God, the gifts had to be "made over to" God. That meant they had to be taken out of the possession of the worshipers and put in God's possession. This explains certain puzzling features of sacrifice—like the slaughter of animals, the pouring out of the blood, and the burning of the animal bodies, the burning of cakes of grain, and the pouring out of wine. These were all symbolic ways of giving things to God and were likely understood to be expressive of providing a banquet for God. As a result these actions were also an acknowledgement of God's divinity, because giving gifts this way only made sense if the recipient were divine.

Such background gives us a perspective on the role of death in sacrifice. When the gift was an animal, death was integral to sacrifice as an essential step in making over the gift to God. This means, however, that it was not the death of the animal that was offered, but simply the animal itself.

In explaining why the blood of the animal is offered to God, the Book of Leviticus says, "For the life of the flesh is in the blood" (Lv 17:11). A little further on it says in a more unqualified way, "The life of every creature is the blood of it" (Lv 17:14). In other words, when the blood is given to God, the very life of the animal is being given to God. Or to say the same thing in even more explicitly sacrificial terms, the pouring out of the blood on the altar is a way of offering the life of the animal as a gift in sacrifice. The burning of the body on the altar had the same significance as a way of offering the animal as a gift to God.

All this tells us important truths about the death of Christ. First of all, Christ's death was directed to God and intended to affect God in some way. As Ephesians 5:2 says, "[He] gave himself [as a] sacrifice *to God.*" We can discuss the question of the recipient of the payment made by Christ's death. Or we can raise an issue about the judge who was satisfied by the punishment Christ underwent. But questions of that sort no longer remain once we speak of Christ's death as sacrificial.

God was the object of the sacrificial death of Christ. What happened in his redemptive work was directed to God in worship and homage and was intended to affect him. To see Christ's death as an expression of God's love for us or as a good example for us to imitate misses the central aspect of his death if it was a sacrifice. A sacrifice is directed to God, not to us.

This understanding of sacrifice also tells us something about why death was necessary for Christ. A death, after all, is not a very good gift—especially not the bloody death of a beloved Son. But the death of Christ on the cross was not an offering of death to God. It was the way Christ gave his life in sacrifice to God.

Christ "offered *himself* without blemish to God" (Heb 9:14). He "put away sin by the sacrifice of *himself*" (Heb 9:26). He "gave *himself* [as a] sacrifice to God" (Eph 5:2). Christ made himself an offering, a sacrifice to God, a gift that was truly pleasing to his Father. We were saved by Christ's blood because we were saved by his life made over to God through a killing which made it a true sacrificial offering.

An Atoning Sacrifice. Christ's sacrifice was not only an act of worship but also an act of atonement. Understanding the meaning of "atonement" or as it is sometimes translated, "propitiation" or "expiation," will shed more light on the nature of Christ's death as a sacrifice. To do this we can look at another "secular sacrifice."

In Genesis 32 we read about Jacob returning to the promised land after an absence of many years. He received a message that his brother Esau was coming to meet him accompanied by four hundred men. Jacob was distressed when he heard the news. He was afraid that Esau was angry with him for how he had treated him before he left and was coming to kill him.

In response Jacob took "from what he had with him a present for his brother Esau, two hundred she-goats and twenty he-goats, two hundred ewes and twenty rams, thirty milch camels and their colts, forty cows and ten bulls, twenty she-asses and ten he-asses." Then Genesis explains, "For he thought, 'I may appease him with the present that goes before me, and afterwards I shall see his face; perhaps he will accept me'" (Gn 32:20).

The Hebrew word translated "present" in the above passage is translated "tribute" in Psalm 72 and "offering" in many sacrificial passages. The word translated "appease" is translated "make atonement" when describing the results of sacrifices. The word translated "accept" is commonly used for God's reception of a worshiper who has offered a pleasing sacrifice.

Jacob gave Esau a gift to make Esau relate to him in a friendly way and accept him again as a brother. Using the English sacrificial terms, we could say that the passage shows us a valuable "offering" of animals given to "make atonement" and to make Jacob "acceptable" to his brother. Because Esau was a human being, the animals did not have to be killed to make them over to him as a gift. Because he was not Jacob's lord, the gift may not have expressed homage. But the transaction was much like a sacrifice.

The English word "atone" is now almost only used in Christian religious language. Its root meaning is to unite or reconcile. In the English Bible it is used to translate a Hebrew word commonly employed to describe what sacrifices did— they atoned. In the Genesis 32 passage the RSV uses the English word "appease" for the same Hebrew word that in sacrificial contexts is translated "atone." "Appease" brings out the relational aspect of atonement more clearly, although it has some unfortunate connotations because it is most often used to speak about what someone does to calm another person's irrational or arbitrary anger.

Jacob does not clearly seem to be repenting for his past treatment of his brother. But he did suspect anger on Esau's part, and he certainly wanted to change Esau's disposition to one of favor or friendliness. He intended his gift to move Esau to treat him well and take him back into a good relationship. A proverb uses the same word to express much the same endeavor: "A king's wrath is a messenger of death, and a wise man will appease it" (Prv 16:14). A gift offered as an atonement, then, is a gift offered to make someone favorable and to establish a friendly relationship.

The word "atone" is also used to describe the effect of a sin or guilt offering. If someone under the old covenant committed certain kinds of serious wrongdoing and wanted to repair the situation, part of what they needed to do was to offer a sacrifice. They needed to confess their sins, acknowledging their guilt as a sign of repentance (Num 5:7). They needed to make restitution where appropriate in order to make amends to the human beings harmed by their actions (Num 5:7). But they needed to complete their repair by bringing an offering to God which the priest would take and "make atonement for him... and he shall be forgiven" (Lv 4:35).

In a sin offering, the gift more clearly includes the element of making up for the wrongdoing or making amends. Nonetheless, it has the same effect as Jacob's gift, namely, disposing God to be favorable and take someone back into a good relationship. When concerned with sin, in other words, "atonement" implies doing what needs to be done to make amends or give satisfaction so that God will be favorable, however much it may be used more broadly in other contexts.

The Hebrew word for "atonement" and its normal Greek equivalents could be translated into Latin by two different words that have given rise to the English words "propitiation" and "expiation." These have two somewhat different meanings, but are related to one another when the concern is sin. We propitiate a person offended by a sin, and we expiate the sin itself. To propitiate God is to dispose him to be favorable and forgive. To expiate a sin is to take it away or blot it out, to make it no longer a matter of offense or a source of bad consequences. Since the same action can do both, "propitiation," "expiation," and "atonement" can be used somewhat interchangeably.

"Propitiation" and "expiation" catch different aspects of any action which truly repairs sin. In the biblical perspective, to expiate a sin involves propitiating God for it, since a sin is never really expiated except by God's action. Only when he forgives and releases someone from the penalties or bad consequences attached to a sin is the sin genuinely expiated. That result usually comes only as a response to something that propitiates God, that is, disposes him to forgive the sin and receive back the sinner in cases where the sin caused a breach of relationship.

This does not mean that God needs to be bribed to forgive, nor that he is reluctant to forgive. He is "forgiving" by nature (Ps 86:5). Nonetheless, God looks for certain actions which express the fact that the sin is being taken seriously and the offense against himself is being repented of. He looks for something, in other words, which is meant to propitiate. Sacrifices do that, so they are able to expiate sin.

Other words can also be used to describe the effect of an atoning sacrifice. "Purification" or, as it is often translated, "cleansing" is especially important. It is used to describe what happens to the sinner as a result of the process of atonement for sin. "Purification" and "atonement" are, in fact, often linked in the Old Testament, as when Leviticus 14:20 says, "Thus the priest shall make atonement for him, and he shall be clean." Purification words are used in the New Testament to describe what happens to sinners who come to Christ. They are made pure or clean.

The meaning of "purification" or "cleansing" is derived from old covenant ceremonial terminology. In the old covenant, people were required to be pure or clean before they could come into God's presence and worship him or relate to him directly in any other way. A variety of things might cause uncleanness or impurity, including leprosy, discharges, and sexual intercourse.

Many of the causes of uncleanness in the old covenant were not moral wrongdoing, but moral wrongdoing was also seen as a kind of uncleanness. For instance, Psalm 51 expresses a prayer of repentance by saying, "Wash me thoroughly from my iniquity, and cleanse me from my sin." In the new covenant, sins are, in fact, the only thing understood to cause impurity or defilement (Mt 15:10-11, 17-20; Ti 1:15). Therefore, for both covenants, when sin is taken away the person who has sinned is cleansed or purified.

Since the terminology of cleansing or purification is derived from old covenant ceremonies, the Old Testament understanding of the sacrificial system provides background for most of the passages where these words are used in the New Testament. Under the old covenant, uncleanness needed to be dealt with by certain rites of cleansing or purification. The cleansing was done by sprinkling with the blood of a sacrifice or by washing with water that often had been mingled with the blood of a sacrifice. These rites symbolically expressed the application of the effect of the atoning sacrifice to the state of the worshiper. Atonement, in other words, allowed the removal of offensive uncleanness in a person. When the uncleanness was sin, the cleansing resulted in guilt being taken away and sin forgiven (Is 6:7).

Whether the New Testament understands the cleansing of sin as only pardon or as something more as well has been much discussed. Some hold that it also involves the taking away of the source of sin by transforming the sinfulness of the human heart. It is clear, however, that the New Testament believed that sins needed to be taken care of by cleansing.

Moreover, when the New Testament speaks about the cleansing of sin—as well as about sprinkling with blood or washing in water—behind such words is probably the understanding that an atoning sacrifice is needed to give effectiveness to the cleansing. As the Letter to the Hebrews puts it, "Without the shedding of blood there is no forgiveness of sins" (Heb 9:22).

The New Testament does speak of Christ's death as atoning the way a sacrifice is: "...but if anyone does sin, we have an advocate with the Father, Jesus Christ the righteous; and he is the atonement [RSV: expiation] for our sins, and not for ours only but also for the sins of the whole world" (1 Jn 2:1-2). It likewise speaks of Christ as making atonement the way a priest would when offering sacrifice. Hebrews says that he became "a merciful and faithful high priest in the service of God, to make atonement [RSV: expiation] for the sins of the people" (Heb 2:17). Since, however, the Old Testament presents sacrifice in general as atoning, simply the understanding of Christ's death as a sacrifice indicates that it is atoning and brings purification or cleansing.

THE RESULTS OF THE SACRIFICE

The Purpose of Christ's Sacrifice. As a sacrifice, Christ's death was his offering of himself to God, giving his life as a gift that acknowledged God as God. Moreover, Christ's sacrifice was intended to be atoning, to dispose God to be favorable and to receive himself and those for whom he offered the sacrifice. Such an understanding highlights the way Christ's offering was directed to God to establish a better relationship with him for the human race. It does not, however, state very fully what his sacrifice was designed to accomplish in terms of a change in the situation of the race.

Sacrifices could be offered for a variety of purposes. Once again, the tendency of modern Christians is to think almost exclusively in terms of sacrifices as offerings that take away sin. Some sacrifices were offered primarily to take care of sin, but sacrifices were offered for other reasons as well: to thank God for his benefits; to pray for what people wanted; to consecrate priests, temples, and altars; to seal covenants; or simply to celebrate God's goodness and express one's relationship with him. The various purposes of the old covenant sacrifices can all cast light on what Christ's sacrifice accomplished, but the New Testament writings see certain ones as being especially significant.

To begin with, Christ's death was a covenant-sealing sacrifice like the one described in Exodus 24 that sealed the covenant on Sinai. This was expressed by the way Jesus interpreted his upcoming death to his disciples at the Last Supper. At the blessing of the cup, he said, "This is my blood of the covenant which is poured out for [the] many" (Mk 14:24).

We do not have to consider the relationship between the cup at the Last Supper and the death on the cross to understand that in speaking of the significance of the cup which was a memorial of his death, he was also speaking of the significance of his death. In speaking of the cup, he was specifically speaking about the pouring out of his blood on the cross. The words in Mark preserve a direct allusion to Exodus 24:8, where "the blood of the covenant" is used to describe the blood from the sacrifice which seals the covenant at Sinai. Christ's death on the cross, then, was a sacrifice which made possible the new covenant relationship with God.

Christ's death on the cross also fulfilled the sacrifice of the paschal lamb. First Corinthians 5:7 states this explicitly, but the context of Christ's death on the cross also makes it clear. He deliberately died at Passover to fulfill the old covenant ceremony. Just as the blood of the paschal lamb allowed the people of Israel to be spared from the destroying angel who executed judgment on the Egyptians, so the blood of the true Lamb of God allows those who believe in him to be spared from destruction and redeemed from the bondage of sin. As a result of his sacrifice, his followers are free to enter into the promised land of the new relationship with God.

Christ's death on the cross also fulfilled the old covenant sacrifices of consecration. Whenever anything was set aside to be used in the worship of God—including the priests, the temple, and the altar—it had to be consecrated. Part of the rite of consecration was the offering of a sacrifice that was atoning (Lv 8:34). That sacrifice made it possible for whatever was to be consecrated to be cleansed and purified and so made fit to come into God's presence. As a result of the rite of consecration, the consecrated person or thing was holy, God's in a special way. Consecration sacrifices were seen as background to Christ's death in Hebrews 9:21.

Finally, Christ's death on the cross fulfilled the sacrificial offering on the Day of Atonement, as the ninth and tenth chapters of Hebrews teach. On this day atonement was made for all the sins and uncleanness of the people of Israel that had not been previously atoned for by specific sacrifices. At the same time the temple with the altar—the place of God's presence—was purified from the defilement due to its contact with unclean people. In fulfilling the offerings on the Day of Atonement, Christ's sacrifice on the cross purified God's people from all of their sin and uncleanness so they could be the place of the presence of the holy God. Moreover, as Isaiah 53 indicates, Christ atoned not simply for Israelites but also for Gentiles, so that their hearts might be cleansed through faith in him and in what he did (Acts 15:9).

The New Testament also describes Christ's sacrifice as a sacrifice for sin (Heb 9:12). These could be offered on any occasion when Israelites recognized specific offenses that were transgressions of God's law and that needed specific acts of pardon on God's part (Lv 4). However, many ceremonies, including the Day of Atonement and rites of consecration, involved several sacrificial offerings, including sacrifices for sin. The sacrifice for the sealing of the covenant also involved an offering for sin according to the Letter to the Hebrews (Heb 9:18-22; 9:24). Atonement for sin, in other words, was an integral part of the great ceremonies of old covenant. It made possible the establishment, restoration, and strengthening of relationship with God.

Moreover, although it is not true to say that every sacrifice is a "sacrifice for sin" in the way described by Leviticus 4, in a broad sense all sacrifices could be said to deal with sin. Every sacrifice is atoning and propitiatory, especially bloody sacrifices (Lv 17:11). Therefore, they all probably have the aspect of dealing with whatever sin or unworthiness there may be on the part of the worshiper, even when not offered specifically to deal with sin. This is a common Christian understanding and seems to be implied in Hebrews 9:15-22. Such an understanding supports the truth that some atonement for sins is normally if not invariably an aspect of all relationship-building between sinful human beings and the all-holy Lord of all.

Christ himself understood his death to be a sacrifice for sin. When at the Last Supper he described his blood as "poured out for many for the forgiveness of sins" (Mt 26:28), he was explaining his coming crucifixion as a sacrifice for sins. As we have seen, he was probably referring to Isaiah 53 which predicted that the Servant of the Lord would "make himself an offering for sin" or an offering for guilt that would "make many to be accounted righteous" (Is 53:10-11). In so doing he would bear "the sin of the many" (Is 53:12)—that is, undergo a punishment for their sins by giving his life as a sin offering. By alluding to Israel 53, Christ also seemed to be asserting he would offer a sacrifice that was not just for a specific sinful action or offense of some individual. It was a corporate sacrifice for sin, a sacrifice for a body of people (Lv 4:13-21). It was, moreover, not just a sin offering for the people of Israel but for the whole human race.

THE SACRIFICIAL UNDERSTANDING

Christ's Sacrifice and Our Sin. To see Christ's sacrifice as an atoning sacrifice for sins gives us some helpful perspectives on his death. As we have seen, "sin" is the word for wrongdoing and failures in relationship to God, and sacrifices are directed to God. Describing Christ's death as "a sacrifice for our sin," therefore, removes the issue from the realm of merely earthly justice and brings it before the throne of God. His death deals with our sins, because it affects God. As a result, the gates of heaven are open to us, the gates of life and blessing in God's presence.

There is a further implication to speaking about Christ's death as a sacrifice for sin. When we considered Christ's death as a penal substitution for our sins, we saw that as a death that was an earthly penal substitution, it would only be a fitting equivalent of something that deserved the death penalty. Otherwise, it would be "overkill." The sacrificial system of the old covenant, however, gives us a different perspective on what Christ's death accomplishes in regard to sin.

First, the old covenant sacrificial system requires atonement to be made and purification to be undergone by people who do not need serious sins taken away. All priests when consecrated needed to have sacrifice offered for their sin, even though some of them were "righteous before God, walking in all the commandments and ordinances of the Lord blameless," as in the case of Zechariah (Lk 1:6). Likewise, the Day of Atonement is for all the sins of Israel. All the people need to undergo it each year whether criminals according to the law or not. In other words, sacrifices for sin, even bloody animal sacrifices, were offered for more offenses than just those that deserved the death penalty.

Behind these facts is the principle that the nearer a person gets to God, the more atonement and purification is needed. Priests to be consecrated needed more purification than ordinary Israelites—not because they had committed worse crimes, but because they were allowed to come closer to the earthly throne of God. Everyone, common Israelite and priest alike, needed purification when they wanted to draw near to the inner sanctuary of the temple, or when they wanted to offer sacrifice to worship God, or have any dealings with holy things. The purity that sufficed for daily life did not suffice for the closeness involved in temple worship. Isaiah needed to have his lips cleansed by fire from the altar—not because he spoke more sinfully than others, but because he was called to be a prophet of the holy word of God (Is 6:7).

The closer someone comes to the holy presence of God, the purer one needs to be and the more atonement one needs. The purpose of Christ's work is to bring his disciples to God (1 Pt 3:18), to bring them into his presence (2 Cor 4:14), to present them to God (Col 1:22). Since their access to God is to be closer and more direct, greater atonement and purification seems to be required for new covenant people than for old covenant people.

These considerations point to Christ's death as effective in dealing with sin in a broader way than just handling death penalties prescribed in the old covenant law. If Christ's sacrifice fulfilled the whole sacrificial system of the old covenant, it should have accomplished what they did in taking away sin and more. Therefore, Christ's sacrifice makes possible the purification of all sin and uncleanness, allowing those who believe in him to come near to God, to come into the true holy place, and to engage in holy worship without being displeasing to God.

This implies that Christ's death atones for less serious sins than those deserving the death penalty, including sins of thought known only to God and perhaps never expressed in external action. This also implies that Christ's death atones for human sinfulness, that inner corruption or weakness—the sinful inclination of our nature that we were born with as children of Adam. That sinfulness is displeasing to God, even though we may not have personally chosen it or affirmed it because it means that we are not yet fully what he wishes us to be and hence not a completely agreeable dwelling place for his holy presence.

Some Christians have viewed the fact that Christ died for even lesser sins or for sinfulness as an indication that in the full light of Christian revelation all sins and sinfulness must be recognized to be deserving of the death penalty. Some Christians simply hold that Christ's death takes care of whatever sinfulness we have—no matter what kind of penalty it deserves—since whatever is adequate for the greatest must take care of the lesser as well. Whichever view is taken, understanding the death of Christ as a sacrifice for sins allows us to see its role as a covering of all of our shortcomings.

Finally, understanding Christ's death as a sacrifice for sins throws some additional light on its pain and degradation. As we have already seen, this aspect of Christ's death can be explained by the penal nature of his death. He was paying a penalty, deserved by others and not by himself, but a penalty nonetheless. He died a death appropriate to someone undergoing such a penalty.

The sacrificial nature of his death provides the same sort of explanation. His sacrifice was not simply a sacrifice to honor God his Father but also to atone for the sins of the human race. The nature of the offering, therefore, affected the way in which he died, just as it affected the way the old covenant sin and guilt offerings were treated (see Lv 6:24-7:10). In such sacrifices, and only in such sacrifices, the bodies of the sacrificial victims were burned "outside of the camp" during the travels of the Israelites in the wilderness and outside the temple later. Such treatment expresses the victim's role in atonement for sin.

At the height of his triumph as the Messiah, Christ could have been suddenly and even painlessly assassinated like Julius Caesar or Abraham Lincoln. Such an ending would have been the fitting completion of a life fully and gloriously given to God in the service of the human race, soon to be vindicated by a resurrection. In such a scenario, Christ's death could still have been a sacrifice.

Instead, he died in disgrace and humiliation, outside the city, with his blood shed and his body destroyed in a dishonored way. This was a manner of death appropriate to a sin or guilt offering, especially to the offering for the Day of Atonement (Lv 6:27-28). As the Letter to the Hebrews says, "For the bodies of those animals whose blood is brought into the sanctuary by the high priest as a sacrifice for sin are burned outside the camp. So Jesus also suffered outside the gate in order to sanctify the people through his own blood. Therefore let us go forth to him outside the camp, bearing abuse for him" (Heb 13:11-13).

COMPLETING THE VIEW

The Third Description. Christ's death was effective in dealing with the sin problem of the human race, because it was not only a payment for our redemption and a punishment undergone instead of us but also a sacrifice offered for us. We are now in a position to see how these three descriptions of Christ's death can be put together to give us a more complete view of what Jesus was doing when he went to his death. The combination of these three understandings, in fact, presents a powerful picture of the importance of Christ's death for us.

To begin with, there is a central point of overlap: Christ is doing what human beings could not do for themselves with respect to their sins. His death made the condemnation of the human race unnecessary. To describe his death as an atoning sacrifice for sins, as a punishment he underwent instead of us, or as a payment that made our release possible is to state the same truth in three different ways. Each makes a contribution, because each sees Christ's work in a different perspective. But they all assert that Christ's death was able to free others from the bad consequences of their sin, and in that respect, they reinforce one another.

Second, these descriptions of Christ's death complete one another. To understand his death as a payment for redemption leaves the question of why a death could be a payment. Adding that Christ's death was a penal substitution provides the explanation that what held human beings in slavery was the fact that they owed a "debt of punishment" and that his death was a penalty Christ underwent to handle that debt. That response, however, leaves the question of how one person's death can count for the penalty another person deserves. Adding that Christ's death was a sacrifice for our sins provides the explanation that the death of Christ was accepted by God as a sacrifice for sins, and so was able to free others.

Third, the description of Jesus' death as a sacrifice removes the chief difficulty we noticed in the other two descriptions—an uncertainty about the "other end" of the action. We saw that there were certain incongruities in seeing God as the "other end" in a payment or penal substitution view. The death of his Son could not be a useful payment to him. Likewise, if he condemned his innocent Son, he would be an unjust judge.

We also saw similar incongruities in seeing Satan as the "other end." Satan does not justly own or reign over the human race. Consequently, if the human race is in Satan's power, it would seem more appropriate for the all-powerful God simply to defeat Satan and liberate those unjustly held in captivity—rather than allow his Son to pay off Satan or to satisfy Satan's blood-lust by dying.

Seeing the death of Jesus as a sacrifice for sins provides a more satisfactory view of the "other end." Jesus laid down his life as a sacrifice for sin. He did not, of course, kill himself. That would have been suicide, not sacrifice. Roman soldiers and Jewish officials—sinners on whose behalf the sacrificial action was being offered—killed the sacrificial victim. But Christ allowed himself to be taken and put to death by those for whom he died. In so doing, he provided himself as a sacrifice that would be acceptable to God for the sins of the human race. God is at the "other end," not as someone bought off or as someone who condemns his Son, but as the recipient of a freely-given offering by his Son.

Of the three descriptions, the sacrificial understanding of the death of Christ is probably the most important. As we have already seen, this is the most common way of seeing Christ's death in the New Testament. More significantly, it gives us the best overall understanding of what happened when Christ died, because it expresses most clearly the "heavenly" perspective of what Christ did. Redemption and punishment are ways of relating that can occur between human beings without reference to God. One can buy a slave from another. A human judge can punish a criminal. But people who do not believe in some god do not offer sacrifices. They may perform magic rites hoping to influence unknown forces, but giving gifts to express homage presupposes belief in a divine being. Sacrifice makes no sense apart from God.

To see Christ's death as a sacrifice, then, is to see it as an action that concerns God himself, his rightful claims as our Lord, his right to be satisfied that defects in our conduct are handled well, his right to be honored and respected. Christ's death offered God an acceptable sacrifice to make amends for human misdeeds which were offensive or displeasing to him. The sacrificial perspective therefore provides the way to focus our understanding of his death on what is most important to its meaning—his offering of his life to God for the sins of the human race.

Even though seeing Christ's death as a sacrifice provides the best overall understanding, the other two develop it in helpful ways. To say that Christ underwent the punishment for our sins makes unmistakably clear a central aspect of why he did what he did. Christ died because sin needed to be repaired. Amends needed to be made. The justice of God needed to be satisfied. In one respect where the sacrificial view is most helpful—in giving us a broader view of the way Christ's death deals with sin—it is potentially misleading. The way it points to our cleansing from all sin and sinfulness, might allow us to miss the requirement of penal justice that Christ satisfied by his execution. That difficulty is avoided by supplementing the sacrificial understanding with the penal understanding, as Scripture does.

Paradoxically, the description of Christ's death as undergoing a punishment for us highlights the personal nature of what he did. He did not find some money and make payment to free us. He did not find a gift and give that. He himself died, so we did not have to. He himself underwent a punishment so we were freed from the need to do so. The Good Shepherd laid down his life for his sheep.

To say that Christ paid for our redemption likewise adds a helpful perspective to the sacrificial understanding of his death. It adds the perspective of a deliverance or liberation from something that not only claims us by right but also has a hold on us. It was a work of liberation from the oppression caused by sin and its consequences. This understanding orients us more naturally to the personal tranformation brought by his death. Christ's redemptive work changes us so that we can live without sin, and frees us from the power of death and Satan so that we can live for God.

In addition, the redemptive understanding also highlights the way Christ's death dealt with the state of the whole human race. The penal understanding focuses us more readily on particular sins and their forgiveness. By and large, the sacrificial understanding does the same, especially when we focus on the individual sacrifices for sin. Only when we look at the Passover or the covenant-sealing ceremonies do we begin to see a clear corporate perspective. Significantly, these are sacrifices which have their origin in the Exodus whose meaning is closely connected to redemption.

It is, however, especially the view of Christ's death as a redemptive payment that lets us clearly focus on the human need to be delivered from a bad or deprived state. The redemptive understanding leads us to see Christ's work in what some have described as a more "dramatic" way than the other two. It helps us to focus on the results of what Christ did for the state of the human race, and thereby makes the description of the Passover and Exodus a natural way to see the crucifixion and resurrection as a whole.

When put together, these three scriptural descriptions enable us to see what it was about the death of Christ that made it effective in helping us. If his death was an atoning sacrifice that paid for our sins by his undergoing a punishment so that we did not have to, it was a death that counted for us. This is what Christ thought he was doing, the way he understood himself to have come to serve (Mk 10:45).

The True Sacrifice. There is one further way in which the sacrificial understanding is the most important one. As we have seen, each of these descriptions is a way of saying that Christ's death was like other more common events. It is like buying people out of slavery, like being punished as a criminal, like being offered as a sacrifice. Yet it was even more than "like" these things. His death truly bought us out of a slavery, truly saved us from punishment, and truly atoned for our sin. It was all those things, although not in the ordinary way. Nonetheless, what happened on the cross was more fully a sacrificial transaction than a commercial or courtroom transaction.

To be sure, Christ's death was not a sacrifice according to the Old Testament ritual. The Son of God was not an animal brought to the temple in Jerusalem and there killed with his blood poured out on the altar. Yet in the Christian view, the Old Testament ceremonies were less truly sacrifices than Christ's death. They existed to foreshadow what was to come (Col 2:17; Heb 10:1). The blood of bulls and goats and the ashes of a heifer do not actually deal with sin. God only agreed to accept them for a period of time in consideration of the obedience of the worshipers who offered them according to the law (Heb 9:13; 10:4). Such ceremonies were, however, instituted by God not only to provide people with a way to find forgiveness under the old covenant order but also to teach them about sacrifice. They were types or preliminary sketches which would enable them to understand what was to come and accept it when it arrived.

Christ was the substance, the reality (Col 2:17; Heb 10:1). Christ's death on the cross was the true sacrifice for sins, the offering for human sin that alone was truly acceptable to God. Despite what we might be inclined to think, Christ's sacrifice was not metaphorical and the old covenant animal sacrifices literal. Rather, the old covenant animal sacrifices were only types and shadows. Christ's sacrifice was literally a sacrifice because it was more truly an offering that God would receive for the cleansing of the human race from sin.

When John the Baptist saw Christ, he spoke as the greatest representative of the old covenant people (Mt 11:11). Look, there is the true Lamb which is provided to take away the sin of the world (Jn 1:29). That one will be the sacrificial offering which is truly an effective sacrificial offering for human sin.

Part Three

The Accomplishment of the Redemption

Introduction to Part Three

IN THE PREVIOUS PART OF THIS BOOK, we looked at the death of the Redeemer. We saw that Christ's sufferings and death were necessary in order for him to redeem us from the predicament caused by our sin. If Jesus had not given his life on the cross, we would not have been redeemed.

We also looked at three descriptions that the New Testament uses to clarify how his suffering and death could be effective in redeeming us. To put them together in one statement: by dying the way he did, Christ offered a sacrifice which God accepted as a compensatory payment so that we would not have to suffer the penal consequences of our sins and the sins of the human race. Or to put it differently, we might say that Christ's sacrifice of himself to God paid the debt for our sins so that we would not have to be punished for them.

Such a statement brings us part of the way to understanding what Christ did as the Redeemer. But for most people, now and in the ancient world, it still leaves the main questions unanswered. Why was the death of one human being an acceptable sacrifice that could free us from the necessity of condemnation? Why did it meet the requirements of justice? Why did it count for others? Why was God willing to receive such a payment?

We could perhaps reply: that is all there is to be said. It is simply a fact that Christ's death was an atoning sacrifice, a compensatory payment, and a penal substitution. We simply need to accept the fact as found in God's Word, believe it, and trust that God's wisdom is true wisdom. In the final analysis, we may still be brought to such a point. Nonetheless, there is more to be said, more that Scripture has to say. But to say more, we have to change our perspective.

Up to this point, we have looked primarily at the death of Christ in itself. While we will still focus on his death, we also will begin to look at the broader picture. It is not adequate to say Christ's death redeems us. His death does not make full sense apart from his resurrection and ascension. His dying on the cross is only one part of what Christ did on earth to save us. The crucifixion may be the most puzzling part to us and so require more thought, but it is not a separable part. It must be seen as a component of all that Christ came to do.

Even more importantly, it is not exactly Christ's actions that redeem us. Christ himself redeems us. His sufferings, death, and resurrection, indeed all of his life and all of his actions, are only significant because they are Christ's. We are redeemed by a person who stood in a special relationship to God, whose entire redemptive work was concerned with God.

This relational aspect of Christ's work is the key to further understanding. Words like justice, acceptability, sacrifice, atonement, mediation, and love are words that concern relationships—especially the relationship between God and the human race. In this case, they concern the relationship of the Redeemer who mediates between God and the human race. Christ is able to save or redeem us because of how he relates to God on our behalf, how he relates to us on God's behalf, how he and God are one, and how he and we are one.

This third part of the book, then, we will focus on what has been called the work of Christ as mediator. We will not, therefore, focus on how Christ imparts the benefits of his work to us. That will be reserved, as much as possible, to the fourth part, when we will consider the way he transforms human beings in redeeming them.

The third part of this book, then, considers the sufferings and death of Christ as part of the Redeemer's work of redemption. In it we will look at the process as an interaction between God, his only Son, and the human race. In doing so, we will consider three "relational" reasons why the death of the Redeemer could be effective for us:

1. He was the New Adam, the great High Priest, and the Son of God;
2. He was obedient to death;
3. He humbled himself.

Each of these reasons is a key to an aspect of why Christ's death as a sacrifice for sins, compensatory payment, and penal substitution was accepted by God for the sins of the human race.

Because Christ was the New Adam, the great High Priest, and the Son of God, he was able to be the mediator between the human race and God. Because Christ died obediently, he was able to give his life as an offering to God, acceptable for the sins of the human race. Because Christ humbled himself, he was able to undergo the humiliation of suffering death in faithfulness to God and be exalted in victory and life and so he was able to overcome sin, Satan, and death. In each of the next three chapters, we will consider one of these three statements about Christ's death.

SIX

The Redeemer
Who Died

T HE MAIN SECTION OF THE BOOK OF REVELATION begins with a vision. John sees an open door in heaven and is summoned by a heavenly voice to come and see "what must take place after this" (Rv 4:1). No sooner had the voice spoken than he found himself in heaven. God was seated on his throne, presiding over his court. God, in other words, appeared before John as the Ruler of the universe, the King of Kings, and the Lord of Lords. He was in the process of determining what would happen to human history.

In God's right hand John sees a scroll, which contains the divine decrees for the future. Once the scroll would be opened, his purpose would be achieved, evil would be destroyed, and the great and blessed consummation would arrive. John's vision, however, comes at a dramatic and somewhat distressing moment. The time is at hand for the concluding act to begin, but something is missing. The angel calls out the great summons: "Who is worthy to open the scroll and open its seals? Let him stand forth and be the blessed instrument of the consummation." But no one in heaven or on earth or under the earth comes forward as worthy to open the scroll.

John begins to weep. He fears that human history will not

achieve the purpose for which God created it, that the present evils will continue. Then one of the rulers in heaven speaks to John. "Weep not," he says. Someone has just conquered, the one who was prophesied as the Lion of the tribe of Judah (Gn 49:9-10) and as the Root or Branch of David (Is 11:1, 10)—the messianic King of Israel. Because he has conquered, he can open the scroll.

As it turns out, John is present when the one who is worthy arrives in heaven: he who died on the cross, was raised from the dead, and was ready to receive "dominion and glory and kingdom" (Dn 7:14) from the eternal Lord of the universe, the Lord God Almighty.

The one who stands forth is an extraordinary personage, a Lion who is a Lamb. This is symbolic language that shows the paradox of a man of great and regal power, a King and High Priest, standing before the throne of God—yet appearing at the same time as a sacrificial victim. Moreover, although he is a human figure, John can see in him divine power and divine omniscience as expressed in the symbols of the seven horns and seven eyes.

Only one was found worthy, our Lord Jesus Christ. He was the one who could open the scroll. He is the one who can bring human history to its decreed consummation, who can establish the kingdom of God, and who can bring to earth the heavenly Jerusalem, the city of God, filled with God's glory and blessing (Rv 21-22).

Why was Christ worthy? He was worthy because of what he did, shedding his blood and paying the price of redemption. But he was also worthy because of who he was. He was not just an ordinary man. Christ was worthy because he was special.

I was once employed in a shipping room. Various attempts had been made to improve efficiency—to no avail. One day the president of the company unexpectedly appeared. From then on the shipping room was different.

Another time, I was in New York City seeing a friend off on an ocean liner to Europe. The area around the dock was crowded, with no parking spaces anywhere nearby, except within a cordoned-off area. My friend's uncle, who happened to be a priest, was driving. An Irish policeman noticed our efforts to find a place, caught sight of my friend's uncle, lifted the chain, and waved us to an empty space while nodding respectfully to the priest.

I recently read an article describing a well-known television talk show. The article explained how the person being interviewed was asserting the evils of abortion. Normally, no one would have been allowed onto that particular program to make such remarks. The guest on the show, however, was Mother Teresa. Her charitable work in Calcutta gave her an access and moral authority that opened up even that show to her.

"It all depends on who you are." The saying is true in many ways, some good, some bad, but the principle involved is an important one for our redemption. Not just anyone could be the Redeemer. It would have done no good for the Jewish high priest or the Roman emperor to have noticed that the human race needed redemption and to have asked for volunteers. No one else in the land of Israel or in the Roman Empire—indeed no one else in all of human history—could have done what Jesus did. Only the one to whom God had given a special position could be the Redeemer.

John's vision in Revelation 5 shows us who the Redeemer was and had to be. He was the prophesied King, the one who was from the royal dynasty of Israel but who was to rule all the nations of the earth as their rightful Lord. He was also the Priest who was himself a sacrifice, able to make the offering that could purchase human beings for God. He was human, but had divine power and omniscience and could be worshiped as the Son of God (Rv 5:13). Only such a person could be the Redeemer.

In this chapter we will consider who the Redeemer was and why that made a difference. We will look at Christ as the Second Adam, the new head of the human race, born of the line of David. We will look at him as the great High Priest after the order of Melchizedek. And we will look at him as the Son of God. Each will give us a different view of why Christ's sufferings and death could have the impact on human history that they did.

THE NEW ADAM

Christ and Adam. The question before us is: who must someone be in order to die for the sins of others and have that death make any difference? Christ's position as the New Adam gives us a first answer. He held a special position in the human race and that allowed his death to have an effect that no one else's could have.

Paul makes several references to Christ's relationship to Adam. The most extended presentation is found in Romans 5, where Adam is described as "a type of the one who was to come" (v. 14), a type of Christ. Paul says of the two of them,

> If, because of one man's trespass, death reigned through one man, much more will those who receive the abundance of grace... reign in life through the one man Jesus Christ.... Then as one man's trespass led to condemnation for all men, so one man's act of righteousness leads to acquittal and life for all men. For as by one man's disobedience many were made sinners, so by one man's obedience, many will be made righteous. **Rom 5:17-19**

The same connection is made in First Corinthians 15: "As by a man came death, by a man has come also the resurrection of the dead. For as in Adam all die, so also in Christ shall all be made alive" (1 Cor 15:21-22). In the same chapter, Christ is called "the last Adam" (v. 45), in contrast to the first Adam.

To see Adam as a type or foreshadowing of Christ indicates an important correspondence between the two in God's plan for human history. In certain respects, the position Adam held and Christ holds are the same. Adam prefigures or foreshadows Christ as the head of the human race, the source of its life.

By calling Christ "the last" Adam, Paul probably means that Christ is the Adam for the end of the age, when he brings into existence a new human race as the fulfillment of God's plan. A more common title among Christians is "New Adam," indicating that Christ brings that newness of spiritual life which is the mark of the new covenant (Rom 7:6). Either way, Christ is a new beginning, the first father or personal source of a new humanity that fulfills the purpose for which God originally created the human race.

Adam is a type of Christ, but in a somewhat different way than someone like David. Christ fulfills David's role of king of Israel by ruling in a "fuller," that is, a more spiritually effective way. Although he fulfills the same role as Adam, in certain respects he reversed what Adam did. Both Adam and Christ were appointed to establish the human race. Adam was appointed to begin it, Christ to renew it. Adam, however, brought condemnation; Christ brought acquittal or justification. Adam brought death through his fall. Christ brought true and unending life through his rising.

At the same time, Christ did not totally reverse what Adam did. He became a son of Adam and took on the humanity Adam began. He reversed the fall of Adam not by annihilating human nature and transforming it into something completely different—but by restoring human nature and bringing it to a new level of life.

A Corporate Effect. The position of the first Adam reveals some important truths about that of the New Adam. The texts comparing the two indicate that the chief reason to see Christ as the New Adam lies in the way Christ passes on the results of his actions and his own life to his spiritual descendants. Just as by eating the forbidden fruit, Adam performed an action that changed the human race, so by giving himself on the cross, Christ performed an action that also changed the race. Just as Adam's action effected the way all his descendants lived because as their father he passed on his life to them, so Christ's action effected all his spiritual descendants, because he too passed on his life.

Behind the way Adam's and Christ's actions could have the effect they did was what could be called the family principle. The family principle explains why the action of ancestors can have moral effects on their descendant. The modern mentality makes it more difficult for us to recognize the family principle than it seems to have been for earlier people, including the recipients of Paul's letters. Our individualistic orientation often leads us to overlook corporate effects, especially coporate moral effects.

According to the family principle, parents in general and especially fathers have a moral effect on their offspring. The fate of children is to some degree determined by what happens to their parents. In traditional societies this has been especially true of the fathers.

For instance, if a father is a criminal, his children and grandchildren share the disgrace and bad consequences of his actions. They might lose some of their inheritance because the father is fined or cannot work while he is in prison. As the offspring of a man who was disgraced or dishonorable, they might lose access to certain positions of responsibility. On the other hand, children prosper if their father prospers. If he is a hero, they are honored. If he receives a reward, their inheritance is increased. A son or a daughter might even be rewarded because of the merit of a dead father who was a war hero.

Because they are part of a corporate entity, family members gain or lose by what happens to the older generation. They are, de facto, bound together, and thus effected by what happens to their fathers somewhat regardless of their own merit. Their personal merit may improve their situation or ward off some of the bad effects of a problematic father. Their lack of merit may also have the reverse effect when they have a good father. But children are not likely to be unchanged by either their father or mother. Even more, their very character, the way they live their lives, the merit they themselves turn out to have, is directly effected by their father. They live with him, are raised by him, and thus turn out to be like him. It is rare to come across a son or a daughter in whom one cannot see to some degree a reflection of the father.

We tend to resist the basic reality expressed in the family principle. Most people now want to be treated "on their own merits." To some extent, such a reaction stems from one of the negative features of modern society, the individualism that makes people want to cut loose from their families and other corporate groupings and be treated as individuals on their own. This individualism is a reflection of what has been called the dissolution of natural community.

On the other hand, the reaction against the family principle also stems from something good, namely the influence of Judaism and Christianity which does seek to limit its effects. The Old Testament teaches, "The son shall not suffer for the iniquity of the father, nor the father suffer for the iniquity of the son." The deeds of each shall be upon themselves (Ez 18:20). Christianity is a religion of new beginnings, where people can turn away from "the futile ways inherited from your fathers" (1 Pt 1:18). It is a religion of new births.

Nonetheless, Christianity does not simply cancel the family principle, nor can modern people eliminate it from society. Children of good Christian parents are more likely to develop strong character and be more open to spiritual life. Sons and daughters of responsible parents are more likely to be good employees. Deservingness and merit turn out to be corporate in a way that God honors, and in a way that seems to be rooted in human nature.

In Adam we see the family principle magnified. As the first father, he simply *was* the human race at one point. What happened to Adam happened to the whole race. Subsequently, the same was true of Adam and Eve together. As we have seen, none of the various views of "original sin" among orthodox Christians completely eliminates the corporate aspect of the result of the first sin.

The human race as a whole has been in a state of separation from God. Corporately, it has failed to comply with the commandments of its sovereign. As a result, it has suffered the bad consequences, including the loss of that full life that God intended for it. According to the beginning of Genesis, this condition is the result of the family principle and of the actions of the first two parents of the whole human race.

The family principle is similarly magnified in Christ and allows him to merit (deserve, earn, pay for) redemption for us. As the head of the new human race, Christ functions like Adam. He passes on his life to that new human race and determines much of what their life is like.

Christ is, however, the New Adam. "New" indicates that there are some important respects in which Christ's effect on Christians is unlike Adam's effect on the human race in general. It is not only unlike Adam's in the fact that the effect of his actions reverse that of Adam's. It is also unlike Adam's in the fact that the operation of the family principle or principle of corporate solidarity is itself strengthened in Christ, rather than lessened.

This increase in the effect due to the family principle is indicated by the section of First Corinthians 15 that talks about Christ as the New Adam. Paul is explaining how a corruptible human nature can be raised from the dead after decaying in the tomb:

> Thus it is written, "The first man Adam became a living being"; the last Adam became a life-giving spirit. But it is not the spiritual which is first but the physical, and then the spiritual. The first man was from the earth, a man of dust; the second man is from heaven. As was the man of dust, so are those who are of the dust; and as is the man of heaven, so are those who are of heaven. Just as we have borne the image of the man of dust, we shall also bear the image of the man of heaven. I tell you this, brethren: flesh and blood cannot inherit the kingdom of God, nor does the perishable inherit the imperishable. 1 Cor 15:45-50

In this passage, Paul tells us that the New Adam is a heavenly man, not just an earthly man. He is, in other words, a human being, but a special one. He also tells us that this heavenly human being is not just a living being like other human beings, but a life-giving spirit. In both ways Paul is possibly referring to what we would describe as Christ's incarnate nature. More probably he is talking about the transfigured, glorified humanity that resulted from the resurrection. Either way, the human Jesus of Nazareth has a heavenly aspect, a "spiritualized" humanity. That humanity is the source of a new human life, one that changes us so that we look more like God and can live eternally.

The heavenly human being, who is Christ, imparts the new life to us directly. We receive spiritual life from the "life-giving spirit." We are given the heavenly image from the "man of heaven." We are not, in other words, connected to Christ the way we are connected to Adam. While we are only connected to Adam through generations of intermediaries, we are connected to Christ directly. We become Christians through a personal union with him. We could even be said to be one spirit with Christ and corporately one flesh with him (1 Cor 6:16–17). We are his body, members of him (1 Cor 12:27). The corporate nature of the human race is therefore heightened rather than diminished through the new creation. We are united with one another more fully, more immediately, and more contemporaneously through our union with Christ and through the one and same divine Spirit in us. If on the basis of the family principle, we inherit our situation as a race and as individuals because of the actions of our ancestors, especially that of Adam in the fall, all the more can the action of Christ count for us if we are united to him and become part of his body. In one way, the benefits of what Christ did on our behalf come to us undeserved. We receive them by pure grace on God's part as part of our new birth in Christ. Yet in another way, what comes to us is not completely undeserved or unmerited, because it is deserved or merited by Christ. He could rightfully pay for new life for his body, undergo the punishment his body deserved, merit a new life for his body.

To use a technical term once again, our relationship in the body of Christ is analogously like the corporate relationship of the human race or a family relationship. It is the same in that as we share in the benefits and misfortunes of the body of Christ, as we do of other corporate entities, both the good and the evil that comes to us is often deserved by what others do. It is different in that the fullness and voluntary nature of our union with Christ make the effect of what he did more complete in us and passed on to us with much more justice.

The Representative of the Race. Christ's position as the new head of the human race provides another important perspective in understanding why his death could count for us. He acted on our behalf in his death, resurrection, and ascension. He was representing the new human race that would come into existence, that would be his body, that was already being drawn together through the calling and formation of his disciples. In considering his death and resurrection, we sometimes miss the fact that Christ acted in such a way and not just as a righteous or godly individual.

In the New Testament Christ is more commonly spoken of as the Messiah, the anointed king of Israel, rather than as the New Adam. His title as Messiah points to his having a position in Israel, and therefore seems to indicate something different than his title of the New Adam. Yet the two titles turn out to indicate much the same position within the human race.

The nation of Israel was not called into a covenant relationship with God only for itself. Israel, as the descendants of Abraham, was to be the source of blessing for all the nations of the earth (Gn 12:3; Gal 3:8-9). That blessing would not reach the nations, however, until a messianic king of Israel would come who would extend his reign over the whole earth. By reigning over them, he would bring the nations God's kingdom or reign, the source of the promised blessing.

The prophesied messianic king of Israel, then, was to be the ruler of the human race. He would confer a better life on human beings and govern them so they could fulfill the purpose for which they were created. To call this Messiah the New Adam is to add the fact that he personally is the source of new life for human beings who come under his rule. Since, however, as the source or head of the new human race the New Adam is also ruler of that race, the position of the New Adam and Messiah are equivalent in many respects.

As the head of the human race, as King, Christ has a representative role. To use an example, if two warring nations decided to make peace, the presidents or their designated representatives would sign the treaty. Average citizens off the streets, even citizens in good standing, would not be authorized to sign. They would not hold a position allowing them to represent the nation as a corporate entity.

Likewise, if one nation wanted to warn another nation that war was imminent unless something changed, the message would not be delivered to just any citizen of the other nation. Once again, the president would communicate that message to the head of the other nation or a personal delegate, in the expectation that the head of state would lead that nation in its response. Only an appropriate leader can represent the nation as a corporate entity.

Christ can represent the human race. As the New Adam and King of Israel, he is the head of the human race. He is the one God appointed to be the ruler of the human race, and even now he functions as the King or Lord of those who accept him for who he is. Consequently, Christ has the authority to deal with God the Father on behalf of the human race. In turn, he also represents God to the human race insofar as God treats the human race through the head of that race. Finally, he leads the corporate response to God of those who accept him.

To say Christ died "for us," therefore, means that not only was his death for our benefit, but also that he died "on our behalf" as our representative. As Paul put it, "One has died for all, therefore all have died" (2 Cor 5:14), because that one could act on behalf of all as the head of those who were united to him. Consequently, the effects of his death can become our own once we become members of his body and "live for him."

THE GREAT HIGH PRIEST

Christ and Priesthood. Christ is not only the New Adam but also the great High Priest. His priesthood gives us a second perspective on who he was and why his sufferings and death could have the effect they did. Christ's role as High Priest is similar to his role as New Adam in some respects, especially in the way both roles allow him to represent the human race. His role as High Priest, however, adds the important aspects of his priestly service and of his priestly access to God.

Of New Testament writings, the Letter to the Hebrews most explicitly presents Christ's role as Priest.[1] It says, "We have a great high priest who has passed through the heavens, Jesus, the Son of God" (Heb 4:14). Priests can only function the way they do because they are appointed by God. "One does not take the honor upon himself" (Heb 5:4). Human beings can become fathers or mothers by begetting or adopting children, or become soldiers by volunteering. But just as they cannot become judges unless appointed by the right person, so they need to be appointed to become priests.

According to Hebrews, Jesus was appointed by God. We can see that fact in Psalm 110, where God speaks to his Son and says, "You are a priest for ever, after the order of Melchizedek" (v. 4). The "order of Melchizedek" indicates that Christ was not appointed to the Aaronic priesthood of the old covenant but to a priesthood that would replace it and would be greater—just as Melchizedek himself was greater than Aaron and even Abraham himself.

Like the head of a family or a nation, a priest is a represen-

---

1. For passages which present Christ as a Priest, see page 302.

tative who can perform certain actions on behalf of others, actions that cannot be successfully carried out by anyone not in the priesthood. In fact, there is a great similarity between the roles of the head of a grouping and the priest. In many cultures the head of a family is often the priest for the family (see Jb 1:5), and the king is often a priest. Under the old covenant the two roles were separate, but were reunited under the new covenant in the person of Christ.

The priest has several representative functions, but that which was most distinctive of his position was the function he performed in sacrifice. The priest was the only one who could present a gift to God (cf. Heb 5:1). Here again our tendency to equate sacrifice with death can make it more difficult to understand the nature of sacrificial action. We commonly understand the role of the priest to be the one who kills the sacrificial offering. Yet for many old covenant sacrifices, this was not essential to the role of the priest. When an individual offered a sacrifice for sin, that person both provided the animal and killed it (see Lv 4:29). In the Passover, the worshiper likewise provided the Passover lamb and killed it. Since these were sacrifices in which the priest did not kill the victim, killing sacrificial offerings is not essential to the role of the priest.

Moreover, killing the animal and offering it to God were two distinct steps in the ceremony of old covenant sacrifices. Killing was only a means to offering. When the worshiper did the killing, he gave the offering to the priest. The priest put some of the blood on the altar and poured the rest at the base. He also burned all or part of the body on the altar. In special ceremonies the blood was sprinkled in the holy place, or in the holy of holies on the Day of Atonement. To perform these actions was to present the gift to God or offer sacrifice.

Only a priest could make the sacrificial offering. He could do so, because he had been chosen to be God's servant. Priests were not menial servants but servants the way the more important servants of a king were. Such royal servants were ministers who took on governmental roles and there-fore attended the king in court where many of the gov-ernmental functions were performed. Even today, many countries still speak of the chief governmental officials as ministers, that is, as servants of the king or queen. Priests, then, were ministers of the Lord who assisted him in govern-ing his people. They were therefore present when people came to pay homage to the Lord and to give him those gifts which expressed their acceptance of him as Lord and were given to handle various aspects of their relationship with God, including the repair of sin.

Old Testament Israelites would not walk directly up to the king of Israel and present him their gift or tribute. They kept their distance from the king as a sign of respect. Likewise, under the old covenant, they would not walk directly up to the altar to present their offering to God. Instead they gave their gifts to the priest. As the minister of God, the priest had special access to God's presence and could approach more closely than ordinary worshipers. He was the one appointed to make the actual presentation of the sacrificial gifts.

Access to God's presence was so important that the status of each type of priest was correlated with their degree of access. The Levites could enter the priestly court of the temple, but not the temple building itself. The priest could occasionally enter the building and come into the holy place, but not go behind the veil into the holy of holies. Once a year, the high priest could enter into the holy of holies, the closest a human being could approach the presence of God under the old covenant. The greater the priest, the closer he could come and the more he could do.

Because of his access to God, the priest fulfilled certain other functions connected to sacrifice besides the presenting of gifts. He also presented petitions. In Old Testament times, most secular petitions were spoken to the minister who then gave them to the king with the accompanying gift. The minis-ter likewise took the response back to the people, often in the form of a promise that the king would act as petitioned or grant the requested favor. In a similar way, the priests interceded for the Israelite worshipers during the sacrificial ceremony, and blessed the people on behalf of God, calling down upon them the benefits obtained by petitions accompanied by sacrifices acceptable to God.

The priestly minister, then, was an intermediary between God and the people. He represented the people to God and God to the people. He was able to do so because of his appointment by God (cf. Heb 5:1). His role was broader than the offering of sacrifice and mediating the results of the sacrifice to the people, but his sacrificial functions were his most important ones. For this he was given special access to God.

Christ's Priesthood and Our Redemption. Christ's position as the great High Priest enabled him to play a special role in our redemption. As a Priest, he had an access to God that allowed him to mediate between God and the human race. The New Testament teaching on his priestly role reveals some important truths about what Christ came to do and what he had to be like to do it.

First of all, the fact of Christ's priesthood tells us that he was a mediator or intercessor for his people. Modern Christians tend to think of Christ simply as one with the power to do whatever he decides. Such a view, however, ignores his priestly role. Christ does act directly to redeem people, but such actions are done on the basis of his priestly work of offering sacrifice.

Christ saves the human race because he has first atoned for the race and made redemption possible for them. On that basis he intercedes for them. In a certain way, his intercession then "entitles" him to act directly to help us. When we speak about something happening "through" Christ, we give expression to our need of Christ's work as Priest and Mediator.

Even more importantly for our purposes, it is because of Christ's position as Priest that his death can have an effect for us. If he were not a Priest, his sufferings would have been of use only for himself. Because he was appointed Priest, Christ was able to offer his death as a sacrifice for others. His action counted for others because a high priest is able to offer atoning sacrifices for sin to God on behalf of those he represents.

Further, Christ's position as a Priest indicates that he needs to be human. Because he was a representative of the people, the priest needed to be one of them. In the case of Christ, this means not so much that he had to be an Israelite, although as the Messiah he was, but that he had to be a human being, because the sacrifice he offered was for the human race.

Hebrews says, "For he who sanctifies and those who are sanctified have all one origin.... Since therefore the children share in flesh and blood, he himself likewise partook of the same nature, that through death he might destroy him who has the power of death, that is, the devil, and deliver all those who through fear of death were subject to lifelong bondage" (Heb 2:11, 14-15). Just as with his role as the New Adam, Christ needed to be a human being for his role as priest.

Finally, it is helpful to see the personal nature of Christ's sacrificial action as Priest. In one respect, his redemptive role is quite different from anything else in the old covenant system because he is Priest and sacrificial victim at the same time. He was a Priest who understood that animal sacrifices would not be enough. He therefore voluntarily "offered himself without blemish to God" (Heb 9:14). He let himself be given up to death on earth so that his blood might be shed for the sins of the world. He then entered the true holy of holies in heaven to present himself in a priestly way as the Lamb who had been slain—the acceptable sacrifice for the sins of the world.

THE SON OF GOD

The Human Son of God. Describing Christ as the New Adam indicates something about his relationship to the human race. He is a human being whose special position within the human race allows him to earn or merit salvation for the rest of the race and to represent it in its dealings with God. De-scribing Christ as the High Priest indicates something about his relationship to both the human race and God. He is the member of the human race who has been chosen by God as his minister to be an intermediary or mediator—acting both on behalf of God and as a representative of human beings. Describing Christ as the Son of God primarily indicates some-thing about his relationship to God.

At one time most Christians would have immediately taken the title of Son of God to refer to the divinity of Christ. He was the divine Son of God, the Second Person of the Trinity, eternally begotten of the Father. Modern Scripture scholars often put the accent elsewhere. Christ was the Son of God as a human being. The two views are not incompatible with one another but, in fact, support one another. In the context of this chapter, we will begin considering Christ as God's human Son and then consider his divine sonship.

The High Priest who saved us and so who had to be "of the same nature" as we are (Heb 2:14) was the Son of God. In fact, the Letter to the Hebrews seems to say that Christ was Priest precisely because he was Son:

> So also Christ did not exalt himself to be made a high priest, but was exalted [RSV: appointed] by him who said to him,
>
> "Thou art my Son,
> today I have begotten thee";
> as he says also in another place,
> "Thou art a priest forever,
> after the order of Melchizedek." **Heb 5:5-6**

The connection between Christ's priesthood and his sonship seems to lie in the understanding of the basis of Christ's priesthood found in the Letter to the Hebrews. He did not become Priest because of a "legal entitlement [RSV: requirement]," succeeding to a position attainable by others (Heb 7:16). Christ was a Priest because as risen Son he had the necessary access to God. He had it because of his relationship with God as his Son, and he had it because he was risen and so with God in heaven.

Christ did not need a further appointment or enablement to be Priest. Having died as a sacrifice for sin, he could freely come before his Father and intercede for blessing and salvation for his body. Such a role is a priestly role, one that a risen Son could fulfill and one that the Father would acknowledge as being according to his will.

The positions of head of the human race and the King of Israel were also connected to sonship. Adam and the line of kings of Israel were to be sons of God because they were to reign on his behalf. God's intention had been that they would be his vicars, ruling according to his laws and with his wisdom and authority. Adopting or appointing them as sons was God's way of recognizing their relationship to him. That meant their rule and his rule would, in effect, be one rule. Consequently, the messianic King and the New Adam—the one who was not only to restore the human race but also bring the kingdom of God—had to be the Son of God.

The Scriptures lay great weight upon Christ's position as the Son of God. We are, however, not able easily to comprehend the importance of the scriptural understanding of sonship because of the major cultural changes that have occurred in family life and in the father-son relationship. For us, the family exists primarily for the children before they become adults. Once young people are able to fully care for themselves, they become independent. They move away from their family of origin, may start a new family, and are on their own. At the same time, although it is not often remarked upon, once the children leave home, the parents are usually on their own as well.

In the ancient world and in the Israelite-Jewish culture in which the two testaments were written, family life functioned much differently. Sons did not typically leave the family relationship when they became adults. While there were a variety of family relationships, some sort of common life, mutual economic dependency, and possession of common property did not normally cease when the sons became adult.

The first-born son, in particular, was expected to succeed to the position of the father. He would usually take over the family farm or family business as heir. He worked with his father as long as his father was able. He commonly either lived with his father or in close proximity. He had a special responsibility to carry on the family. In the parable of the prodigal son, the father says to the eldest son, "Son, you are always with me, and all that is mine is yours" (Lk 15:31). He meant what he said literally, and not just as an expression of sentiment. For these reasons, in the Scripture the father-son relationship was thought of more as a relationship between adults than between an adult and a child.

Moreover, there was understood to be a type of identity between a father and a son, especially between a father and the first-born son, and above all between a father and an only son. The Jews had a saying: "The son is the father," and on that basis they would treat the son the same way as the father. They knew the son would some day take the father's place. In fact, the son would represent him even before the father's death. When in the parable of the vineyard, the owner sent his son after sending his servants, he expected his son to receive the same respect he would. Sending his son, the heir, was like coming himself (Mt 21:33-43; Mk 12:1-12).

When the Scriptures speak about Adam or about the king of Israel or about Christ as sons of God, they have in mind this stronger form of father-son relationship. To be a son of God means to be in a special relationship of partnership with God, with a closeness that is constant, because a son can always have access to the Father. It also, however, indicates a special identity with the Father, since sons, especially the first-born, take the father's place and act on his behalf and with his authority. All this is true of Christ as the human Son of God in his relationship with his Father.

The Divine Son of God. To say Christ is a Son in his humanity is to assert much the same as what is asserted by calling him New Adam and great High Priest. To say that he is a divine Son adds considerably more. As the prologue to the Gospel of John says, "The Word [who was God] became flesh and dwelt among us, full of grace and truth; we have beheld his glory, glory as of the only Son from the Father" (Jn 1:14; cf. 1:1). Christ is the unique Son of God, the only-begotten Son of God, Son of God in a way no mere human being could be.

Since this is not a book on the incarnation, we can only consider the incarnation in its relationship to the redemption. It is artificial to separate the incarnation and the redemption. As it says in the Nicene Creed, "Jesus Christ, the only Son of God... came down from heaven for the sake of us men and for our salvation." Yet the doctrine of the incarnation contains many special questions, some exegetical, some theological, that would take us far beyond the scope of this book.

There are not two sons of God, the divine Son and the human Son. There is one Son of God, our Lord Jesus Christ. His role as Redeemer has the effect it does in large part because of his position as Son of God, at once divine and human. Nicholas Cabasilas, the Byzantine theologian (born A.D. 1322), put it this way in Book I of *The Life in Christ*: "It was man who should wrest the victory for himself, but only God who was able to do so."

The role Christ came for is a human role. As the Scriptures emphasize, the New Adam, the High Priest, needed to be a human being to represent the human race before God, to offer the redeeming sacrifice, and to represent God to us. Nonetheless, the Redeemer needed to be something more than human in order to succeed.

As Christian teachers throughout the centuries considered the redemption, the emphasis on the divinity of the Redeemer grew. Some of that heightened stress on the divinity of Christ was no doubt a result of the controversies over the Trinity and the incarnation in the fourth through seventh centuries. More, however, came simply from meditating on

Christ reconciling the world to himself..." (2 Cor 5:19). God is the agent who brings about redemption.

The importance of God's being in Christ is perhaps most easily grasped when we consider what he does to liberate us. The Son of God came into the world to establish the kingdom of God, to bring the human race out of slavery to sin, Satan, and death and to confer new spiritual life. All of this he did, and still does, by acting with a divine power that is his own. In part four of this book we will consider the results of the redemption in us and the way God is in Christ, transforming the lives of human beings.

Yet it is also important to see that God was in Christ on the cross itself. In the sufferings and death of the Christ, his weakness and humanity is at its most obvious. Nonetheless, here too God was at work in Christ, "Not counting our trespasses against us" (2 Cor 5:19). In this part of the book, where we are primarily considering the accomplishment of the redemption through Christ's earthly, mediational work, we will mainly consider the divine sonship in regard to why it was important for making Christ's suffering and death effective. In so doing, we will see why much of the traditional emphasis on the divinity of the Son comes from considering the magnitude of the task of offering a sacrifice that could count for our sins.

The "job requirements" for redemption from sin are affected by the greatness of the person sinned against. After all, human beings disobeyed and disrespected the Lord God of heaven and earth, the one who created the human race out of nothing, the one who blessed the human race even before it could deserve anything and who chose it to be his son. They turned to believe and follow his rebel enemy and in so doing left their allegiance to their rightful land.

Among most if not all human cultures, crimes against the king or the government are recognized as greater than crimes against private individuals. Treason against the sovereign of a nation, *lèse majesté*, is among the greatest of human crimes and usually if serious enough, unpardonable. But it is outdone by usually if serious enough, unpardonable. But it is outdone by treason against God, the Lord of the whole universe. Satisfaction or atonement, therefore, needs to be weighty enough to deal with the rejection of the omnipotent Creator of all.

Something needed to come from outside of the human race to deal with the situation, yet without simply eliminating the human role in overcoming its own evil. The work of redemption had to be human, but one invested with a greater effectiveness than a merely human work would have had. For this God provided a solution. He "heightened" the human sonship, which made it possible for the Redeemer to be a representative of the race to be redeemed, by joining it to a divine sonship. Or to state the same truth in a more familiar way, God sent his only Son into the world to take on a human nature from the line of David—the descendant of Abraham and the descendant of Adam himself—in order to be at once the human and divine Son able to come before the throne of God as such.

Here the doctrine of the incarnation and the closely-related doctrine of the Trinity provide an important understanding for us. For much of the work of redemption, especially the work of imparting the results to us, the one we recognize as God the Father would have sufficed. He could have taken on human nature and worked through that nature to communicate divine life. He could have acted in Christ to destroy the enemy and free us from weakness, to teach and rule over us in a form that would be more accessible.

However, to take on the priestly work involved in redemption, to stand in the place of human beings as their representative and to relate to God on their behalf offering sacrifice and interceding for them, we needed someone else. This is not the role of a father but of a son. There therefore needed to be some unfathomable distinctness in the being of the one God—a hypostasis or person who could be fully divine and therefore fully one with the Father, and yet relate to the Father with some kind of otherness. The crucifixion understood as a sacrifice leads us to the doctrine of the Trinity

Divine sonship was needed. The divine sonship of Christ invested what was a human work with a greater worth and effectiveness. A priest was needed who could come before God's throne. Who could come before God's throne more readily and more closely than the one who is God's own Son by nature? An intercessor was needed. Where could an intercessor with more influence with God be found than God's only Son with whom he is well-pleased? A sacrifice was needed—though one of greater value than the animals used in the old covenant, one equal to the race to be redeemed and of enough worth to God to outweigh the offense. But where could a sacrifice be found of more worth to God than his only Son?

A divine Priest, intercessor, and sacrifice could accomplish what a merely human priest or intercessor and animal sacrifice could not. A divine Son was needed to offer an effective redemptive sacrifice. That someone human could come before God as a divine Son is a grace that could not be asked for or imagined (Eph 3:20). But this was perhaps the only way for a necessarily human work to have sufficient effectiveness with God.

A Son For a Slave. Something else was also needed, something we can easily lose sight of by focusing on the Son offering sacrifice to the Father. That perspective only lets us see the Father as the object of what Christ did to redeem the world, the one to whom the sacrifice was offered. There is, however, a complementary truth: the Father was himself personally involved in the sacrifice.

As we have seen, a sacrifice was given by the worshiper and presented to God by the priest. The word "give" was the word used for what the worshiper did in providing the sacrificial victim. The redemption was effective because of the way in which Christ was able to come as Son and Priest before his Father and present the sacrifice of himself. It was also effective because of the way in which he was able to give himself as a sacrificial victim.

a sacrificial victim.

Yet it was not just the Son who gave himself as a sacrificial victim. The Father also gave his Son. We find this truth expressed in the New Testament's presentation of the work of redemption:

> For God so loved the world that he gave his only Son, that whoever believes in him should not perish but have eternal life. Jn 3:16

> In this is love, not that we loved God but that he loved us and sent his Son to be the expiation for our sins. 1 Jn 4:10

> He... did not spare his only Son, but gave him up for us all. Rom 8:32

Christ's death as a sacrifice for sins then, was not only the Son's action but also his Father's action. Moreover, in giving his Son, the Father, in a certain way, gave himself. The way Christ's sacrifice can also be his Father's gracious work is rooted in the relationship between Father and Son.

As we have seen, the traditional and scriptural understanding of sonship involves a certain identification. When the son comes, the father comes. When the son acts, the father acts. The son is an extension of the father. The greater the love between them, the more this is so. This would be true for Christ and his Father if Christ were only a human Son of God, but it is heightened in a way we can only dimly grasp by the fact that Christ was also the divine Son of God, one in being with his Father.

Centuries before he sent his only Son into the world to die for his errant, rebellious creatures, God taught them the significance of what he would do. In Genesis 22, we read about an incident in the life of Abraham, marvelous in its original significance but even more marvelous in its completion in Christ. This incident, sometimes called the "binding of Isaac," gives us a living image of the way God the Father loved the human race through his Son.

Abraham marked the beginning of God's plan to repair the fall and restore the human race. The call of Abraham with its promise of blessing is a type of God's call to every human being. Abraham's response of obedient faith is likewise a type of every human being's reception of salvation. Although he lived almost two thousand years before Christ, yet Scripture says that the gospel was preached beforehand to Abraham (Gal 3:8), the gospel of the blessing that would be given to the whole human race.

In Genesis 22, we see God instructing Abraham on how the blessing would come. Abraham had not only received the covenant promises of God but also the promised child. Isaac was, in a way, the fulfillment of the promise. As Abraham's natural son, he was the one through whom God had promised that the blessing would be given. Then God tested Abraham, as he had Adam after having blessed him. God commanded Abraham to take Isaac, his only son, the son he loved, and offer him as a sacrifice. This was a test, as we are told, of Abraham's fear of God, his willingness to submit to him. This test was even greater than the call to leave his home. God asked Abraham to make Isaac a burnt offering.

The burnt offering was the kind of sacrifice in which the gift was completely burned with nothing given back to the worshipers. It was an expression of full adoration, complete consecration to God which expects no blessing in return. Abraham therefore was called not exactly to destroy his son, but to give him to God completely and in a way that meant he could not keep him for himself. Because of the nature of this particular burnt offering, Abraham was being called to offer a gift that expressed even more than complete consecration. He was being called to offer the son through whom his life would be passed on, the son that was supposed to be the means of fulfilling God's promised blessing, and therefore to offer himself.

Abraham obeyed. As he raised the knife to slay his son as a sacrifice, an angel stopped him. He indicated a ram caught in a thicket that would substitute for his son. This, according to Abraham's unwitting prediction earlier in the narrative (Gn 22:8), was the lamb which God himself would provide for the sacrifice. As a result of his obedience (Gn 22:18), God once again blessed Abraham in fullness.

Yet the ram Abraham offered was not the Lamb which God would provide to bring the fullness of blessing to the human race, but only a foreshadowing. Two millennia later, John the Baptist, the last representative of old covenant revelation, pointed out the true Lamb: "Behold the Lamb of God, who takes away the sin of the world" (Jn 1:30). The true Lamb, the Lamb given by God, was Christ.

God tested Abraham to an extent that is fearful. He was asked to give himself completely to God by offering his own Son. And yet, although Abraham probably did not realize it, the test was also a pledge. The test did not only concern Abraham's son but God's Son as well. God was planning to provide a Lamb, not just for Abraham or for Isaac or for their descendants, but for the whole human race. That Lamb would be adequate for the sins of the whole world because he would be God's own Son.

What God asked Abraham to do, he was prepared to do himself. "God so loved the world that he gave his only Son" (Jn 3:16)—"gave" in the sense of "gave to be a sacrifice." In the praise of the Passover mystery during the Easter celebration of the early Roman church, the amazing fact is proclaimed that "to pay for a slave, God gave a Son."

It is perhaps not so evident to us who no longer experience slavery, nor the kind of family life which made sons, especially an only son, so valuable to a father, but that is something no one would have thought of doing. One might give slaves to redeem a son, but never a son to redeem a slave. But because a whole race that was meant to be a son was at stake, a son was required. And a Son was given, a divine Son, God's only Son.

The story of Abraham and Isaac, then, is a story about

Jesus Christ and his Father. The death of Christ on the cross is the death of God's only Son, given for the sins of the world. He was a Lamb that freely went to the slaughter, like Isaac "opened not his mouth" in protest (Is 53:7). His sacrifice, therefore, was the offering made by the Son of God who was the head of the human race on behalf of the race as a whole. But at the very same time, because of the human-divine relationship of sonship between Christ and his Father, in the gift of a "Lamb" the Father gave himself.

As we contemplate the sacrifice of Abraham as a human being called to express his complete dedication to God, we can grasp what it means to send a son to his death. That in turn will also help us to contemplate the awesome truth of God's costly commitment to a race of creatures that compared to himself—and to his Son—are relatively insignificant. To pay for a slave, he gave a Son, his only Son.

SEVEN

The Obedient Son

A CCORDING TO MANY SCRIPTURE SCHOLARS, Paul's Letter to the Philippians contains a hymn to Christ which praises his humility in redeeming us:

> Though he was in the form of God, [he] did not count
>   equality with God a thing to be grasped,
> but he emptied himself, taking the form of a servant,
>   being born in the likeness of men.
> And being found in human form he humbled himself and
>   became obedient unto death, even death on a cross.
> Therefore God has highly exalted him and bestowed on
>   him the name which is above every name,
> that at the name of Jesus every knee should bow in heaven
>   and on earth and under the earth,
> every tongue confess that Jesus Christ is Lord, to the
>   glory of God the Father. Phil 2:6-11

The hymn begins by considering Christ. "Form" here does not mean external shape, but something more like "the very nature of God," as translated in the New International Version (NIV). The hymn begins, then, with Christ as the divine Son, in "the glory which [he] had with [his Father] before the world was made" (Jn 17:5).

We are perhaps to think of Christ together with his Father,

"who sits above the circle of the earth, and its inhabitants are like grasshoppers" (Is 40:22). As insignificant as human beings are in comparison, he had compassion on them in their predicament. Perhaps they looked to him like ants might look to us after their anthill had been run over by a lawn mower: in confusion and turmoil, their home damaged by something they could not even comprehend.

Then this divine Son—the image of God after whom the first human being was created (2 Cor 4:4; Col 3:10)—did the very opposite of Adam. Rather than reaching out to become "like God," Christ did not even hold on to the glory and greatness he already shared with his Father. Instead he emptied himself, put aside his position, and took a lower place, the place of a servant or slave.

"For us men and for our salvation, he came down from heaven and became man" (Nicene Creed). The Son of God came down from heaven to earth, both in the sense in which the incarnation is a descent and in the sense in which a great king might take the maid's place if she were too sick to serve the meal. He put aside his royal robes and put on an apron, so to speak. "For you know the generosity [RSV: grace] of our Lord Jesus Christ, that though he was rich, yet for your sake he became poor, so that by his poverty you might become rich" (2 Cor 8:9).

The humility of the Son of the King of the universe did not stop there. Perhaps we would be impressed by a prince who strolled the streets and chatted with the villagers, stopping to inquire after the health of the street cleaner. Christ did not come to be served; he did not even come to visit. Rather, he voluntarily came to serve (Mk 10:45).

Although himself the commander of the armies of heaven, Christ came to take orders. But he did not even come to take the orders given to soldiers sent out on a difficult and certainly fatal mission. That would be a glorious service. Rather, he came to die like a criminal—in fact, like the worst of criminals in the most degrading and painful death of all: crucifixion.

Such was the humility of the Son of God. He came to serve his own servants. "By this we know love, that he laid down his life for us" (1 Jn 3:16). He came to obey his Father. "I do as the Father has commanded me, so that the world may know that I love the Father" (Jn 14:31). In so doing, he made himself an example to us. "I have given you an example, that you also should do as I have done to you" (Jn 13:15).

Paul introduces the above hymn with the exhortation, "Have this mind among yourselves, which you have in Christ Jesus" (Phil 2:5). Paul thereby is holding up Christ as an example of someone who loved his Father, counting his Father as higher than himself and obeying him faithfully. He also is holding Christ up as an example of someone who loved his brothers and sisters, being among them as one who served (Lk 22:27). In short, Christ fulfilled the commandments summed up, in, as he himself taught, love of God and love of neighbor (Mt 22:37-40). And in his death on the cross, he gave the fullest example of love, both of God and of neighbor.

Paul had a practical goal in quoting this hymn to Christ. He was exhorting the Christian community at Philippi to remain united in the midst of persecution. Christ is presented as the model of one who brings about unity. By his obedience, Christ maintained unity with the one higher than himself, his Father. He established unity with others by looking to their interests and serving them. For those who accepted him, Christ's obedience and service was reconciling, peace-producing, as love is. His aim, in fact, was "to unite all things" (Eph 1:10) by what he did.

The requirements for a death that would restore the human race were high. Not any kind of death would do. As we saw in the last chapter, it had to be the death of a special person. The one who died to redeem us had to be the New Adam, the great High Priest, and the Son of God. He had to have a special kind of relationship to God, and to us, to offer an effective redemptive sacrifice.

As we will see in this chapter, the way Christ died also was important. His death had to be a special kind of death. The death of the Redeemer had to be an act of love, the fulfillment of the law of love of God and neighbor.

Maximus Confessor expresses this truth in *The Ascetic Life:*

> Our Lord Jesus Christ, being God by nature and, because of His kindness, deigning also to become man, was born of a woman and made under the law, as the divine Apostle says, that by observing the commandment as man He might overturn the ancient curse on Adam. Now the Lord knew that the whole law and the prophets depend on the two commandments of the law—*Thou shalt love the Lord thy God with thy whole heart, and thy neighbor as thyself.* He therefore was eager to observe them the way a human would, from beginning to end.

Since Christ came for our sakes, it is much easier to see how his death was and had to be an act of love of us. This chapter will consequently focus more on the way it was and had to be an act of love of God and therefore an act of obedience. Only as an act of obedience could Christ's death be a payment, a substitution, and a sacrifice that could accomplish our redemption. In looking at who Christ was in the last chapter, we considered mainly the relationship between the Father and his divine-human Son as an objective reality which came about through the incarnation. In this chapter we will see how that relationship was lived out and how Christ and his Father "worked together" to redeem the human race. This will allow us to see why it was his "obedience unto death" that saved us.

THE IMPORTANCE OF OBEDIENCE

Sonship and Obedience. Christ came to bring the human race back to a good relationship with God. "In the beginning," the relationship God wanted for the human race was one of sonship. He created Adam to be his son, living in his presence and ruling over creation on his behalf, bringing it to the full glory he had in mind.

The hymn in Philippians 2 seems to contain an implicit contrast between Adam and Christ. Adam, the first head of the human race who was created as the son of God, out of pride or self-exaltation sought to become equal to God. Christ, the new head of the human race who had been sent as the Son of God, humbled himself in obedience for the glory of his Father. His obedience, along with its inner source, humility, was integral to Christ's work of redemption because without it, a relationship of good sonship is impossible.

Obedience is an old-fashioned virtue not highly esteemed in this new age, not even much considered, much less well understood. For most modern people, it is only a necessary restraint on the adult exercise of freedom which is considered to be the goal of human life. Obedience, when necessary, is a matter of maintaining good order so that we do not damage or unnecessarily interfere with one another. The paradigm of such obedience is respecting the traffic rules that protect our vehicles and lives, while fundamentally going where we ourselves wish to go.

The personal obedience that accepts someone else's direction is seen as only for the immature. Because they are not fully capable of handling their own lives, children often need the will of an adult imposed upon them. It is assumed that the sooner young adults can think for themselves, make up their own minds, clarify their own values, and arrive at their own choices, the better off they will be and the better their lives will go. Even though this is today's prevailing approach, the Scriptures take a different view of obedience.

To begin with, scriptural obedience is not primarily a matter of obeying commands, especially not just obeying commands that concern particular external actions. "Don't cross the street by yourself." "Stop your car when the light is red." To be sure, obedience is sometimes a matter of obeying such commands. If we disregard directives from an authorized source, we may receive a ticket or fine or jail sentence for our disobedience. Nonetheless, for the Scriptures, obedience was more of a relational orientation.

To describe obedience as a relational orientation means it comes into existence out of a desire to be in a certain kind of relationship in a good way. This view of obedience is most powerfully expressed in the Book of Deuteronomy, especially in Moses' discourse in chapters 5-11. Obedience is presented as an expression of the love of God. That message was summed up in the Shema, the daily confession of the devout Jew, which put keeping the commandments (Dt 6:2) in the context of the love of God: "Hear, O Israel: The Lord our God is one Lord; and you shall love the Lord your God with all your heart, and with all your soul, and with all your might" (Dt 6:4-5).

The obedience taught by Moses and the rest of the Scripture is the obedience that comes from a desire to be in a relationship of sonship with God. It is a matter of loving God as Father. Obedience, to be sure, is not an expression of love in every relationship. Fathers do not love their children by obeying them. Often a father loves his child best by refusing to obey him or her, instead insisting that the child change a particular behavior or approach to life. In a father-son relationship, however, the son's love is expressed in obedience. Because the father is the head of the family, a good son is an obedient son.

This scriptural view of obedience can only be comprehended against the background of the scriptural understanding of family life. Since as we have seen, in the ancient world the father and the son often lived and worked together as long as the father lived, obedience was an adult matter. For us, the son's obedience primarily comes into play when he is a child. It allows the father to effectively restrain his son from harmful behavior, to order his life in helpful ways, and also to train him to live more capably. That obedience comes to an end when the son reaches adult age. Ironically, the active father-son relationship and the obedience that goes with it often stops at the point when a son could be of most help to the father and to the family.

In scriptural times, the son's obedience was what made it possible for him to live and work in a unified way with his father during a whole lifetime and to represent the father when appropriate. In large part this meant taking on his father's mind about how life was to be lived and how various matters were to be approached, the way his father had done with his own father before. If all went well, his adult obedience involved relatively few directives and little if any need for restraint on the father's part. A son that accepted and carried out his relationship obediently was a strength to the family and continued the family way of life.

Godly Obedience. The Scripture, then, primarily treats obedience in terms of an adult who wants to live with God and be something of a partner with God as his son or daughter. It is the obedience of someone who receives directives willingly when they come and even seeks them when needed, but who mainly knows what the Father wants and is oriented to doing it when possible. Such an adult obedience enables us to represent the Father and handle all things "to his glory." Although our obedience to God as the all-wise, all-good Creator of the universe has to be even fuller than an Israelite would show his father in scriptural times, we are called to an obedience more like that of an adult Israelite than that of the modern child. Appreciating that fact is important in helping us move from a position of distant respect or childish dependence to one of adult partnership with God.

Obedience can be described as "keeping the commandments" (1 Cor 7:19). This too could be misleading unless we see that God's commandments are not primarily directives to perform particular external tasks. "Do not murder" or "love your neighbor as yourself" cannot be fulfilled by simply performing a limited set of actions, although they can certainly be broken by even one action of the wrong sort. They are instructions meant to form and orient our whole lives.

Consequently, true keeping of the commandments involves taking on the mind of the Father in an adult way. Obedience is most full when we value what God values, when we try to understand his purpose for our lives and cooperate with it, when we walk in his ways, trying to live as he would if he were in our circumstances.

Such obedience can also be described as taking up our adult obligations. For many modern people, the epitome of doing something freely is to do it "of ourselves," without obligation, much less compulsion, but to do it simply because we want to. But for Jews and Christians in scriptural times, and even until fairly recently, obligation and willingness were not set at odds in this way. Those things God commanded were precisely the best, most important things for human beings to do—love of God and neighbor, not murdering, stealing, bearing false witness. The wisest human beings, therefore, were the ones who freely chose and wanted to do whatever God commanded.

If obedience, then, makes possible a good relationship of sonship with God, Christ had to be obedient. He could not be in a bad relationship with God or be a bad son and be a Redeemer. Not only would God not have accepted him as a Redeemer, Christ would have himself needed redemption.

The New Testament has many ways of saying that Christ had to be and was obedient. Many passages stress his sinlessness (2 Cor 5:21; 1 Pt 3:18; Heb 4:15). Others say that he had to be unblemished and pure or holy the way priests were (Heb 7:26), or unblemished the way a sacrificial offering was (1 Pt 2:19, 27; Heb 9:20). He had to be someone with whom God was pleased and in whom he delighted (Mt 3:17). An obedient relationship with God was a condition for his success as the Redeemer.

The importance of obedience for Christ, however, goes

beyond its place as a qualification for the Redeemer. Because it is the response of sons and daughters who love God as their Father, obedience is, in a way, the purpose of life. Christ was not obedient in order to qualify for being the Redeemer, the way a wrestler might follow a strict diet in order to meet the weight requirements for an upcoming match. He was obedient because he loved his Father and wanted to take up his role as Son in a way that would be pleasing to him. He was not obedient so he could be the Redeemer, but he was able to be the Redeemer, because he was obedient.

AN ACT OF OBEDIENCE

Two Passages from Scripture. While obedience is more than specific directives, they can still be of major significance. A soldier may fulfill his role simply by patrolling an assigned piece of terrain, doing what he was trained to do. But if that soldier is commanded to attack a specific enemy position, his value as a soldier depends completely on what he does in response to that directive. It also determines whether he is obedient or not. To be genuine, inner orientations like obedience need at times to express themselves in actions.

Christ's whole life was lived in obedience. Nonetheless, it was by a specific action that he saved the human race—going to death on a cross. That action had to be an act of obedience. There are a number of passages in Scripture that speak of Christ's death on the cross as an act of obedience.[1] We have already considered Philippians 2:6-11. Two others are especially helpful for giving us a perspective on Christ's death as obedience.

The first one is found in the Letter to the Hebrews. In concluding a discussion of how the sufferings and death of Christ replaced the old covenant sacrifices, Hebrews 10 quotes verses 6-8 from Psalm 40:

---

1. For a list of passages which describe Christ's redemptive work as an act of obedience, see page 303.

Consequently, when Christ came into the world, he said,

"Sacrifices and offerings thou hast not desired,
but a body hast thou prepared for me;
in burnt offerings and sin offerings thou has taken no
pleasure.
Then I said, 'Lo, I have come to do thy will, O God,'
as it is written of me in the roll of the book." Heb 10:5-7

According to Hebrews, these verses from Psalm 40 are properly understood as words spoken by Christ to express his purpose in coming into the world. The juxtaposition of the two lines quoted from the psalm is seen as significant in regard to his death. They express Christ's intention to replace the old covenant sacrifices by an action which fulfills God's will, although nothing in the psalm describes the nature of that action. In other words, according to Hebrews, Christ saw a particular action—his own undergoing suffering and death—as the way God intended to have the old covenant sacrifices be replaced by a new and effective sacrifice that would accomplish the sanctification of the human race.

Even more, according to Hebrews, Christ acknowledged that this offering of himself as a redemptive sacrifice was the reason for his becoming human. His Father had prepared a body, a way for his divine Son (Heb 1:3) to share in the same nature as those to be redeemed (Heb 2:14). Christ was thereby eligible to be their Priest. He accepted his Father's wish in the words, "Lo, I come to do your will." He came, in other words, to perform the specific action of giving his own life, because it was willed by his Father as the sacrifice for sins that would save the human race. He came for a particular obedience.

The second passage makes the same point in a somewhat different way. Romans 5:18-19 says, "Then as one man's trespass led to condemnation for all men, so one man's act of righteousness leads to acquittal and life for all men. For as by one man's disobedience many were made sinners, so by one man's obedience many will be made righteous."

Here we have the action Christ came to perform contrasted with Adam's. The action of Adam must be the eating of the fruit of the forbidden tree. Christ's action must be his dying for us, giving his life in a sacrificial death (cf. Heb 5:6–11). The Hebrews 10 passage we just read saw Christ's death only from the perspective of God's desire to replace the old covenant sacrifices. The Romans passage presents it as reversing what Adam had done to cause the current predicament of the human race.

Romans describes Christ's action in a way that indicates it met the requirements of reversing what Adam had done. Restoration of the human race certainly could not have been accomplished by an act of sin, a new attempt to make human beings become "like God" (Gn 3:5). But it had to be more than not sin. It had to be a deliberate act of righteousness, just as Adam's had been an act of sin. It had to be a deliberate act of obedience just as Adam's had been an act of disobedience. To "make up for" what had occurred, the action of Christ had to partake of an opposite character.

Obedience and Sacrifice. On the night in which he began his final sufferings and death, Christ turns to his Father. He stands before him as Adam, Adam in a new way. He has been appointed by his Father to overcome the failure of the first Adam and to begin anew the human race.

He stands before him as a Priest, a Priest of a special sort. He is to offer a sacrifice, because sacrifice is needed as part of a relationship with God. But sacrifice was also needed because of the past. The first Adam had a clean slate. Christ is representing a race with a record—a record that indicates not only that it does not deserve the blessing God wishes to give but deserves to be set aside as a failure. His sacrifice needs to atone for that record.

Finally, Christ stands before his Father as his Son, able to speak directly with his Father and confident of enjoying his favor, but needing to do something for those with whom he has become a brother so that they may be restored to the relationship of sonship.

On that night Christ prays a prayer of self-giving. He presents himself as a willing sacrifice for the sake of the disciples who are with him and of those who would come and be part of the restored human race. To use sacrificial language, Christ "consecrates" himself as a sacrificial victim (Jn 17:19). He does so in obedience and love, because that is the way to be pleasing to God and therefore the way to make an offering that is an atonement for the human race.

To understand the connection between sacrifice and obedience and love, we need to see the expressive or representative nature of sacrifice. A gift is important in sacrifice. If we do not give something worthwhile, we have not actually offered sacrifice. Nonetheless, the sacrificial gift is not as important in itself as in what it expresses.

The first-fruits offering illustrates this truth very clearly. This offering was a return for the harvest. The first-fruits of each harvest were given back to God as an offering to acknowledge his generous sovereignty over the whole harvest and to thank him for his provision of food, the means of life. The offering was not an attempt to repay God, but it represented and expressed the gratitude of the people.

There may have been gods who wanted a payment for what they did or who simply wanted the sacrifices themselves, but the Old Testament tells us the true God was not one of them. "If I were hungry, I would not tell you; for the world and all that is in it is mine. Do I eat the flesh of bulls, or drink the blood of goats?" (Ps 50:12-13). God did not accept sacrifice because he needed a gift of food, but because the gift expressed the intention of his people to have the right sort of relationship with him.

The story of Saul and the Amalekites portrays the representative nature of sacrifice in a way more clearly applicable to the death of Christ. Saul was commanded through a prophecy to defeat and utterly destroy the enemies of God and his people, even foregoing the normal spoils of war. But

Saul and the people took the best of the spoils and returned with it "to sacrifice to the Lord your God." The reason seemed commendable. What could be more worthy than to offer God sacrifice?

But their action, in fact, destroyed the very rationale of old covenant sacrifice. A sacrifice that involved disobedience could not be an acceptable sacrifice. As Samuel replied to Saul: "Behold, to obey is better than sacrifice, and to hearken than the fat of rams" (1 Sm 15:22). Sacrifice could not substitute for obedience, nor could it make disobedience acceptable or even pardonable, because sacrifice was intended as an expression of obedience. It was a gift given to God in homage or submission. God primarily wanted an obedient people, and their gifts were useless to him if they were not an expression of obedience.

As we have seen, when Christ died on the cross, he was offering his life as a sacrificial gift to his Father for the sake of the human race. His death, the pouring out of his blood, was the way to offer his life. But the representative nature of sacrifice indicates that his offering was not just a grudging tribute or the necessary payment for getting something he wanted. Rather, Christ's death on the cross expressed a whole life given over to God in love and obedience. His offering, therefore, had to be an act of love and obedience to express the relational meaning of the sacrifice. It had to be an act of love of God and neighbor to express a life given over to obeying God by keeping his commandments.

Because he died to save others, Christ's death on the cross was the ultimate expression of loving his neighbor. "Greater love has no man than this, that a man lay down his life for his friends" (Jn 15:13). "... Christ loved us and gave himself up for us [as] a fragrant offering and sacrifice to God" (Eph 5:2). His very love of neighbor was part of what made his death pleasing to God.

In the face of the need of the human race, Christ's death was obedience to God at least because it was a willing response to the commandment to love our neighbor. Christ, however, indicated that his death was obedience in an even more direct way. The night before he died he said, "I do as the Father has commanded me so that the world may know that I love the Father" (Jn 14:30). In other words, Christ died for the human race because that is what the Father commanded him, and following that command would be an expression of love of his Father.

Moreover, the very fact that Christ offered his life in willing obedience made his offering pleasing to his Father. He said, "I lay down my life for my sheep.... For this reason the Father loves me, because I lay down my life.... This command [RSV: charge] I have received from my Father" (Jn 10:15-18). This statement not only indicates that Christ died because his Father commanded him to do it, and that his Father was pleased with his sacrifice because it was an act of obedience. It also indicates that God was especially pleased with his obedience because it was not just external. Christ obeyed by making his aim the same as his Father's in giving the command. He died out of love for those whom the Father loved, whose need motivated the Father to send his Son and so provide a Lamb that could save them.

How could God find the bloody death of his Son pleasing? What kind of gift was that? What we have considered so far gives us a partial answer to these questions. The truth, of course, is that God did not find the suffering and death of his Son pleasing in themselves. He found pleasing the full offering of his Son's life to him, expressed in an act of obedience, because it was so difficult. The fullness of his Son's gift and his complete willingness to take on his Father's love for his creatures made Christ's death highly pleasing to God.

MAKING AMENDS

Repairing Sin. When Christ stood before his Father on the night before he died, he gave his life as an act of love for his

Father and for those his Father loved. That act was an act of obedience, because to love his Father, he did what his Father wanted. Such an act of obedience is the kind Adam could have given by refusing to eat the forbidden fruit. Such obedience is expressed by all true sacrifices. Christ, however, stood before his Father to offer a particular kind of sacrifice, a sacrifice for sin. Therefore, his sacrifice had to be an act of the particular kind of obedience appropriate to a sacrifice for sin.

As we have seen in Romans 5, Christ had to reverse specifically what Adam did. He specifically had to undo the first sin that created the current predicament of the human race and made it habitually given to disregarding its Creator and disregarding true righteousness and goodness. Christ, in other words, had to provide a positive act of righteousness that would counter the original trespass, an act of obedience that would counter the original disobedience. And the only way to counter it was to "make up for it."

Here we are at a consideration which has been easily understood in other ages but not always well understood today. To return a human relationship that has been violated to its original footing requires some repair. Moreover, when someone accepts responsibility for having damaged or violated a relationship, repair of that relationship involves repentance.

Repentance is the process of changing direction, changing one's inner orientation or attitude and turning to a new course of action. In restoring one's good relationship with God, repentance has to involve returning to obedience. Repentance, therefore, is the process of coming to willing obedience, making a firm decision to obey in the future in areas where there has been previously disobedience and wrongdoing.

As a change of direction and attitude, repentance involves a turning from the past. That turning involves a regret or sorrow for the past, a rejection of evils committed or of the neglect of obligations. Repentance also involves the desire to restore a relationship that has been damaged or ignored and to remove all offense that has been given. In most cases, the expression of real repentance is the desire to "make up for" what has been done or left undone.

We can see the importance of making amends most clearly in cases of serious wrongdoing. A repentant thief should want to make restitution. According to Old Testament law, as we have seen, the thief needs to not only return what was taken but needs also offer some additional compensation. A repentant slanderer should not only take back the slander but also make an attempt to reestablish the reputation of the person slandered.

Often restitution or repair is not possible. A repentant murderer, for instance, cannot restore the life of the innocent victim, but nonetheless should wish to do something else to express repentance and make any compensation possible. If people do not want to see the damage or harm they have caused made up for, they have not really repented and are not in a good position to live the relationship well.

The same understanding also affects the conduct of judges. They will not normally let a wrongdoer go completely free if there is no restitution possible. The wrongdoer will be expected to undergo some punishment, not simply as a matter of deterrence from crime in the future but to show that the repentance is real. Consequently, simply to let people off when they have done something seriously wrong is not a service to those who are truly repentant and wish to make up for what they have done. Nor is it a service to those who may desire to repent but need help in changing their orientation. These truths of human experience serve as background to Christ's death on the cross.

Christ's Obedience and Sin. As the representative of the human race, Christ desired to "make up for" human sin. Sin is wrong not simply because it harms other human beings or ourselves, not simply because it has bad consequences, but also because it is a violation of our relationship with God. Sin is unsubmissiveness to our Creator and as such disrespectful and dishonoring of him.

Insofar as sin is an offense against God, it should be repaired in regard to God. If Christ were truly to represent a race that needed to be in a good relationship with God, he had to take on its sin as sin. He had to bear the consequences of sin as an affront to the head of the universe and make satisfaction for it.

Christ had to approach this task in a way fitting to what he was trying to accomplish. Personally innocent though he was, divine though he was, Christ nonetheless was putting himself at the head of a race that needed to repair its relationship with its Creator. And he needed to do that in a way that expressed what they needed to express in order to come back to their Creator. He had to express obedience, but a somewhat different type of obedience than that of a Son who always does what is pleasing to his Father (Jn 8:29). He had to express more the kind of obedience that would be shown by a penitent criminal who turned himself in and asked what he could do to set things straight.

Such an obedience involves, first of all, a spirit of willing acceptance of what the judge or authority says. A daughter may be punished by her father for deliberately disobeying a command. If she takes the punishment defiantly, the relationship difficulty caused by her disobedience will not be remedied. The father may decide "enough is enough" and cease disciplining his daughter. He may hope that he asserted his authority adequately and has deterred future external violations. But the father knows he still has a rebellious child on his hands and will not be satisfied with her attitude.

A criminal arrested for mugging may be given the maximum penalty of the law. He may actually only regret letting himself get caught and leave prison determined to be more careful in the future. He might even resolve not to steal again for fear of further imprisonment. Penal justice may have been adequately satisfied and may even have succeeded in deterring future crime. A wise warden, however, would still be inclined to say he was returning a thief to society, and a wise neighbor would justifiably feel uneasy about living next to him.

The Jewish teachers, at the time of Christ, raised the question of what it would take for a condemned murderer to be forgiven and eligible for life with God in the age to come. Being put to death would not suffice because the murderer would be put to death anyway. They concluded that the murderer needed to add confession and repentance, including a willing acceptance of the death penalty.

All these examples express a truth familiar to Jewish and Christian teachers through the centuries. Undergoing a penalty is not enough to restore a relationship that is broken or damaged by wrongdoing. The punishment must also be accepted in the right spirit, willingly accepted as a way of satisfying the authority who imposed it. It must be accepted as a way of "making up for" the wrongdoing. Only punishment willingly undergone is truly reconciling.

This truth also applies to the death of Christ understood as penal substitution. Since Christ was not a sinner who needed to repent and did not receive a penalty he deserved, it does not apply in exactly the same way. On the other hand, as the representative of the human race, Christ did need to undergo the punishment in a similar spirit in order to restore the relationship of the human race with God. Although needing no personal repentance, he did need the corresponding attitude of submission and willingness to satisfy God in order to represent a race that did need repentance.

Acceptance of the Penalty. The obedience required to make up for the sin of the human race did not only involve the right spirit. It also required undergoing the actual penalty determined by God. It would not have been appropriate for

Christ to scale Mount Ararat painfully in the middle of winter and say to his Father: "There is the repair for the sins of the world." It would not even have done for him to raise an army, heroically conquer an Arabian tribe, and then say to his Father: "I thought I would do this and offer it to you for the redemption of the race."

As the representative of the human race, Christ needed to offer the acceptable sacrifice, the one God willed for the redemption of the human race (Heb 10:9). The New Adam needed to present himself to God in humility and be told what sacrifice would do.

On God's part, the determination of what needed to happen was not just automatically decided. A personal element was involved—difficult to describe adequately, but important to understand. If we were to approach God as our teacher and ask if Penang, Malaysia, is on the other side of the globe from Ontario, Canada, his response to us would be an automatic yes. The response would follow from the facts of the case. If we were to approach God under the old covenant law to redeem a kinsman who had fallen into debt slavery and pay him the amount our kinsman owed, the transaction would be relatively automatic. What we gave would handle the matter and the decision would come straightforwardly. The redemption of the human race, however, is a different matter. Both in its penal aspect and in its sacrificial aspect, the decision on God's part is less automatic because it involves considerations of personal relationships.

First, in view of the peril aspect, God has to decide what will satisfy him for the sin of the human race. There is no penal code in existence that specifies the cost of the redemption of a race from sin. There are, however, objective considerations for determining a fitting way to repair what has happened, even though they may involve matters of judgments beyond our full understanding. We intuitively know, for instance, that had the Huns ever been brought to justice for their atrocities, it would not have been just to let them off scot-free.

However, the disobedience of a whole race to its Creator is an even greater matter. Here we have no experience. We are similar to children who do not yet comprehend the seriousness of the offense given by some adult wrongdoing, like a man running off with his brother's wife.

Only God can determine what would be adequate for an offense against the King of the universe, what would suffice to repair the breach between the Creator and his errant creatures. As we have seen, "satisfaction" is the traditional word for what a judge or ruler needs to be given in such a situation. We need to give God—the one who understands the full gravity of the affair—satisfaction as he determines it.

Much the same element is present in the sacrificial aspect of Christ's work. A sacrifice is a special gift. Sometimes we think that gifts of any sort can be given, because by definition they are not required but come from generosity. Yet there are requirements for good gift-giving. To give someone a dirty piece of clothing on their birthday, even if useful to them once washed, is not to provide a good gift. It is an insult, or at least a sign of negligence. For a wealthy uncle to give a stingy gift at the wedding of a niece will likewise not endear him to the family. Moreover, with a gift, it is important to consider the personal factor of what the individual recipient would find an appropriate or useful gift.

Similarly to offer God a swine in sacrifice, or to keep the good lamb and offer him the lame one, is not a successful sacrifice (see Mal 1:6-14). The scriptural word which designates the way a sacrifice has to meet the requirements of the recipient is "acceptability." A sacrifice has to be "acceptable" to God.

The redemptive work of Christ, then, has to give his Father satisfaction and be acceptable to him. Christ as the head of the human race had to repair the relationship between that race and its God in a way God would find adequate. Therefore, he had to do what God wanted.

The sacrifice decided upon by God, as we know, involved

suffering and death. As the fall involved a transgression that had the death penalty, the redemption meant the voluntary acceptance of a death. As the most serious crimes involve "life for life," so a repair of all human crimes meant "life for life." As all human sin involves choosing one's life for oneself rather than giving it in obedience to God and service to others, so the deliverance of the human race meant the giving away of one's life in obedience to God and in service to others.

What God decided on was not suffering, the shedding of blood, and a painful death as something valuable in themselves whose "payment" would automatically make satisfaction to an impersonal order of justice. What he sought was an action that was a personal and moral reparation fitting to what was being repaired.

What God decided on, Christ freely offered for the race of which he was a member. His own life was the offering he gave to repair the damage that had been done. This offering God found acceptable, because what he received was something that in his eyes far outweighed the damage of human disobedience and dishonoring of himself. He received the full obedience and love of his Son, expressed in a way that was appropriate to repairing what had happened.

God received the gift of the New Adam, a gift offered out of Christ's desire to compensate for the failure of the race he represented, a gift that would express its repentance and desire to be obedient in the future. God received therein a fitting payment made, punishment undergone, and sacrifice offered for the sin of the human race.

THE FATHER'S LOVE

"How will it ever be made out a just or reasonable thing that God should treat or suffer to be treated in such a manner the man whom the Father called his beloved Son with whom he was well-pleased?" These are the words of Boso, the honest seeker after truth in Anselm of Canterbury's famous treatment of the incarnation and redemption. They state one of the chief objections to the scriptural teaching about the atoning death of Christ.

Boso's objection has been taken up by many who disbelieve in this doctrine or at least wish to relegate it to the category of outdated myth. It also, however, finds an echo in Christians who hold the doctrine at the center of their faith, but find the view it gives of God the Father somewhat scandalous.

The problem is raised most acutely by a certain way of visualizing the action of God, one that easily arises from the view of penal substitution. God the Father is seated on his throne as judge. The human race stands before him ready to be condemned. His Son is brought as a substitute. In his capacity as just judge, God condemns his Son to death for the sins of the human race. Christ is sent off to be crucified.

The intensity of this picture is increased, as Boso indicates, if we add the feature that the Son was chosen by the Father as a substitute. It is intensified even more if we imagine, as suggested by many Christian meditations on the crucifixion, that Christ then experienced the Father abandoning him and treating him as someone worthy of hell.

Such a picture has the obvious appeal of dramatizing penal substitution and the teaching of Isaiah 53, as well as conveying some sense of the awesomeness and greatness of Christ's sufferings. This dramatization has the great disadvantage, however, of putting the Father in the position of the judge who unjustly condemns the innocent one and who treats his Son cruelly or at least distantly and severely. While such a visualization can be helpful for devotional purposes as a dramatic picture of Christ, it does give us a distorted image of God the Father. The Father's role in the redemption cannot be adequately presented in such a framework.

Another picture is one in which the Father and the Son are working together to resolve the predicament of the human race. Such a view is provided by certain passages in the Scriptures. These are a few of the clearest examples and go along with the passages cited at the end of the last chapter:

> In this is love, not that we loved God but that he loved us and sent his Son to be the expiation for our sins. 1 Jn 4:10

> But God shows his love for us in that while we were yet sinners Christ died for us. Rom 5:8

> All this is from God, who through Christ reconciled us to himself and gave us the ministry of reconciliation; that is, God was in Christ reconciling the world to himself, not counting their trespasses against them.... 2 Cor 5:18-19

> And walk in love, as Christ loved us and gave himself up for us, a fragrant offering and sacrifice to God. Eph 5:2

> The life I now live in the flesh I live by faith in the Son of God, who loved me and gave himself for me. Gal 2:20b

We can see God's motives in these passages. He desired to save his human creatures because he loved them and wished to rescue them from the fate that had befallen them because of sin and Satan. We also see a unity of action between God the Father and his Son. God was in Christ, acting to save the world. God gave his Son to be a sacrifice. The Son gave himself. Christ laid down his life as an offering for sin. But at the same time he was the Lamb of God, the one God provided to take away the sins of the world. Any picture which sets God and his Son against one another misses the unity of purpose and action between them in a way that can only be inadequate and even distorting.

We see a different picture by looking at the Lamb on his way to be sacrificed. The Gospel of Mark tells of Christ on the way to Jerusalem:

> And they were on the road, going up to Jerusalem, and Jesus was walking ahead of them; and they were amazed, and those who followed were afraid. And taking the twelve

again, he began to tell them what was to happen to him, saying, "Behold, we are going up to Jerusalem; and the Son of man will be delivered to the chief priests and the scribes, and they will condemn him to death, and deliver him to the Gentiles; and they will mock him, and spit upon him, and scourge him, and kill him; and after three days he will arise. **Mk 10:32-34**

Shortly before this the transfiguration occurred when Christ appeared transformed in his resurrection glory. At that time the Father spoke from heaven: "This is my beloved Son; listen to him" (Mk 9:7). Shortly afterward, Christ explained to his disciples the way he would be a king by saying, "The Son of man also came not to be served but to serve, and to give his life as a ransom for many" (Mk 10:45).

We do not see here Christ being led passively to his Father for trial. Instead we see him purposefully, even fiercely, setting off to lay down his life as a sacrifice for the sins of the world, with the complete backing of his Father.

In order to comprehend this historical picture adequately, we need to keep a few truths clearly in mind. First, Christ and his Father were united in their determination to see the reign of God established on earth as it is in heaven and sin eliminated from the face of the earth. Consequently they were united in their hatred of sin and their determination to rid the world of it.

Christ is the one who confronted his opponents and "looked around at them with anger, grieved at their hardness of heart" (Mk 3:5). He is the one who said, "Whoever causes one of these little ones who believe in me to sin, it would be better for him if a great millstone were hung round his neck and he were thrown into the sea. And if your hand causes you to sin, cut it off; it is better for you to enter life maimed than with two hands to go to hell, to the unquenchable fire" (Mk 9:42-43). He is the one who denounced the scribes and Pharisees, forcefully cleansed the temple, and prophesied judgment on those who resisted his message. This is the Savior who taught that he would return as Judge, separate the sheep from the goats, and judge the same way his Father would.

The Son of God was on a mission given him by the Father. He wanted to save those who were willing to be saved, to rescue them from the coming judgment, to restore them to true life. In this he was representing "the riches of [God's] kindness and forbearance and patience" which is "meant to lead you to repentance" (Rom 2:4). But Christ likewise expected to represent God's judgment on "the day of wrath." Providing a way of escape from judgment—a way of forgiveness and redemption based upon an atoning sacrifice for the sins of the world—was one way of taking away the sins of the world. Judging the impenitent was another. Christ's act of grace and mercy to the condemned prostitute ends in the command, "Go, and do not sin again" (Jn 8:11).

Christ and his Father were one in the redemption of the world. This oneness was rooted in the way they were one in being before all ages, as the Nicene creed tells us. They were also one through the obedience of the Son in the human nature he took on. Christ loved the will of his heavenly Father and identified himself with it so that he could represent the Father and allow the Father to act through him.

The Son's moral oneness with the Father led him to lay down his life in sacrifice for the sins of the world because it was his Father's will. His sacrifice was at the same time something willingly given as it needed to be and something the Christ "must" do to accomplish his task.

Because of the relationship between the Father and the Son, for the Father to send the Son was like coming himself. "In this is love, not that we loved God but that he loved us and sent his Son to be the expiation for our sins" (1 Jn 4:10). Both in deciding upon the incarnation and in giving the incarnate one to be an offering on the cross, the Father saw that the world was reconciled to himself and did something that amounted to coming to do it himself.

People in earlier times, like Boso, were scandalized at the

Father's lack of justice in not using his power to defend his Son from ill treatment. They needed to see the willingness, even the desire, of the Son to voluntarily take on the service and accomplish the mission. Modern people, on the other hand, tend to be more scandalized at the Father's lack of compassion or feeling for his Son, his willingness to let him undergo such pain.

This is perhaps a point of sensitivity that many modern people cannot be completely freed of. Nonetheless, it helps to see that there is a true nobility to the commander of an army sending troops off to certain death that the nation might be saved—regretting the necessity of doing it, but even more regretting that he himself was not the one to go. To suffer and die for a great cause is a great privilege. There is a true nobility to the mother, on being told of her son's death in the line of duty, both weeping and at the same time rejoicing to have the privilege of having raised a son for such an honor. There is a true nobility to the communities of Christians who eagerly hoped that some of their members would die martyrs and envied the ones chosen.

Too soft a compassion is a sign of moral decline. Sparing someone the necessity of suffering and dying is often sparing them the privilege of moral greatness and so depriving them of one of the greatest human goods possible.

Why then did the Father not go himself? If this is understood as a question as to why Jesus of Nazareth, the Son of God, died rather than God the Father, the most obvious answer is only somewhat helpful: he was the one to die because it took a human being to die. An unincarnate one who is God cannot die.

Answered another way, the question is very enlightening. God the Father did not die because only a Son could do what needed to be done. It was a son, Adam, and his descendants with him, who had disobeyed God, his Father. They had refused God the honor and submission that was his due. If someone was to make up for it, it was only appropriate for a

Son to do so, because the repair for disobedience should be an act of obedience and submission. The way to make up for disobedience and dishonor should be to offer a recompense, a life given in obedience and submission. That is something that a Son who was human and a fitting representative for the human race could do. That is something that a Father who was the Creator of all and the unbegotten one in the Trinity could not do.

We might then ask whether God could not have found another way. Could he not have freed the human race from sin without an atoning sacrifice for sin from his Son? Could he not have devised a way of simply writing off the debt and proclaiming an amnesty? Could he not have received repentant sinners back without all the work and suffering involved in the payment of a price?

Different answers have been given to the question of whether God could have freed the human race without the sacrifice of his Son. Some have said that God could not have done so once he had created the world the way he did. The moral law is so written into the universe that disobedience and dishonor of God require some sort of atonement or satisfaction. Pardon is only just if it is done on the basis of an atonement. Otherwise pardon amounts to God's decision that human actions, even ones of great moral weight, are not to be respected and taken seriously. They can be forgotten or dismissed with no further ado. There is much to be said for this answer.

Another answer is commonly given. Yes, God could have done so, and it would even have been just. God can simply pardon whomever he wishes to. But does he not need to punish sin or require satisfaction in order to uphold the moral order of the universe? As we experience, families without discipline are families in which children grow up weak in character and in which family life is weak in committed love as well as justice. Would not the human race turn out the same as such families if salvation was by simple pardon? There is much likewise to be said for this answer.

There is still a further answer. Yes, God might have simply pardoned the human race and overlooked sin. Yet it was still more gracious for him to give the human race a chance to make up for sin and restore the relationship. To have sinned is degrading enough. To be forced to receive a pardon with no chance of doing anything to make up for what one did is still more degrading. Allowing atonement is itself an expression of grace.

All three of these answers may in fact be true at the same time, if they are not presented, as they were above, as absolute and therefore incompatible. If we do not try to ask what God could have done, but ask why he did what he did, each answer may express part of his approach to the redemption. Such a response would say that God acted with greater justice, better fatherly discipline, and more consideration for human dignity by deciding on an atoning sacrifice for sin than by simply pardoning sin.

Yet an even more helpful approach avoids a question which amounts to a "could we not have gotten out of this somehow" response. Instead imagine God the Father asking his Son, the New Adam, the new head of the human race: how would you like to see this handled? Would you prefer the chance to make up for what your people have done?

I believe the answer would be, and was, that he would prefer a more fitting way to deal with sin and a more worthy response from someone who is the Son of such a Father. In this, his judgment and the Father's would have been one.

EIGHT

Humility and Victory

A S ADAM CONFRONTED SATAN, so did Christ. At the very beginning of his public ministry, right after being anointed
with the Spirit as the messianic King and proclaimed as God's
Son, Christ encountered Satan himself. We read about that
encounter in the fourth chapter of the Gospel according to
Matthew:

> Then Jesus was led up by the Spirit into the wilderness to
> be tempted by the devil. And he fasted forty days and forty
> nights, and afterward he was hungry. And the tempter
> came and said to him, "If you are the Son of God, com-
> mand these stones to become loaves of bread." But he an-
> swered, "It is written,
> 'Man shall not live by bread alone,
> but by every word that proceeds from the mouth of God.'"
> Then the devil took him to the holy city, and set him on
> the pinnacle of the temple, and said to him, "If you are the
> Son of God, throw yourself down; for it is written,
> 'He will give his angels charge of you,' and
> 'On their hands they will bear you up,
> lest you strike your foot against a stone.'"
> Jesus said to him, "Again it is written, 'You shall not tempt
> the Lord your God.'" Again, the devil took him to a very
> high mountain, and showed him all the kingdoms of the

205

world and the glory of them; and he said to him, "All these I will give you, if you will fall down and worship me." Then Jesus said to him, "Begone, Satan! for it is written,

'You shall worship the Lord your God and him only shall you serve.'"

Then the devil left him, and behold, angels came and ministered to him. Mt 4:1-11

To be tempted is to be tested by an inducement to do evil, to sin. For a righteous, godly person, then, a temptation is also an attack on what he values most, living in a way pleasing to God and so attaining the purpose for which he is made. Christ began his public ministry by undergoing such an attack. The first Adam had to face Satan in combat and in so doing brought the human race down in a great defeat. The New Adam also had to face Satan. Upon the outcome of that encounter hung the promise of a new future for the human race.

"The Testing" or "The Trial" is recounted at the beginning of the Gospel for a reason. It was a prelude to the rest of Christ's earthly ministry, which in turn was the prelude to his heavenly ministry of redeeming the human race. He did not come for a peaceful ministry of teaching winning truths, speaking gracious words, blessing children, and being commended by all—however much these things formed part of what he did. "The reason the Son of God appeared was to destroy the works of the devil" (1 Jn 3:8). Christ came for a kind of war, and the initial campaign was to fight on earth to reach an assured position of heavenly power and authority. That war was first manifested in the event we call the temptation.

The encounter in Matthew 4 was a fight, but one that did not involve physical force. The temptation was an ethical or moral fight where the battlefield is the will or heart, the inner place where human beings make decisions. In this case, the battlefield was the heart of Christ.

The issue Christ faced was his role as the human Son of God. How would he conduct himself in the position he held? His identity had been manifested to the world by the heavenly voice at his baptism: "This is my beloved Son, with whom I am well pleased" (Mt 3:17). Like Adam, the New Adam had to maintain the position that was his by the grace and choice of God.

The issue of his position as the Son of God was clearly stated by the tempter: "if you are the Son of God." Christ was tempted to prove himself. He was first tempted to prove himself as the specially favored one of God by an act of power as great as Moses performed when he provided bread in the wilderness. He was then tempted to prove himself by an act of "faith" in God that would prove God's special protection. At the end, he was presented all the kingdoms of the world and the glory of them and tempted to receive them, not from God but from "the ruler of this world" (Jn 12:31): "All these I will give you if you will fall down and worship me."

The temptations were subtle in a certain way. Like the temptation faced by Adam and Eve, Satan tempted Christ with something God in fact wanted him to have. By God's intention Christ would do great acts of power, including making bread in the wilderness. He would receive striking protection from God. He would become the ruler of the whole world.

But the nub of the temptation for Christ was the same as for Adam and Eve. Would he take the path of obedience? Would he follow the instructions of God, trusting God to bring him where he wanted him to be? Or would he reach out and exalt himself, making use of the power and position God gave him but not in God's way?

Christ won his initial combat with Satan. But it was only the first round. As the Gospel of Luke tells us, "When the devil had ended every temptation, he departed from him until an opportune time" (Lk 4:13). The account we describe as the temptation of Christ only reveals in a more vivid way the struggle Christ was undergoing all during his public ministry. Further temptations from Satan are described at those points where Christ is forced to turn away from establishing a messianic kingdom of earthly glory and takes instead the path that would lead to the cross (Mt 16:23, Lk 22:53, Jn 12:31-32; 14:30).

The path Christ took could be summed up in his own words: "Everyone who exalts himself will be humbled, and he who humbles himself will be exalted" (Lk 14:11). To translate the saying into more literal English, "Everyone who raises himself will be lowered, and he who lowers himself will be raised."

This principle was applied to Christ's death and resurrection in the Philippians 2 passage that we considered at the beginning of the last chapter. The New Adam, the Son of God, humbled himself in obedience to the point of death. This self-humbling, this self-lowering, resulted in an exaltation, a rising. *Because* "he humbled himself and became obedient unto death, even death on a cross. *Therefore* God has highly exalted him and bestowed on him the name which is above every name, that at the name of Jesus every knee should bow, in heaven and on earth and under the earth, and every tongue confess that Jesus Christ is Lord, to the glory of God the Father" (Phil 2:8-11).

In Hebrew idiom the word "lowering" or "going down" can refer to defeat, just as "exaltation" or "going up" can refer to victory. Christ's death on the cross was a going down to go up. It was a defeat that resulted in victory, a falling in battle that resulted in rising in triumph. Christ's path followed his own paradoxical instruction: the way to go up is to go down. It had to in order to overcome the fallenness of this world.

In this chapter we are going to look at Christ's victory over the enemies of the human race, a victory that was accomplished through lowering himself or humbling himself. In one way we have already done that in the last chapter. The chief enemy of the human race is sin. Christ defeated sin definitively in his own person by keeping the command-ments to the end, at the cost of his own life. He did so through the humility of obedience and service. He defeated sin, in other words, by never sinning.

Yet as most if not all of us experience, there is more to sin than simply some action we do or do not do. There seems to be a power behind sin, a power that makes it difficult not to act disobediently and transgress God's commandments. Externally, as Scripture tells us, that power comes from Satan and "this world," this place of exile, this house we live in that makes it hard for us to serve God. Internally, that power is the weakness of the flesh that makes us prey to death. Together they determine much of what happens to the fallen human race and produce the pattern of sin we have already observed.

Christ defeated sin itself, but he also defeated those spiri-tual forces that hold human beings enslaved to sin. He defeated Satan and death in his own person and so put him-self in the position to defeat Satan and death by freeing other human beings from sin. He won this victory by following the paradoxical principle of going down to go up. Christ humbled himself, let himself be put down in defeat, to win the victory over the main enemies of the human race. He let himself lose to Satan in order to win over him. He let himself be put to death in order to defeat death.

This is a chapter about the victory of Christ—on the cross itself. It concerns the way his humility led to spiritual victory because it led to the action of God on his behalf. To gain insight into the paradox of Christ's statement about going down to go up, we must insert "by God" into it. "Everyone who raises himself will be lowered *by God,* and everyone who lowers himself will be raised *by God.*" To state it more gener-ally, the key to spiritual victory over the fallenness of this world is the action of God and the way to bring about that action is submission to God and his plan.

SPIRITUAL WARFARE

The Enemy. The conflict Christ faced was a moral and there-fore internal one, but Christ had an external opponent. He did not only have to deal with desires or tendencies inside himself that might lead him to wrong choices. He was deal-ing with a being outside himself leading him to sin. He was encountering Satan.

When modern people think of Satan's activity in human life, what often comes to mind is possession. From time to time we hear about dramatic exorcisms, attempted liberations from the mysterious control a demonic force has over an indi-vidual. Or some, most commonly Christians, think more of Satan's activity as special influences of evil spirits or "holds" that such spirits can have upon people, holds that need to be broken by a process of "deliverance." Others associate Satan with curses, hexes, spells, and malign and hidden influences that come from witchcraft, voodoo, or spiritualism.

All these, however, are only special works of the devil, not what he is mainly about. When John says, "The reason the Son of God appeared was to destroy the works of the devil," the context makes clear that "the works of the devil" are com-mitting sin. In regard to the human race, Satan is mainly interested in getting people to sin.

Satan is behind what we have been calling the sin prob-lem. Since what God commands is goodness itself, sin is moral evil. Satan is behind the moral evil of the universe because he himself has become morally corrupt and passes on his own way of life. But he is also behind the moral evil of the universe in a further way. He attempts to get human beings to choose moral evil so that they sin, that is, enter into disobedience to God. As the leader of a rebellion against God, Satan entices human beings to disobey God as a way of joining them to his own kingdom. His strategy is similar to the way modern governments sometimes win over spies or traitors. They first get them to commit a crime, so that the traitors have a personal interest in being free of the authority that would punish them if caught.

The existence of the organized rebellion that is the kingdom of Satan is not always clearly recognized. Not to have it recognized works to his advantage. Sins that he is trying to bring human beings to commit often do not look like sins. As Paul puts it, "Satan disguises himself as an angel of light," and "his servants also disguise themselves as servants of righteousness" (2 Cor 11:14-15). Sin can appear to be humanitarian or philanthropic. Agents of evil can be disciplined and self-controlled, even courteous and affable. If the result of their actions, however, is to take human beings away from honoring and obeying God, they are advancing the kingdom of Satan and ultimately furthering evil.

The New Testament writings present Satan and demonic forces as waging a fight for control of the human race. New Testament passages about warfare and fighting in the Christian life do not refer, for the most part at least, to physical combat. They refer to a moral or ethical combat. Behind sin, in the common New Testament view, lies not just human weakness and ignorance, nor simply human perversity, but something more than human. "We are not contending against flesh and blood" (Eph 6:12), said Paul about opposition to the Christian message.

We are not just contending with the human forces we can see. We are confronting evil spiritual forces as well. We are, in fact, confronting "the wiles of the devil." We are up against a struggle designed to lead us either to give up serving God or, if possible, to turn to disobedience to God. That struggle is primarily conducted by deceit, temptation, and unacknowledged influences working upon us. Satan is "the father of lies" (Jn 8:44). In this age, his main tactics are persuasion to sin, what we might call propaganda. As we know, such propaganda is often most effective when it is least overt.

There is, however, another important truth about Satan's power: he seems to have not only influence but also authority in this world. The New Testament writings speak of the work of redemption as freeing people from Satan's power or authority (Acts 26:18) or delivering them from the kingdom of darkness (Col 1:13). Christ even spoke of Satan as the ruler of this world (Jn 12:31). Paul especially spoke of the greater evil spirits in words that indicate they have ruling power. They are principalities and powers, thrones and dominions, world rulers of this present darkness (Eph 6:12).

Satan's rule seems to be real, but there is no indication in the New Testament that it is just or lawful. He is a usurper. God, however, seems to respect his rule and allow it to continue. He clearly does not allow it because he wants what Satan wants. He allows it because he lets those who rebel from him conduct their own affairs in the way they choose. As Paul indicates, that is in itself a punishment because a life of sin leads people into destructive habits and inevitably leads to death (Rom 1:12-22). That death is not just physical but spiritual as well, separation from God and loss of true life. Those who die in such a state go down to the place of the dead and there find themselves under the rule of Satan. He is most justly not the ruler of earth but the ruler of the nether regions, of hell, of those who live in separation from God.

Although Satan is the ruler of hell, in this age he is also the ruler of this world, of the current state of human affairs. Through the fall, he has obtained dominion over human beings, even before their final death, because they are spiritually already dead. Human beings who choose sin rather than God de facto choose to have Satan as their ruler. By that choice, they leave the blessing and protection that come from being in God's kingdom and go out into a world of Satan's making. The consequences of sin, therefore, include subjection to the rule of Satan and other demonic beings.

From God's point of view, allowing Satan's sway over fallen human beings is just. After all, they chose him and believed his message. Moreover, it was only fitting that sin should have such consequences. The obedience God teaches is obedience to what makes heaven possible—love of him and love of one another. A life of ingratitude and rebellion toward one's Creator, a life of loving oneself first, in itself creates hellish conditions.

Nor is it strange that those who choose to turn away from God find themselves under a ruler who turns out to be a tyrant. A ruler of such beings and of such a place naturally embodies the characteristics that make up its nature: Satan is a being of malice and that malice shapes the way he rules.

From God's point of view, Satan's authority is like that of a jailer. A jailer would have no authority over anyone if there were no crimes. His authority comes into existence because of the crime of those he rules. In a similar way, where slavery functions legally as a way of dealing with insolvent debtors, slave masters would have no authority over anyone if they did not fall into debt they could not repay. Satan is a kind of penal slave master who acquires dominion over his subjects because of their debts. Since he himself induced them to contract those debts, they also can be seen as his captives, but they became captives by their own decision.

Like the company stores in mining towns during early capitalist exploitation, the control Satan gained was accomplished with a certain legality. He managed to persuade Adam, after all, to choose to contract the debt of sin. Human beings are held by a certain legal justice, no matter how great the malice with which their captor acted. God, then, was faced with the captivity of his creatures to a ruler who would not give them up freely and so had to be defeated. Nonetheless, their captor also had a certain claim in justice that had to be dealt with properly. Simple force would not do.

The Personal Struggle. It is for this war of liberation that Christ came. His sufferings and death issuing in resurrection were a battle, the turning point of the war for the soul of the human race. As Paul tells us in Colossians 2:15, the cross was the place where Christ "disarmed the principalities and powers." There he triumphed over them.

We do not often view the crucifixion as a victory. One current of popular devotion, in fact, makes the cross seem like a great misfortune which was simply reversed by the resurrection. Nonetheless, the New Testament contains many passages where the crucifixion is seen as a combat with Satan from which Christ emerges victorious.[1] In fact, when the sufferings and death of Christ are seen in that light, we can more easily see them precisely as redemption. On the cross, Christ was delivering human beings from an oppressive enslaving force, one from which they could not free themselves.

During the last day of his life, we find Christ in the garden of Gethsemane, in a situation very similar to the temptation. The Gospel of Matthew describes it this way:

> Then Jesus went with them to a place called Gethsemane, and he said to his disciples, "Sit here, while I go yonder and pray." And taking with him Peter and the two sons of Zebedee, he began to be sorrowful and troubled. Then he said to them, "My soul is very sorrowful, even to death; remain here, and watch with me." And going a little farther he fell on his face and prayed, "My Father, if it be possible, let this cup pass from me; nevertheless, not as I will, but as thou wilt." And he came to the disciples and found them sleeping; and he said to Peter, "So, could you not watch with me one hour? Watch and pray that you may not enter into temptation; the spirit indeed is willing, but the flesh is weak." Again, for the second time, he went away and prayed, "My Father, if this cannot pass unless I drink it, thy will be done." And again he came and found them sleeping, for their eyes were heavy. So, leaving them again, he went away and prayed for the third time, saying the same words. Then he came to the disciples and said to them, "Are you still sleeping and taking your rest? Behold,

---

1. For passages which speak about Christ's death as a combat with or victory over Satan and his kingdom, see page 303.

the hour is at hand, and the Son of man is betrayed into the hands of sinners. Rise, let us be going; see, my betrayer is at hand." Mt 26:36-46

The fact that Christ is in a garden is probably typologically significant. He is the New Adam encountering Satan in a garden as was paradise. But Gethsemane is a garden of grief in the middle of the fallen world rather than a garden of delight in the world as it was created.

Christ is going through what is often described as "the agony in the garden." When we hear the word "agony" we primarily think of pain or suffering. That is an aspect of what Jesus went through, but the word in origin means a struggle or a contest like a wrestling match. The agony in the garden refers to Christ's combat.

Even though Satan is not explicitly mentioned, Jesus is there in combat with him. The three times Jesus returns to prayer are probably connected to the three times he had to undergo temptation by Satan in the desert. If that is so, "the agony" is something of a repeat of the temptation. The scene in the garden may be itself an encounter with Satan. Or it may be a preparation for the real struggle with Satan on the cross when Jesus was given over to the power of darkness (Lk 22:53)—just as the temptation in the wilderness was a preparation for the struggle with Satan that was his public ministry. Perhaps it was both at the same time.

In the Garden of Gethsemane, Satan has the initiative. He wants to turn back the initial incursion of the Son of God, primarily by working through the Jewish and Roman leaders.

In the wilderness Satan tempted Christ to use the power he had for his own worldly success. He tempted Christ to set up a kingdom over this world, an empire that would embrace "all the kingdoms of the world." Satan no doubt made such an endeavor seem good. If Christ actually controlled all the world, could he not see to it that the human race would live in a better way? This was a test, however, as to whether Christ would turn aside from the path on which his Father had set him.

In the Garden of Gethsemane, Jesus faced a different type of temptation to turn aside. If events continued on their present course, he would go to his death the next day. He knew he would face crucifixion, the death reserved for insurrectionists, those claiming to be messiahs and seeking to establish a Jewish kingdom independent of the Romans.

Jesus knew what crucifixion was like. The Romans crucified people on the roads entering cities so that the sight would deter others from committing similar crimes. Crucifixion was a cruel, degrading death, deliberately made to be a torture. Moreover, such a death would involve the humiliation of being an apparently failed messiah. It would be a seeming defeat at the hands of the very ones he had challenged—the worldly authorities and behind them the ruler of this world, Satan himself. It was no doubt such death which was before Christ's eyes in the Garden of Gethsemane.

Yet he was still free. Instead of staying at the garden where Judas and the temple police would find him, Jesus could take the Gethsemane road away from, rather than toward Jerusalem. He could then escape across the Jordan to safety. The temptation he faced in the garden was the temptation not to die, not to lay down his life, and therefore not to obey his Father.

When Christ prayed to his Father, he was troubled by fear and sorrowful at what lay ahead. Yet he also knew why he would have to undergo such a death. He had come to serve, to give his life as a ransom for the many. Christ had come, as he had just told his disciples, to pour out his blood for many so that they could be part of the new covenant and receive forgiveness for their sins. He "must" suffer and die. His Father had given him a command to do so in order that those who believe in him should not perish but have eternal life.

Christ was free not to die—only too free. That freedom was probably itself the source of the testing. When we have no choice, there is not as much of a struggle to endure suffering. We usually swallow what we have to take with some measure of resignation. When we could get out of a difficult situation but believe we should undergo it, then we face a test. Jesus faced such a test in Gethsemane.

The victory of Christ was expressed in the prayer, "Not my will, but yours be done." In praying such a prayer, Jesus rejected the course of action any human would have wanted to take, and instead accepted the full purpose of God. That prayer was probably a plea for help to go through what faced him. It was also a willing acceptance of God's will and a desire to see the human race served as a result of what he would do. In the Gospel of John, in a scene that corresponds to the agony in the garden, Jesus expressed the same willingness to do the will of God, "Now is my soul troubled. And what shall I say, 'Father, save me from this hour'? No, for this purpose I have come to this hour. Father glorify thy name" (Jn 12:27-28).

Losing to Win. Christ then began what is sometimes called "his passion." "Passion" in this sense means the suffering he knew he must undergo for the salvation of the human race from its sins. His passion was an ordeal, a true humiliation, but one that he went through with a great deal of self-mastery and personal dignity. Christ knew what he was about because he had made a decision in Gethsemane. He died well, in a way fitting for an unblemished lamb.

The Gospel of John records the last words of Christ on the cross: "It is finished" (Jn 19:30). By these words he did not simply mean that his sufferings were over and now he would die. He also meant that he had completed the task for which he came. His words registered victory rather than defeat. Christ had succeeded in putting aside "my will", his own human will that recoiled from such an ordeal, and had instead embraced "your will," his Father's will. He had been obedient to death. The Son of God had therefore succeeded in dying in such a way that his sufferings and death could be a payment for the redemption of the human race.

In the death of Christ, Satan was defeated. As the Letter to the Hebrews puts it, "We see Jesus, who for a little while was made lower than the angels... so that by the grace of God he might taste death for every one.... He... partook of the same nature [as those he was to save], that through death he might destroy him who has the power of death, that is, the devil, and deliver all those who through fear of death were subject to lifelong bondage" (Heb 2:9, 14-15).

Not only was Satan defeated but so were all those who share in his rule. Colossians says, "God made [you] alive..., having forgiven us all our trespasses, having canceled the bond which stood against us with its legal demands; this he set aside, nailing it to the cross. He disarmed the principalities and powers and made a public example of them, triumphing over them in it [RSV: him]" (Col 2:13-15).

Both passages speak about Christ's death as a defeat of Satan. The first says he "destroyed" Satan, although that translation is misleading because it seems to imply that Satan went out of existence after Christ's death. The word rather probably indicates that Satan lost his ability to inflict death, spiritual, eternal death, on the "many sons" who belonged to Christ (Heb 2:10-13). Once Christ died, Satan did not lose all power over the human race, nor all power to inflict death. He did, however, lose his ability to hold in bondage those who belonged to Christ. That power was destroyed by what Christ did. Christ "tasted death" so that no one else would have to die eternally.

The Colossians passage provides an explanation for why that was. On the cross the debt due to sin was canceled and we were forgiven our trespasses. As a result, Satan's power due to our indebtedness to the punishment of sin was taken away. His power can no longer affect those who are "in Christ" (Col 2:10-12). The death of Christ on the cross was the greatest defeat Satan suffered, the reversal of the great victory he won when he induced Adam to fall.

When Christ fought and defeated Satan, clearly he did not defeat him by physical force. He was crucified in weakness

(2 Cor 13:4), in what looked like a defeat from a human perspective. He was humiliated in the eyes of all, treated like a great criminal, apparently ending his life as a failed messiah.

Christ's way of fighting was paradoxical. To fight, he refused to fight. He refused to defend himself, not so that he could be a pacifist but so that he could be a sacrificial Lamb set apart to be slain. He deliberately chose to "endure the shame" of defeat (Heb 12:2) in the confidence that his very defeat would be victory, that his very lowering would be a raising up. In the eyes of a fallen world, this makes no sense. It only made sense from a heavenly perspective, which allows for the Messiah to make his life an offering to overcome sin.

At the same time, Satan, who looked like he was achieving his greatest victory, was undergoing defeat. In the words of many Christian writers, he "overreached himself." He was like a commander who seems to be winning a battle and charges deep into the ranks of his enemy—only to find that he has fallen into a trap and is surrounded with no hope of escape.

At the very moment Satan seemed to be achieving his greatest triumph, he was being most completely defeated. Because the whole human race was under the sentence of death as a consequence of the fall, he could have put anyone else to death with justice. Instead, Satan put to death the sinless Son of God, the one who was truly innocent, and who therefore did not deserve to undergo the penal consequences of sin. Christ's death, consequently could be an expiation for the sins of others. Satan went too far and so produced the one event which would deprive him of his hold over the whole human race.

Did Satan know what he was doing? How could he have allowed this to happen? The answer seems to be that he did not know what he was doing. As Paul put it, "None of the rulers of this age understood this; for if they had, they would not have crucified the Lord of glory" (1 Cor 2:8). Ignatius of Antioch, a man who lived in the time of the apostles, described Satan's ignorance this way: "Now, Mary's virginity and her giving birth escaped the notice of the prince of this world, as did the Lord's death" (*Ephesians, 19,1*). Leo the Great (died A.D. 460) stated it this way, "And in order that he might set the human race free from the bonds of deadly transgression, He hid the power of His majesty from the raging devil, and opposed him with our frail and humble nature" (*Sermon LXII, 3*).

Satan seemed to understand enough to know that Jesus was the Messiah and the Son of God in the sense in which kings of Israel were sons of God. But he had defeated would-be messiahs and kings of Israel before. He did not seem to reckon with the fact that this King was God's Son in a more than human way. Satan did not seem to understand at all the "secret and hidden wisdom of God" (1 Cor 2:7), that is, God's plan to restore the human race to a glorified life that only became obvious with the resurrection.

Satan was tricked—not tricked in a mean way, but outwitted by a plan conceived in divine wisdom. Perhaps even more accurately, he was outwitted by his own pride. Satan was so set on his own exaltation and dominion that he could not imagine the willingness of his divine adversary to lower himself to the complete humiliation of giving his life for the sake of his creatures. He had no way of reckoning on the humility of God.

A Trial of Justice. The crucifixion was a contest of justice between God and Satan. Traditionally the Book of Job has been used to provide a perspective on the sufferings of Christ. It is now often overlooked, but nonetheless it is still illuminating.

Christian teachers throughout the centuries have seen Job himself as a type of Christ. The Book of Job narrates a contest between God and Satan. God is holding court as the King and Judge of human affairs. Satan comes before God in the role of "adversary," something like a prosecuting attorney. He enters into debate with God, because if he can establish his case as just or righteous, he can get his way. God is willing to argue, because he will only reign in justice or righteousness and because he wants it to be seen clearly that justice is done.

God points out Job, a blameless man who fears God and refuses to do evil. In God's view, Job is the example of a man who proves that sin is not all-powerful and that righteousness can prevail. Satan's reply to God is, "Does Job fear God for nothing?" He is making the claim, in other words, that Job does not serve God because he truly is a servant of God. Rather, Job serves God because he gets what he wants from doing so. He is merely a hireling. He was, so to speak, bribed by God to behave. Implied in Satan's position is the claim that no human being serves God for the sake of serving God.

As we know, God allowed Satan to afflict Job, depriving him of every human good, and although Job complained, he remained steadfastly righteous. Job's endurance was a reply to Satan, an imperfect one but a reply nonetheless. God's full reply to Satan, however, did not come in the Book of Job. It came in Jesus, the truly righteous servant of God. It came in the way Christ underwent "the afflictions of Job" in his sufferings and death. In his crucifixion, Christ was God's response to Satan. His death showed God's justice in a way the world and Satan could see (cf. Rom 3:25-26).

The crucifixion is God's counter-statement to Satan's most fundamental accusation against the human race. It is first of all a statement that the human race is capable of being what God asks it to be. Jesus underwent the sufferings of Job, not for personal reward but for the sake of the glory of his Father. He had nothing to gain personally. After all, he began with heavenly glory in the presence of God (Jn 17:5; Phil 2:6).

Being rich, Christ impoverished himself for the sake of others and therefore for the sake of God who sent him to serve them (2 Cor 8:9). He went through sufferings great enough to make human life seem valueless, and he did so willingly to the end in order to accomplish his mission. He showed that human nature could keep the commandments of God. In so doing he victoriously refuted Satan's accusation.

Even more, the very path of the crucifixion and of the redemption is a counter-statement to Satan. In the way Christ died, he lowered or humbled himself. He voluntarily underwent the humiliation of defeat and degradation as a criminal. As a result he offered his Father an act of humility for the redemption of the human race. This was not only a fitting sacrifice in atonement but also a stunning counter-statement to the pride with which Satan fell, and which he taught to Adam and Eve to induce them to fall.

In the Gospel of John, Christ describes his "lifting up" as the judgment of Satan, "the ruler of this world" (Jn 16:11; 12:31). "Judgment" here means "condemnation." This probably does not mean that Satan was personally condemned at that point for his rebellion against God. Rather Christ is referring to the way in which Satan is deprived of his power. He is condemned the way a corrupt governor might be removed from office or the way a defeated king who had usurped his power might be deprived of his authority.

With the crucifixion of Christ, Satan lost his rule or power over those members of the human race who would choose to belong to Christ. But when he was deprived of that position, Satan was deprived in full justice. God pointed to his Son and said, "See my servant. He was obedient and faithful to death. You are without excuse, as are all who have chosen your path. You could have obeyed. Had you obeyed, you would not have lived in constant humiliation but rather in glory as he will. You deserve to have no power over human beings, and so you will have none over those who come to my Son to be set free from you."

THE HUMILITY OF THE REDEEMER

The way to live is to die. The way to be victorious is to undergo defeat. The way to go up is to go down. This principle is paradoxical, but it describes the path Christ took. That same principle applies to our own lives. The way Christ died is not just the source of our redemption but also a pattern that should shape our redeemed lives in this fallen world.

Scripture states this truth in various ways. "Christ suffered for you, leaving you an example, that you should follow in his steps" (1 Pt 2:21). "Have the same orientation [RSV: this mind] among yourselves which is yours in Christ Jesus who... humbled himself and became obedient unto death, even death on a cross" (Phil 2:5, 8). "Walk in love, as Christ loved us and gave himself up for us, a fragrant offering and sacrifice to God" (Eph 5:2). "For I have given you an example, that you also should do as I have done to you" (Jn 13:15). "Take up [your] cross and follow me" (Mt 16:24).

We are to imitate Christ (1 Cor 11:1). Yet if we do not understand what this means, imitating Christ could get us into a great deal of trouble. It does not mean imitating him in his power or authority, claiming to be king and messiah, relating to others as their lord. Denouncing people the way Christ denounced the Pharisees, for instance, may be appropriate under certain circumstances when we have an authorization from God similar to the one Christ had. It is not, however, supposed to be something we do whenever we come across someone not behaving well simply on the basis of following Christ's example.

If we look at all the passages in which we are urged to imitate Christ, we find that they concern his sufferings and death.[2] We are called to imitate him in his lowliness or humility, not in his messiahship, or his divinity, or his exaltation. We are to imitate him in the way he chose to go down in order to go up.

Here again we could make a mistake, less dangerous than the previous one but distorting nonetheless. We could decide that imitating Christ in his sufferings was the key to handling all circumstances in life. We could "open not our mouths," never reproving wrong or explaining ourselves when falsely accused. We could become pacifists simply because Christ

---

2. For a list of passages which speak about Christ's death as a moral example to be imitated, see page 303.

told his disciples in Gethsemane not to use the sword to defend themselves.

All these responses have their place and have their place on the basis of the imitation of Christ, as indicated by Peter's exhortation to slaves with masters who mistreat them (1 Pt 2:18-25). But Christ's approach to his passion is not a universal rule for handling every situation, as demonstrated by his own previous conduct.

We are most especially called to imitate Christ's humility in the willingness to undergo sufferings for the kingdom of God. We are called to willingly undergo loss of reputation, loss of possessions, physical harm, and even death because of our faithfulness to God. The summons to take up our cross and follow Christ is the summons to follow a master who provokes opposition from the kingdom of darkness and a fallen world—but who steadfastly refuses to give up obeying his Father because of that opposition.

We are, however, called to imitate Christ more broadly—in the way he loved God and neighbor. We are to have the servant-love Christ manifested in the way of the cross. He humbled himself to become a servant. As a servant, he was obedient to God and he gave his life to serve those his Father sent him to. He loved in humility.

Humility points us away from making our own good and our own glory our aim. To be sure, when we are humble, we do not lose our desire for happiness or excellence. In fact, God intends them for the human race. Christ, in fact, came to bring us to glory (Heb 2:10). But the way to go up is to go down. God does not put our glorification into our own hands. Our fallenness means that we cannot seek our own glory and fully seek the good of others at the same time. We need to correct for the self-centered tendencies of our fallen nature. God's plan, therefore, is that we please him by loving others as Christ loved us, and leave our glorification to him. The way up is the way of reliance on God.

When our human fallenness has been completely overcome in the glorified life, loving others as ourselves may be easy, even effortless. In this life, however, there will always be resistance to overcome, both internal and external. In this life, there will always be personal cost. We will have to choose to suffer losses to live consistently for the welfare of others. In no other way can the fallen world be overcome in our own lives in this age. That is why the new covenant formulation of the second great commandment for disciples of Christ is "love one another as I have loved you" (Jn 15:12). That reformulation does not change what we are asked to do. Rather, it describes the only path that will allow us to do what we are asked to do: going down to go up, suffering defeat to achieve victory, dying to live.

Humility would have been important for the human race even if human beings had not fallen. Adam and Eve would have had to show humility towards God by obedient submission and by gratefully receiving his gifts and blessings as his creatures. They would have had to show humility towards one another by daily servant-love. That humility would have made it possible for human life to reflect the glory of God.

But for the New Adam, humility inevitably involved humiliation—personal suffering, defeat, and death. These are not in themselves God's desire or purpose for the human race. Rather, they are the necessary way for anyone who fulfills God's purpose and keeps his commandments to succeed at living a godly life in a fallen world dominated by sin, Satan, and death. The path of the cross understood as the path of love is a model of the end of human life, a model of the kind of love God wants human beings to live for all eternity. The path of the cross understood as the path of suffering is a model of the means to that end, a model of the way to love in this fallen world.

The path of the cross is also a path of faith and hope in God. It is not exactly a human, earthly strategy. Humble, humiliated service and death is not the normal way great earthly victories come about. Only when we recognize that God and his action is the key to overcoming the fallen state of the human race, can we follow Christ's path of humility, and only when God acts is that path of humility redemptive and victorious. Therefore, that path can only be followed by having faith and hope in God because of what God did in Christ. As First Peter explains: "Through him you have confidence in God, who raised him from the dead and gave him glory, so that your faith and hope are in God" (1 Pt 1:21).

We tend not to think of Christ as a man of faith and hope because of his divinity. But his path of humiliation to exaltation could only be taken in faith and hope. I once had the experience of watching a neophyte learn hang gliding. We were on the top of a cliff and I overheard him being instructed. I thought the veteran in effect said that the way to soar aloft was to jump off the cliff. When I looked at the neophyte with his eyes gazing downward over the cliff, and his face turning whiter and whiter, I was sure that was what he thought the instructions amounted to as well.

As it turned out, whatever his instructor had told him worked. The young hang glider jumped off the cliff and began to soar. But I was convinced that no matter how sure I was that jumping off the cliff was the way to fly, I would have "sweated blood" if I were to try it.

Even worse would have been knowing that the way to soar was not only to jump off, but to crash on the rocks and die in pain a few hours later with the assurance that I would then wake up, find myself free to soar wherever I wished, and experience an indescribable joy and gladness that I had done what I did. Even if I was sure of what I had to do, my human nature could not have accepted it peacefully.

Divine though he was, Christ's human nature was "like ours in all things except sin." He was able to take the way down, to suffer and die in great humiliation. But it was very costly. And it was a step he could not have taken without reliance upon his Father.

Part Four

Redeeming
the Human Race

Introduction to Part Four

THE REDEMPTION OF THE CHILDREN OF ISRAEL from Egypt came through a victory that God won. He himself came "down to deliver them out of the hands of the Egyptians and to bring them up out of that land to a good and broad land" (Ex 3:8). He brought them out "with a mighty hand and an outstretched arm, with great terror, with signs and wonders" (Dt 26:8). In the Exodus, "the Lord... has triumphed gloriously" (Ex 15:1), as the Israelites sang in "The Song of Moses." The redemption of Israel from Egypt was a victory that God himself won in a struggle with Pharaoh, the Egyptian army, and the gods of Egypt (Ex 12:12).

"In Christ God was reconciling the world to himself" (2 Cor 5:19). God "came down" once again to deliver his people, only this time he became human and redeemed human beings in the person of Jesus Christ. Christ too won a victory "with a mighty hand and an outstretched arm, with great terrors, with signs and wonders." But as we have seen, that victory was begun in an unusual way. He first laid down his life on the cross, in order that human beings could have the blood of the true Passover Lamb sprinkled upon them and so be saved from the destroyer. He then could lead them into the good land of true freedom.

If we say that Christ defeated the forces which make for human destruction, we could be referring to three somewhat distinct events: what happened on the cross, what happened in the resurrection, or what happens when human beings become Christians and so are personally redeemed. We might add to that what happens as the result of the Second Coming and the consummation of all things, but at the moment, we will leave such future events to one side. We could, of course, be referring to the result of all three events at the same time. In fact, most commonly that is what we do.

The victory of Christ, then, occurs in stages. The first stage occurred on the cross and is the stage we have so far mainly considered. His death on the cross was a real victory—a moral one. He endured death in full faithfulness to God and thereby offered the sacrifice of his life. It was a paradoxical victory, because at the moment of breathing his last, his enemies—death and Satan—were in possession of the field and seemed to be the victors. Yet, in fact, he had defeated them because his death robbed them of their power.

The second stage occurred in the resurrection. On the third day after he died, he was raised from the dead and ascended to the right hand of the Father. In rising again, he achieved a victory in his own person. As a result, his own new humanity existed free of death and of any subjection to this world and to Satan.

The third stage occurs as individuals become Christians and receive from Christ new life and freedom. Christ's victory is achieved in them because they are liberated from the power of death and Satan to become the possession of Christ. By the power of God in Christ, they become "the spoils" (Is 53:12) of battle.

It is probably most natural for us to speak about a victory when someone obtains the results of the struggle—when an army is driven away or a city conquered. Similarly, it is natural to speak of a redemption when a slave is actually freed from an oppressive master and comes into the possession of a good master. We therefore most naturally connect Christ's victory with the resurrection and redemption with the point at which human beings are freed from bondage.

Yet we speak of the victory on the cross and redemption through the cross. When we do, we express the truth that the sufferings and death on the cross made the victory of the resurrection and our redemption possible. Christ's resurrection to glory and our redemption from bondage would not have occurred if Christ had not died the way he did. Even more, once he had died, the resurrection and our redemption could be assured. The obstacle had been taken away. Now God's plan could unfold in and through Christ the Lord.

In the first part of this book, we considered the predicament of the human race as a result of sin. It was unable to achieve the purpose for which it was created. Then in part two we looked at what made the death of Christ the kind of death which could have a beneficial effect on other human beings. It was a sacrifice which made a compensatory payment so that the human race would not have to suffer the penal consequences of sin. In part three, we considered the reason why the death of Christ was accepted by God for our sins.

Christ's death was able to make a difference for our sins, first of all, because of who he was. He was the New Adam, the great High Priest and the Son of God himself, and so he was able to be the mediator between God and the human race. His death was also able to make a difference for our sins because in dying obediently he gave his life fully in love of God and love of us. It was given in response to what his Father wanted in order to make amends for the sins of the human race. In that way, his death was an offering that was acceptable to God. Finally, by undergoing the humiliation of defeat and death the way he did, he overcame Satan by depriving him of any claim over the human race.

Since the death of Christ—valuable as it was—was not an end in itself, but the means to an end, we now have to look at that end. That end was twofold. It was something that happened in Christ's person, so he could be the Redeemer of the human race. It was something that happened to us through Christ so we could be a redeemed race. This provides us with three final reasons why the death of Christ was able to redeem us:

1. He defeated death;
2. He was exalted over all;
3. He gives forgiveness of sins and new life to those who come to him.

In this final part, we will look less at Christ's death and more at what came afterward. In the first two chapters we will look at his resurrection and ascension. In so doing, we will look at what difference his death made for himself. Then in the last two chapters we will look at his giving of the Spirit and the Second Coming. In so doing, we will look at what difference his death made for us.

NINE

Defeating Death

TOWARD THE END OF HIS EARTHLY MINISTRY, Jesus led Peter, James, and John up onto Mount Tabor, the Mount of Transfiguration. By then the Jewish rulers and many of the people had clearly turned against him. On behalf of the disciples, Peter had just recognized Jesus as the Messiah, only to be told of his coming suffering and death. To Peter, such a thing should not happen. The Messiah predicted in Scripture was victorious, the King over the whole earth. For Peter and the Jewish teachers, success was the Messiah's proof of identity. An executed messiah was a disproved messiah.

On Mount Tabor something happened to Jesus. He was transfigured or metamorphosed. Without becoming a different person or a different type of being, he was transformed into someone so glorious as to be almost unrecognizable. He was then joined by Moses and Elijah, the representatives of the old covenant law and the prophets, themselves glorious as well. Anticipating the future, they "spoke of his exodus [RSV: departure], which he was to accomplish at Jerusalem" (Lk 9:31). When Jesus came down from the mountain, he reaffirmed that he would be put to death. Jesus then began a journey, a passage from this world of bondage to sin to true spiritual freedom in the promised land. It was a personal exodus, one that involved he himself going through suffering to glory. Yet it was an exodus that he went through for our sakes.

233

Jesus was a King, but he did not stay at home in the capital and send his generals off to war. He went into the battle as a captain. Nor did he direct his troops from behind. He himself led the way and those who fought with him would follow in his path. His name translated into Hebrew was Joshua (Yeshuah or Yehoshuah). Jesus was the true Joshua, leading God's people into the promised land by going first.

His personal exodus followed a certain path. He went down to go up. He underwent the defeat of suffering and death to reach the victory. He died, but by that death he defeated death and reached a new life. He rose in glory, in the state he had briefly entered on Mount Tabor as an anticipation of what was to come.

In this chapter we will look at the death of the Messiah from a different perspective. We will look at that death as the transition to a new state, the glorified state. We will therefore see that death as the destruction of the old order of sin and death and the inauguration of the age to come.

THE VICTORY OVER DEATH

Death As an Enemy. For many people, Christ's death would have been an even finer example of nobility if the story had ended there. He would then have been the tragic hero left dead on the battlefield, one who fought bravely to the end only to suffer personal defeat at the hands of a physically superior but morally inferior force. He could have left behind an example of unparalleled moral greatness that could itself have inspired a new human race. As a result of efforts that to him seemed like a failure, the kingdom of God could have been brought into existence.

Such a death would have been higher tragedy, no doubt, but it would not have been Christianity. Christianity is not tragedy, nor was Christ a tragic hero. No godly man can ultimately be a tragic hero. Christianity is based on hope, that confidence in God which gives assurance that even apparent earthly defeat is not final.

The story does not end with the grave, nor can it be understood apart from God. Earthly humiliation and defeat, if undergone in obedience to God, are the prelude to a success that lasts eternally. Christ's death was not a tragic end but a transition to something better. "Was it not necessary that the Christ suffer these things and so enter his glory" (Lk 24:26)?

Christ's death was the defeat not only of Satan and sin but also of death itself, because it forever altered the nature of human death. Sin and Satan were the source of our bondage, but death was as well. As Hebrews says, "he himself partook of [flesh and blood] that he might destroy him who has the power of death, that is, the devil, and deliver all those who through fear of death were subject to lifelong bondage" (Heb 2:15). Fear of death creates bondage because death, in its current reality, is an enemy.

There is a fear of death that comes from seeing death as annihilation. Many have recognized the desire for self-preservation to be the most basic and powerful of human desires, so instinctive that human beings almost invariably avoid danger to their life. The willingness to relinquish life by suicide or even to welcome the end through sickness or defeat in battle is a sign that someone has reached a very low ebb, almost dead already through psychological or physical suffering. Death, then, is the destruction of what human beings prize the most—life.

The recognition of an afterlife adds to this common fear of death. It does not usually take it away. It adds the fear of a future life that might be filled with misery or possible terrors. Any recognition of God or of gods adds further to that fear because it raises the possibility of finding oneself facing divine or demonic beings who are unfriendly. Such a fear is much the same as the Christian fear of hell.

Fear of an unknown and unfortunate fate at the end of earthly life is common to the human race. It is even common among human beings in modern society where many profess to disbelieve in an afterlife—but who at the near approach of death discover that they are not so sure. There is much to be said for the view that all human beings somewhere inside do believe in an afterlife, and without an assurance of a good afterlife, approach death with a dread that is greater than the simple dread of annihilation. It is the dread of a destruction that takes away all that makes life worthwhile, but without the elimination of existence or consciousness. Most human beings are under the bondage of such a fear of death.

Christians recognize such a bondage as genuine rather than illusory, because the fear of death is well-grounded. Paul explains the danger presented by death when he cryptically says, "The sting of death is sin, and the power of sin is the law" (1 Cor 15:56). A sting causes pain or harm if it is severe enough. Death has a sting because it inflicts harm by delivering people to hell and to Satan who is its ruler.

Sin is a sting because the sin of the human race leads to hell. The law gives sin such a power. Paul here seems to be thinking of the law as God's decrees which penally condemn sin and legislate the punishment of sinners. Because human beings sin, they are under a just and lawful heavenly condemnation. Human beings who die in such a state face an existence that is objectively to be feared.

Many Christian writers, especially those in the Eastern tradition, have seen death and the fear of death as the source of many of the misfortunes that afflict the human race in this life as well—including sinfulness itself, the fundamental source of human unhappiness. Because of the fear of death human beings seek to preserve their lives, sometimes to the point of murder, stealing, and idolatry, actions which seem to promise a more secure life. The fear of death, then, produces in human beings a bondage to certain emotions or "passions" which control them and lead to sinful actions. It therefore provokes the very condemnation and destruction they fear.

Death, in short, is not just a normal, natural human condition. It is a moral disease because of the way it affects human beings. What may have been intended by God as a natural transition to a better state, a life more fully in his presence, has become death as we know it. It is fearful without an assurance of God's help in the face of an unknown and dangerous future. It produces sinful responses as people desperately attempt to avoid it.

Two Views of Christ. To understand how Christ's death was a victory over human mortality, we have to look at him in a somewhat different way than we have so far. We most naturally think of Christ as a person who is distinct from God and who relates to him in a somewhat external way, especially when we read the synoptic Gospels. He looks up to heaven and speaks to his Father as someone spatially outside of him and in some sense above him. When he relates to human beings, he does so with the power God has put at his disposal and the wisdom and knowledge which God has taught him. When he dies, rises, and ascends, he leaves the earthly Jerusalem and goes "up" to some location that is not in our spatio-temporal world but apparently still has some spatial relationship to it.

In such a view the relationship between Christ and God is somewhat external. It affects Christ "inside," because any relationship of significance affects people internally. Yet the relationship between God and Christ remains external in much the same sense as two human beings have a relationship to one another.

There is another view of Christ in relationship to God which we also naturally take, especially when we read the Gospel of John or consider the way in which Christ acts on earth after his resurrection. We think of God as being in Christ. When we see Christ, we see God. When he acts, God acts. When he speaks, God speaks.

In such a view, Christ has divine power and wisdom, not so much as something made available to him from the outside, but as something inside of him. Even more, that divine power and wisdom is his own. He possesses it, has intrinsic title to dispose of it, and uses it at will. In fact, he can give human beings divine life, not just as a gift he gets God to give but as his own life that he is able to share with them.

When we take this second view of Christ in his human nature, we see him in relationship to God with a certain lack of distinctness or externality. Because of the oneness of being of Father and Son and because of the incarnation of the Son, the relationship between God and Christ is interior to Christ's being, something in him. In fact, the relationship between God and Christ is interior to his human nature.

The same two ways of seeing Christ's relationship with God can also be found in our own relationship with God. We too look up to him, speak to him, and relate to him as a being external to ourselves. Yet as Christians, we experience God dwelling in us, giving us new life, and acting through us. Because he is a spirit, God can be inside of us and affect us internally in a way no merely human being can.

From our own experience, we know that the two aspects of our relationship with God are just two different ways of seeing the one relationship of personal union. God is both outside of us and in us. He is even, in a certain sense, a part of us because his presence in us enters into our ability to live and act as Christians.

To be sure, there is a notable difference between our relationship to God and Christ's. The divinity Christ experienced inside of himself was his own. It belonged to him in a way God's presence inside of us does not belong to us. To use the technical phrase, Christ's divinity belonged to him by nature, not by grace. Yet there is enough similarity between the two that our experience of God can help us intuitively understand that the two ways of viewing Christ's relationship to God are not incompatible alternatives but go together.

So far, we have considered the sufferings and death of Christ mainly in terms of his external relationship with God. He offered the redemptive sacrifice for the sins of the world to his heavenly Father. We did consider his oneness with God when we looked at his obedience and his willingness to die for the sins of the world. Even so, it was still the external unity of two persons united in their aim and approach.

To understand Christ's personal victory over death, we need to consider his relationship to God as a more internal unity. We need to consider the divine presence in the humanity of Christ, how God acts in and through Christ's human nature to redeem the world. We need to understand more fully the scriptural truth that God was in Christ, "reconciling the world to himself" (2 Cor 5:19).

Dying to Defeat Death. At Easter, Christians proclaim that Christ has defeated death. Most commonly if we speak about people defeating death, we mean that they came close to dying but did not, probably because they fought to stay alive. Christ, however, died. He defeated death in a more definitive way than by staying alive when his life was threatened. He defeated death by dying and coming back to life by his own power.

Christ did not just defeat death for himself, but he defeated death for other human beings as well. His death and resurrection make it possible for others to survive their own deaths and as a result of dying come into a life that is better than the one they had before. In this chapter we will consider how Christ overcame death himself, and in subsequent chapters how he defeats death in the lives of others.

Freedom from a captor like Satan is freedom from an external oppressor. Freedom from death is freedom from an internal weakness. Death may originate from an outside cause like a blow or gunshot or fire. But death does not occur until the human organism loses the power to sustain life.

Life takes constant effort, as human beings discover when their lives are threatened by disease or injury and they find themselves in a "fight for their life." Overcoming death, then, involves the strength to sustain life. Defeating death by dying and coming back to life involves a special strength, a more than normally human strength. This strength Christ had.

In the description Paul gives us of Christ's redeeming work in Philippians 2, he tells us that Christ began his attack on death by lowering or humbling himself. "Though he was in the form of God, Christ Jesus did not count equality with God a thing to be grasped, but emptied himself, taking the form of a servant, being born in the likeness of men." This description refers to what we now would call Christ's incarnation. The first step, then, to defeat death was for Christ to enter into the human condition so that he could change it.

Paul describes Christ's incarnation as a self-emptying or self-lowering, because he wishes to describe how Christ's death—a further step of self-lowering—led to his exaltation. The fact that the Philippians passage goes on to describe Christ's resurrection and ascension as an exaltation indicates that the incarnation by itself does not fully constitute his self-lowering, since Christ will still have a human nature, a glorified human nature, after his resurrection and ascension.

Christ's self-lowering was not simply his taking on the condition of humanity, but his taking on a human condition in which he was deprived of something that would be present once he was raised from the dead and glorified. His self-lowering, in other words, was his willingness to take upon himself humanity in its fallenness. Exactly what he took on of our fallen human nature, when, as Paul says he came "in the likeness of sinful flesh" (Rom 8:3), is a complicated question. He clearly became subject to human weakness (2 Cor 13:4), suffering, and death. But at the same time, he was able to remain without sin and in full union with God. How ever these two facts go together, Christ willingly entered into and personally took on something of the fallen, low state of humanity. Before his resurrection, there was something missing in him that could have been there without making him something other than human.

To understand fully what was missing, we need to consider what happened to Christ in his exaltation or resurrection.

After his resurrection, Christ was "glorified." As we have seen, the scriptural word "glory" means greatness or power, even more than it does exterior radiance or splendor. Moreover, it can be used to indicate a greatness or power that things have in their own makeup, not just something conferred on them externally. "Glorification" then, can refer to an inner strengthening or empowerment.

When Christ was glorified, he did not cease to be human or become human to a lesser degree. Rather, his human nature was given a new power or capacity. He was capable of acting in ways he could not before. He could appear in rooms without opening doors. He could ascend to heaven by his own power. Even more importantly for our purposes, he was free from the power of death. "Christ being raised from the dead will never die again; death no longer has dominion over him" (Rom 6:9). When he was glorified, his human nature became transformed or metamorphosed so that he had a greater or more glorious type of human life, one with fewer limitations. Most especially, his human nature had a greater power over its own life, so it lacked the limitation of intrinsic mortality.

Before his glorification, however, Christ did not lack all glory. He had a glory with his Father before the world was made (Jn 17:5, 24), and therefore a glory that was uncreated. That divine glory is in him now (2 Cor 3:18; 4:6), and it was in him on earth even before his resurrection. Because of the presence of that glory, when we see him we see God in him (2 Cor 4:6; Jn 14:9). Even though he took on the weakness of unfallen human nature, Christ had a power inside of himself capable of taking away that weakness. It was hidden or veiled to a certain extent, but it was there. Christ's death and resurrection, then, was a transition from a state of humiliation which involved a divine glory present in a "weak human nature" to a state of exaltation, which involved a human nature transformed by that glory.

When the Scripture describes that transition, it most

commonly says that God raised him from the dead (Acts 2:24, 32). The change is described as coming from an action from outside of Jesus which rescues him from death. Yet Paul also describes that change as Jesus himself rising (1 Thes 4:14). In the Gospel of John, Jesus asserts that "I have power to lay [my life] down, and I have power to take it again" (Jn 10:18). As the Son of God, Jesus could not only count on God's power to raise him up. He could also count on that power as something in him, something he could employ even though dead.

These two types of statements are two ways of seeing the same truth. God did raise his Son but did so by acting through the divinity which was "in" Christ, which he and his Son shared. In a similar way, when God raises us from the dead, our resurrection will be due to his Spirit in us which will communicate life to us "from the inside" (Rom 8:11).

Jesus in the Gospel of John used an image to describe his death which sums up the truth we have been considering. He said, "Truly, truly, I say to you, unless a grain of wheat falls into the earth and dies, it remains alone; but if it dies, it bears much fruit" (Jn 12:24). A seed can be very hard and look much like a little stone, lifeless. But once it falls into the ground, a process of change happens that could be described as a death. The seed dies to its old mode of existence. That death, however, is not the end. Something inside of the seed, something that was there all along, is released and begins to live in a new way. It transforms the seed into something greater, a plant capable not only of growing but of giving rise to other plants like itself. Death can be life-giving—depending on what is inside when the dying begins.

Inside Christ was divine glory. Once he died, the shell of his "weak" human nature began to crumble. Rather than leading to the complete dissolution of his existence, that crumbling led to freedom for what was inside to "come out." The kernel of the seed—the glorious life inside—began to act not only in his human spirit and soul but also in his body.

The bonds of death could not hold him (Acts 2:24). His "indestructible life" (Heb 7:16) manifested itself. Or as Melito of Sardis, an early second-century writer, put it in his Paschal Discourse: "By his Spirit, which was incapable of dying, he dealt man's destroyer, death, a fatal blow."

The death of Jesus, then, was a victory over death itself. The very act of dying was itself the way death was overcome. "He destroyed death by death" (Byzantine liturgy). Jesus underwent a human death and proved stronger because of the indestructible glory within.

THE GREAT CHANGE

Scripture describes the transition from the life we live now to the life that God intends us to live in strong language. It is a change of worlds or of ages. We simply cannot live in the age to come in our current condition. It would be too much for us. The "eternal weight of glory" (2 Cor 4:17) would crush us.

"Flesh and blood cannot inherit the kingdom of God, nor does the perishable inherit the imperishable.... This perishable nature must put on the imperishable, and this mortal nature must put on immortality" (1 Cor 15:50, 53). A transition has to occur at our death, so that we are fitted to live in the heavenly, eternal environment of the new world.

Christ himself had to make that same transition. We do not fully understand the incarnation until we see that, sinless though he was, he entered into the condition of human fallenness. He came to lead the way out of that condition, across the Red Sea of human death to the promised land of true immortality where "what is mortal may be swallowed up by life" (2 Cor 5:4). In so doing, he had to himself overcome death.

Two main reasons have been given to explain why Christ had to die to overcome death and both probably have truth. First, it was not until Christ died that he offered his life for the sins of the human race and finished his work of satisfaction. That death atoned for the state of the human race, lifted the curse on Adam and his descendants, and took away the sentence of condemnation which allowed Satan to have power over human beings. Now he was free to cast aside the limitations the fall had placed on humanity, including on himself as someone who was one with the human race.

Second, Christ also had to die to overcome death because the old form of human nature was an obstacle to the new life coming through. It was ordered in a way that was self-seeking, intent on preserving itself rather than trusting itself fully into God's hands and allowing God's life and power to permeate it completely.

Even Christ's sinless human nature shared in that weakness, at least in the effects of that weakness, as was manifest at Gethsemane. He could control it, sometimes at the cost of a struggle, but there was something to control. What was needed was a kind of death—not the death of annihilation, but the death that involves a dissolution of the old. Once the old died, the glorious life within Christ could reconstitute his humanity on a new basis.

When Jesus rose, he did not simply return to the state he was in before his sufferings. He rose in a glorified state, because the divine glory within replaced the weakness of his humanity with a more powerful ability to live and act. He himself had made the passage that we needed to make after him in order to reach our heavenly inheritance.

TEN

Exalted over All

I N THE VISION IN THE FIFTH CHAPTER OF REVELATION when John found himself before the heavenly throne of God, the scroll that would unfold God's plan for the human race was sealed. He was pointed to the one worthy to open the seal: Jesus Christ, the Lion of the tribe of Judah, the Root of David. Christ was worthy because of who he was. But he was also worthy because of what he had done.

The elder said to John, "[He] has conquered, so he can open the scroll and its seven seals" (Rv 5:5). Because he has won a victory, he can fulfill God's plan. When Christ was given the scroll by God, those in heaven sang a song of praise to him. This was a "new" song, that is, a song to celebrate the new conditions created by Christ's victory:

"Worthy art thou to take the scroll
    and to open its seals,
for thou wast slain and by thy blood
    didst ransom men for God
from every tribe and tongue and
    people and nation,
and hast made them a kingdom and
    priests to our God,
and they shall reign on earth." Rv 5:9-10

The scene itself is striking. The Lion is standing before the throne of God, closer to the divine majesty than the greatest of angelic beings. Apparently he is standing in the heavenly Holy of Holies, at the holiest point in the universe. But the Lion is "a Lamb, standing as though it had been slain" (Rv 5:6).

The phrase is an odd one: Dead lambs do not stand. John seems to mean that he saw the Lamb standing and therefore alive, it was possible to see that he had been slain. His wounds, the signs of his death, were visible. His standing posture probably indicated his priesthood, because priests stand before God when they serve him. The Lamb, in other words, was standing before God, risen and victorious, but as the one who had died for the sins of the world. He was now in God's presence as the High Priest, seeking the salvation of the world.

All of this is picture language. The same figure cannot be a Lamb and a Lion. Nor will Christ look at us with seven eyes, as in the next phrase. But in some way that we cannot fully understand, he is and has been and will be in God's presence as the Priest who was a sacrificial victim and as the King who conquered by being defeated. The visions of the Book of Revelation cannot be drawn without grotesqueness, because they are a fusion of different pictures, all of which have significance. But the details all reveal something about the heavenly fulfillment of the death of Christ on earth.

When did the events in John's vision occur? Some have thought that heaven was opened to him at the moment when the risen Lord arrived before the throne of his Father. The dialogue with the elder seems to indicate that the worthy one arrived while John was looking. Others have thought that the pause between the question and response only indicates that John did not at first know what to look for, but Christ was there all along.

In either case, there is agreement that the vision is meant to dramatize the importance of the position Christ attained through the resurrection and ascension. Only after the arrival of the Lamb in heaven can God's plan for the human race unfold, because only then has the work been accomplished that made it possible. Both aspects are important. Something has been accomplished on earth: payment and victory. And the one who did it is now in the place where the events of human history are determined—before the throne of God presenting what he has done.

John does not record any words of the Lamb. From that some have concluded that Christ did not say anything. He did not need to. His wounds and his risen humanity were enough. He simply needed to present himself in God's presence since what he had done was well enough known to God. Others have held that he did speak, and the words of his intercession were echoed back to us in the song of praise. Christ certainly interceded, with or without words, since the role of a priest involves intercession on the basis of the sacrifice being offered. The Letter to the Romans says that, "[It is] Christ Jesus who died, yes, who was raised from the dead, who is at the right hand of God, who indeed intercedes for us" (Rom 8:34).

Ascended in the presence of God, Christ must have communicated something like this: "Here I am, Father, having completed the task you sent me to do. I have suffered and died for this race. I have paid the price. I have given my life completely. Now look upon these wounds, the sign of my life given to you as an offering. Look upon the sacrifice, which I know is acceptable to you, and be gracious to those below. Accept them as well. Cleanse them. Pour out your blessing upon them, the gift of your Holy Spirit. Take them for yourself, holy to you. Free them from their bondage and bring them to yourself. May this offering I have made achieve the result for which it was given."

In this chapter, we are going to look at the resurrection and ascension of Christ. His death cannot be understood in isolation, no matter how useful it is to focus on it more extensively in order to understand its meaning. Explaining it all by itself is like describing a journey without mentioning the destination, or like saying to a child how good it was to make the last mortgage payment without her realizing that meant the one who made the payment then owned the house. Christ's death is only one step in a process, part of a transition from an earthly existence to a heavenly one. His resurrection and ascension complete that transition by bringing him into the heavenly place from which he could be the Redeemer.

The Scriptures describe the resurrection and ascension of the Lord as an exaltation. Both words indicate a going up, one a rising up from a fall, the other a climbing up from a descent. The resurrection and ascension, then, are the conclusion of the process we looked at in the previous chapters. Christ went down, he lowered or humbled himself. But he did so that he might be raised up. Raised on high, the Redeemer could bring about the effects his humbling was intended for.

The word "exaltation" in Hebrew idiom is used to refer to a state of power or greatness or rule. A king is high or exalted. Anyone else is lower in rank by comparison. "Exaltation" can also be used to refer to victory. A victor is exalted or set on high, while the defeated opponent is humbled or brought low. But "exaltation" can also refer to going up to heaven because heaven is as high as someone can go.

Christ's resurrection and ascension were his exaltation in victory to a position of authority and power, his exaltation to a heavenly place. From there he could exercise a heavenly priesthood and a heavenly kingship. Or to put it in another way, Christ was then in the kind of relationship with God that allowed him to bring about the redemption made possible by the sacrifice he offered in humility upon the cross.

The resurrection and the ascension, then, are the conclusion of an exodus. They complete the passage of the Lord himself from a fallen or low state to an exalted or heavenly one. They also make possible our exodus from bondage to spiritual freedom and the enjoyment of our heavenly inheritance. In this chapter, we will look at what the resurrection and ascension resulted in for the Lord. In the next chapter we will look at what it resulted in for us.

EXALTATION AS PRIEST

Earthly and Heavenly. The Letter to the Hebrews gives us an image of Christ's resurrection: "Christ has entered, not into a sanctuary made with hands, a copy of the true one, but into heaven itself, now to appear in the presence of God on our behalf" (Heb 9:24). As a result, "we have [a perfect] high priest, one who is seated at the right hand of the throne of the Majesty in heaven, a minister in the sanctuary and the true tent which is set up not by man but by the Lord" (Heb 8:1-2).

Hebrews tells us that the earthly temple in Jerusalem was made by human beings to be a copy of the true temple (Heb 8:5). Israelite workmen were able to make it as a copy because God revealed the "pattern" to Moses. We might say God showed him a model from which a blueprint could be made. The true temple is heaven itself, and the true holy of holies is before the very throne of God.

Christ was not an earthly priest. He would not have been allowed into the court of priests in the earthly temple, much less the earthly holy of holies. Nor would he have been interested in trying to enter. His was a new covenant priesthood rather than an old covenant priesthood, meant to be exercised in a heavenly way rather than an earthly way.

Christ's death on the cross was an earthly event with heavenly consequences. It happened on earth, because that is where Christ died. The consequences are heavenly because God's reception of Christ's death as the payment and atonement for the sins of the human race made the redemption possible. Christ the Priest made the connection between earth and heaven. Yet how that connection happened is not easy to state with accuracy.

Some Christian teachers stress that Christ's death was a sacrifice completed on earth. Usually they also say that he was likewise a Priest on earth offering his life to the Father on the cross, an earthly altar.

Perhaps the strongest support for this view comes from the Gospel of John. At the moment of his death, "knowing that all was now finished" (Jn 19:28), Christ said, "It is finished" (v. 30). He bowed his head and "gave up his spirit" or perhaps "gave over the spirit" (v. 30). Then in an unusual event, blood and water, the two instruments of purification, flowed from his side (v. 34). It seems likely that in these details John is describing the death of Christ on earth as the sacrifice that achieves the redemption of the world through purification from sins and the gift of the Spirit. From this passage many Christian teachers have developed the phrase "the finished work of Christ" (on Calvary).

Other Christian teachers speak of the resurrection and ascension of Christ as the completion of the sacrifice of Christ on the cross. Some of them go so far as to speak of the heavenly sacrifice of Christ, not meaning that he offered two sacrifices but that the earthly sacrifice was somehow completed in heaven.

They usually base what they say on the Book of Hebrews. They point out that Hebrews says Christ would not be a Priest on earth, but that his priestly ministry must be in heaven (Heb 8:4).

Moreover, he must have had something to offer in heaven if he were to minister as a Priest (Heb 8:3-4). In addition, Hebrews says he is now appearing in the presence of God on our behalf (Heb 9:24). They also observe that the high priest on the Day of Atonement poured out the blood on the altar and then took it into the holy of holies to sprinkle it before the earthly throne of God. The Letter to the Hebrews seems to connect this second step with Christ's ascension into heaven (Heb 9:11-12, 24).

Both positions are based on truths and have much to be said for them. To discuss them adequately would go beyond what is possible here. Properly understood, they may not, in fact, be incompatible with one another. They do, however, certainly stress two different truths. One position stresses that the earthly death of Jesus on the cross was the full satisfaction for the sins of the world. Nothing further was needed to pay for the redemption of the human race, nor did he in any way die again or offer another sacrifice. The other position stresses that his death on the cross was only effective as it was presented to God in heaven, and that presentation in some way is the work of Christ as the heavenly Priest. Both truths have a place in the full understanding, even if it is difficult to find the best way to speak about how they can be combined. Moreover, even if we take the strongest view of the completion of Christ's sacrifice on the cross, there are many features of the resurrection and ascension that can only be understood as connected to sacrifice and can best be described in sacrificial terms. Three sacrificial terms are especially important: acceptance, intercession, and blessing.

Acceptance. "Acceptability" translates a Hebrew word commonly used in sacrificial contexts to indicate that someone or something meets with God's approval. He therefore "accepts" or receives it. In English, to say that someone is "acceptable" to God is somewhat grudging. It is a word we might use in the process of hiring a new employee to indicate that someone is merely still in the running. The scriptural word is more positive. It indicates that someone or something actually meets with God's favor or approval and is something he wants.

Both people and sacrifices could be acceptable to God. In fact, sacrifices were intended to make people acceptable to God. Leviticus describes a sacrifice this way: "If his offering is a burnt offering from the herd, he shall offer a male without blemish; he shall offer it at the door of the tent of meeting, that he may be accepted before the Lord; he shall lay his hand upon the head of the burnt offering, and it shall be accepted for him to make atonement for him" (Lv 1:3-4).

The result of sacrifice, then, was to make the worshiper accepted by God, established in friendship with him. In order to do that, however, the offering itself had to be accepted by God, and therefore it had to be acceptable to him. This passage mentions three requirements for the acceptance of a sacrifice. It had to be a male animal of the right sort, without blemish, and offered in the tent or temple ordained by God.

Christ himself fulfilled all these requirements for the new covenant. He was the Lamb provided by God, without the blemish of sin, and offered in the true tent of heaven. But because he fulfilled the requirements of sacrifice in an unprecedented way, the acceptance of his offering could not be presumed, as the Israelites in the Old Testament had presumed the acceptance of old covenant sacrifices.

A similar situation of uncertainty occurred when Solomon built the temple to replace the tent of meeting. When it came time to offer sacrifice there, the Israelites needed some attestation of God's acceptance of the new temple and therefore of sacrifices offered there. Second Chronicles describes what happened: "When Solomon had ended his prayer, fire came down from heaven and consumed the burnt offering and the sacrifices, and the glory of the Lord filled the temple" (2 Chr 7:1).

The fire that consumed the sacrifices and the glory that filled the temple served a similar function. Like the pillar of fire and the pillar of cloud in the wilderness, they were visible manifestations of the presence of the Lord. The cloud of glory that filled the temple indicated that God accepted the temple and made it his house. The fire that came down upon the sacrifices indicated that God accepted the sacrifices and took them to himself. This special manifestation of God's action indicated to the people of Israel that the new temple was the place chosen by God as the true temple where sacrifices could be acceptably offered.

In a similar way, the resurrection of Christ was the manifestation of the acceptance of Christ's offering. He had been put to death outside the temple. As he lay dead in the tomb, the glory of God came upon Christ in a new way. God's presence and power filled him the way the cloud filled the temple, entered into him and transformed him, as the fire had consumed the offering. By his glorification, Christ's humanity was taken by God and so became holy in a new way, holy as a sacrificial offering. In fact, as a sin offering it became "most holy" (Lv 10:17). At the same time, his humanity was transformed in such a way that it could enter heaven and function in a heavenly mode.

The resurrection and ascension were the heavenly reception of the sacrificial victim. They were either the actual acceptance of the sacrifice or else the manifestation of that acceptance. The sacrificial Lamb was now God's in a new way, a gift given in sacrifice and received by God. It was therefore manifestly able to make the worshipers for whom it was offered acceptable to God.

Intercession and Blessing. The next two sacrificial terms are best treated together: intercession and blessing. Most sacrifices were offered for some benefit the worshipers wished to receive from God. This may not have been true of the burnt offering, which symbolized a complete giving to God with nothing received in return. It was, however, true of the sin and guilt offerings by which Israelite worshipers sought forgiveness for their sins. It was also true of the peace or communion offerings which were offered along with petitions for some favor, as a thanksgiving for some favor granted, or simply as a free expression of love to God and desire to strengthen their relationship with him.

The offering of sacrifices involved both intercession and an impartation of a blessing. We have a description of the high priest Simon offering sacrifice in a service from about 200 B.C. This account concludes by saying,

And the people besought the Lord Most High
　in prayer before him who is merciful,
till the order of worship of the Lord was ended;
　so they completed his service.
Then Simon came down, and lifted up his hands

> over the whole congregation of the sons of Israel,
> to pronounce the blessing of the Lord with his lips,
>   and to glory in his name;
> and they bowed down in worship a second time,
>   to receive the blessing from the Most High. Sir 50:19-21

As this passage makes clear, both intercession and blessing were part of the sacrificial ceremony. As the gift was being given to God, intercession was being made. In a certain sense, the sacrifice was itself intercessory, because the prayers that accompanied the sacrifice only put into words the purpose of the gift. Sacrifice was a way of seeking God's grace and blessing.

At the conclusion of the ceremony, the priest imparted a blessing. Behind this was a conviction that an acceptable sacrifice would bring blessing. Since the priest knew how to offer an acceptable sacrifice, he simply pronounced the closing blessing upon the worshiper, confident that God's blessing would be given. The verbal blessing expressed the actual blessing that resulted from an acceptable sacrifice that a duly ordained priest had offered.

Both aspects are present in Christ's priestly service. As a Priest, he makes intercession before God for his people. He is in heaven "now to appear in the presence of God on our behalf" (Heb 9:24). "He is able for all time to save those who draw near to God through him, since he always lives to make intercession for them" (Heb 7:25). We will not be condemned by "Christ Jesus who died, yes, who was raised from the dead, who is at the right hand of God, who indeed intercedes for us" (Rom 8:34).

There is, in other words, an ongoing priestly intercession of Christ, and it has our redemption as its object. He intercedes for us that we might be blessed as a result of his sacrificial offering. That offering makes us acceptable to God. His intercession may or may not be verbal, but the very presence of the Lamb who has been slain for us before the heavenly throne of God is itself a presentation of the sacrifice on the cross to the Father. In view of that sacrifice, God is gracious to us.

We should not necessarily think of the intercession of Christ as a set of actions by which he responds to our prayers for particular favors. Every time one of his followers prays, he probably does not get up from his throne and ask his Father to grant the favors being sought. His intercession is rather a single eternal intercession that we be acceptable to God and that we receive forgiveness of our sins and the new life for which his sacrifice was offered. That intercession puts us into a relationship with God which allows us to make petitions for particular favors and be heard by God (Jn 16:23-24).

As a Priest Christ also imparts a blessing. At the end of the Gospel of Luke there is a description of the risen Christ which probably shows his priestly blessing. He manifested his resurrection by appearing in the midst of his disciples. He then explained the crucifixion and resurrection, concluding with the prediction of the outpouring of the Holy Spirit: "'And behold, I send the promise of my Father upon you; but stay in the city, until you are clothed with power from on high.' Then he led them out as far as Bethany, and lifting up his hands he blessed them" (Lk 24:49-50). It is probably not an accident that Jesus blesses his disciples in a priestly way and does so right after promising the Holy Spirit, since the gift of the Spirit embodies what Christ's sacrifice was meant to bring.

The Holy Spirit, as Paul says, is the promised blessing (Gal 3:14). He is the fulfillment of the promise of the reversal of the fall that had been pledged to Abraham and his faith, because the gift of the Spirit brings about the reversal of the fall in those who receive him (Gal 3:6-14). The Spirit is the source of the new life (2 Cor 3:6), the first installment given as a guarantee of the full possession of the heavenly inheritance (Eph 1:13-4). He brings the initial presence of the kingdom of God (Rom 8:18-25). The Holy Spirit, in other words, brings all the blessings of the new covenant, given as a result of Christ's sacrifice.

The Holy Spirit, however, could not be given to Christ's disciples until his sacrificial gift was presented in heaven through his resurrection and ascension. John said of the situation before Christ's death, "The Spirit had not been given, because Jesus was not yet glorified" (Jn 7:39). Christ's blessing of his disciples described in Luke 24, then, was the action of the risen Lord. He had probably already ascended initially (Jn 20:17), and was calling down that gift which would surely be given to his disciples some days later. Christ's blessing was an action of the High Priest appointed by God, who knew that he had offered an acceptable sacrifice and knew that he was authorized to call the blessing of the Holy Spirit down upon those who belonged to him.

However we state the relationship between the earthly and heavenly aspects of the sacrifice of Christ, his death on the cross is the cause of the blessing and salvation Christ came to bring. The cross on earth was the point of atonement and satisfaction. Sin came into existence on earth and was atoned for on earth. But the change in relationship with God and the consequent change in human lives is heavenly and eternal, because God dwells in heaven and in eternity. Christ makes the connection in his priestly ministry. He is before God, presenting the acceptable sacrifice, the offering of himself, and on that basis interceding for his people. Since his sacrifice is the one God wanted, Christ's intercession is heard and the blessing of new life is given.

EXALTATION AS KING

Christ is not only exalted as Priest, he is also exalted as King. He is a royal Priest who combines in his person both roles. His kingship too is heavenly. He reigns in heaven in a way that he could not on earth. In his kingdom, under his heavenly rule, is true life and prosperity. His exaltation, then, is also an exaltation to a position of effective kingship.

The word "ascension" indicates that Christ's work was completed by his "going up" to God. The same event can also be described as Christ's enthronement or his being seated at the right hand of the Father. There is a connection between the two ways of describing what happened to Christ at his ascension, because the royal throne was always the highest seat in the audience hall. The spatial placement expressed the role of the king. Often the seats of others in authority were also elevated, but never higher than the royal throne. In the same way, the royal palace was on Mount Zion—the highest point in Jerusalem, right below the temple, the palace of God. Heaven itself, of course, was also understood to be "on high," much higher than the highest position on earth.

Peter's sermon on Pentecost expressed this connection between resurrection and ascension and between ascension and enthronement. In it, he explained the outpouring of the Holy Spirit as the sign of the messianic age. Speaking of Psalm 16 as a prophecy of the resurrection of Christ, he said,

> "This Jesus God raised up, and of that we all are witnesses. Being therefore exalted at the right hand of God, and having received from the Father the promise of the Holy Spirit, he has poured out this which you see and hear. For David did not ascend into the heavens; but he himself says,
> 'The Lord said to my Lord, Sit at my right hand,
>   till I make thy enemies a stool for thy feet.'
> Let all the house of Israel therefore know assuredly that God has made him both Lord and Christ, this Jesus whom you crucified." Acts 2:32-36

The way Peter passes from Christ's resurrection to his being seated at the right hand of God indicates that he sees the resurrection and ascension as two aspects of the same event. He then quotes another messianic psalm to indicate that the Messiah, who would die but not be held by death, would ascend to the right hand of the Father (Ps 110). That in turn would indicate that the crucified one was both Lord and Christ.

The phrase "to sit at God's right hand" can only be understood in terms of a royal audience. The King of the universe takes his seat on the royal throne (Dn 7:9-10) to govern his realm. When God holds audience, his Son—"one like a son of man" (Dn 7:13-15)—will sit beside him on his right hand, the position of next greatest honor and authority. For the Son to be seated at God's right hand, then, is to be enthroned as King, King of the universe. As a result, Christ will share the position of his Father as divine King and reign in union with him, subordinate to him but with divine authority and power.

To say that Christ is the King of the universe is to say that he is Lord of all. No other authority in the universe is equal in right or power, nor is there any that can withstand him. "The God of our Lord Jesus Christ... made him sit at his right hand in the heavenly places, far above all rule and authority and power and dominion" (Eph 1:17, 20-21). At the same time, to say that he is King indicates that Christ is in a personal relationship with his subjects, especially his loyal subjects. He cares for them in justice, defending the cause of the poor, giving deliverance to the needy, and crushing the oppressor (Ps 72). In his kingdom is life.

While Christ's kingship is like an earthly kingship, it is a heavenly kingship, because though human he is the heavenly Son of God. In the resurrection, he was given a new kind of life that allowed his human nature to function in a heavenly way. He was thereby enabled to take a position as human that he had previously held as divine. He "returned" to the glory he had with the Father before the world. But in the process of doing so, that glory had transfigured his humanity in such a way that someone who was human could share the divine throne.

Having someone human on God's throne does not mean that the universe is ruled by a human being rather than God or ruled in a merely human way. "By nature" Christ was united to his Father, so that not only was his divine nature one in being with the Father, but his human nature was also united with his divine nature in oneness of person, and therefore with the Father's divine nature. By his self-lowering or humiliation, Christ's human nature had proved itself fitted for such an exalted position, because it was the human nature of a fully obedient servant, willing even to surrender his own life in great suffering for the sake of doing the will of God (Heb 5:8-9). Christ's human nature was also fully ready for such a position, because it had died and so left behind any of the restrictions that went with sharing in the life of fallen humanity. As a result, that human nature was now glorified—a perfect expression or image of the divine nature, no longer weak but strong with divine power or glory.

When Christ reigns with God the Father, therefore, the Father does not have to share his glory with any other (Is 42:8; 45:20-25). Not only is the Son fully united with his Father so that they share the same glory of their natures, but also his humanity is that of a servant, fully set on the glory of his master, transfigured so as to be a fully responsive instrument of divine action and reflection of divine glory. God, in short, can speak and act in and through the humanity of Christ without any diminishment of his glory. Therefore Christ reigns to the glory of his Father (Phil 2:11).

The Victory of the Redeemer. The enthronement of Christ is the true victory, but not in the sense of winning a combat. That was done as Christ, the obedient servant, resisted the temptations of fear, pain, and disgrace to successfully lay down his life in humility and humiliation. That was also done as Christ—the Son of God in "the likeness of sinful flesh" (Rom 8:3)—gave up that flesh to death, so that in dying he might trample down death.

Humiliation, however, led to exaltation. Dying led to rising again in new life. Christ's enthronement was victory in the sense of taking possession of the battlefield and the kingdom. As Satan, sin, and death lay defeated, God's kingdom was proclaimed and Christ began to reign. He was exalted in victory to a position of rule. "To this end, Christ died and lived again, that he might be Lord both of the dead and of the living" (Rom 14:9).

As a man on earth, Christ went about preaching and teaching, healing and casting out demons. As he did so, people gained considerable freedom. Christ was therefore Redeemer during his earthly ministry. Nonetheless, he was not able to be the Redeemer in a full way until after his resurrection. As millions of people would come to believe in Christ, we have only to imagine long lines of people waiting for his personal attention to realize the impracticality of an earthly ministry as the main means of our redemption.

More seriously, even though Christ's earthly ministry brought many individuals into contact with divine power and healing, the gates of paradise were still closed, the banishment from the garden was still in effect, and the condemnation of Adam still stood. Therefore, the full blessing could not be given. Christ could not do for people all that he came to do until he had completed his priestly work by giving his life as a sacrifice for sin and presenting that sacrifice to his Father. For that he needed to be a heavenly Priest.

Likewise, Christ could not reign as King on earth. The title belonged to him. As Son of David he was the rightful King of Israel, anointed by God with the Holy Spirit and power (Acts 10:38). Even more, as the divine Son of God, he was the natural Lord "of all" the whole human race and all the angelic beings as well. Nonetheless, the usurper who was ruling as prince of this world and holding its inhabitants captive had not yet been judged and cast out (Jn 12:31; 16:11). Nor had Christ been enthroned and given the position that was his by right.

All that changed with the resurrection and ascension. The Messiah entered into his glory, and could do so because he had suffered (Lk 24:26). He had paid the price, taken upon himself the curse, and offered the sacrifice (Lk 24:26). He had removed the barrier, pierced the veil, and entered the most holy place. He had ascended on high, had sat down at the right hand of the Father, and had been proclaimed Lord of all.

Christ had done what was needed to make available the fullness of redemption, blessing, and heavenly access. There was no longer anything to prevent him from fully taking away the sins of those who came to him and imparting to them the new life. As Lord to the glory of God the Father, Jesus could be the Redeemer of the whole human race.

This description, however, is still too external to provide a full picture. In the process of taking his new position, Christ himself had changed. He was glorified or transfigured by the power of God. As a result, the fullness of redemption was in him because the new, redeemed life was his in completion. Christ was fully united to God in oneness of being. But he was united to God in a new way in his human nature as well. As a result, the power and life of God filled his human nature the way God wanted. Christ had become a glorified human being, one who not only had a more direct access to God's heavenly presence but who also was able to transmit God's life and power more freely and directly.

THE PERSON OF THE REDEEMER

At the beginning of this chapter, we looked at the vision of Christ as the Lamb standing before God as Priest and sitting on the throne as King. That was the prelude to what the royal Lamb would do in bringing human history to its fulfillment and accomplishing the complete victory. The Book of Revelation continues on to unfold the "war of the Lamb."

Those visions are preceded by letters in which the risen and ascended Lord speaks to the seven churches who represent the whole church of the redeemed and who are living on the battlefield. Those letters are preceded by a different vision of the Lord—the Lord in the midst of his people, the Lord as he is now.

> Then I turned to see the voice that was speaking to me, and on turning I saw seven golden lampstands, and in the midst of the lampstands one like a son of man, clothed with a long robe and with a golden girdle round his breast; his head and his hair were white as white wool, white as snow; his eyes were like a flame of fire, his feet were like burnished bronze, refined as in a furnace, and his voice was like the sound of many waters; in his right hand he held seven stars, from his mouth issued a sharp two-edged sword, and his face was like the sun shining in full strength.
>
> When I saw him, I fell at his feet as though dead. But he laid his right hand upon me, saying, "Fear not, I am the first and the last, and the living one; I died and behold I am alive for evermore, and I have the keys of Death and Hades." Rv 1:12-18

John saw the Lord glorified, standing in the middle of the seven golden lampstands which represent the seven churches that stand in the true temple of God, the people of the new covenant (Ex 37:17-24). He saw, in other words, the presence of the Lord on earth now, in the middle of his people. The same Lord who is with God in his heavenly throne room is also on earth in the middle of his people, bringing the heavenly presence and reign and blessing into their lives. In his person, he unites heaven and earth.

The Lord appeared as "one like a son of man," as a human being. This phrase is taken from Daniel 7 and indicates the heavenly man who was given kingship over the earth (Dn 7:13; Mt 27:64). He was clothed in priestly garments, appearing as Priest as well as King. His hair was like the hair of the ancient of days (Dn 7:9), a symbol that indicates that the glory of the Father was present in him as the incarnate Son. His appearance was angelic, like the powerful heavenly messenger who came to Daniel (Dn 10:6)—a vision so fearful that Daniel was overcome, as John himself was.

The Lord announced himself to John as the eternal one, the first and the last who had entered into time to die. He now is eternally alive, but not because he is divine. He is alive in a human nature that has died and come to life (Rv 2:8) so that it can die no more. Because of his victory Christ now has the keys to death and hades, opening new life to those who come to him and sharing with them his victory and his throne (Rv 3:20-21).

The redemption is not simply an event. It is a person. It is the Lord who has himself gone through the exodus of the human race, and so has in his own person the fullness of redeemed humanity. Christ is the incarnate one, but the incarnation was not simply intended to be the bare union of divinity and humanity in one person. The incarnation was intended to be the means to the transformation of humanity into a glorified state. As a result, the life, goodness, and power of God would be manifested in human nature. In the person of the Redeemer, humanity is divinized in the sense of "made godlike." Redemption begins with the transfiguration or transformation of the Redeemer. He is now in the midst of his people, able to share with them what he himself has become.

ELEVEN

New Life in Christ

S HORTLY BEFORE JESUS' DEATH, he received an urgent message that Lazarus was dying—someone he loved, a close sympathizer, possibly a disciple, possibly also a member of the Sanhedrin. Martha and Mary seemed to expect Jesus to come quickly and heal their brother.

Jesus gave an enigmatic response: "This illness is not unto death," but for the glory of God as a means to glorify God's Son (Jn 11:4). Jesus' statement was probably understood by his disciples as a prediction that Lazarus would recover. The fact that he was in no hurry to leave may have even confirmed such an understanding in their minds. But two days later Jesus told them that Lazarus had died and that therefore he would go to Lazarus' home at Bethany.

Bethany was very near Jerusalem, in the area under the direct rule of the Jewish governing authorities who had shown every intention of putting Jesus to death if they could. The disciples saw no point in running such a risk now that Lazarus had died. But the fact that Lazarus had died seemed to especially make Jesus want to go.

On their arrival, Jesus was met by Martha. By then Lazarus had been dead four days. She knew that Jesus had delayed, despite the urgency of her message. Her plaintive greeting—perhaps reproachful, perhaps simply regretful—was, "Lord, if you had been here, my brother would not have died." Jesus replied, "Your brother will rise again" (Jn 11:21-23).

Like many Jews, Martha believed in the resurrection of the dead and so answered, "I know that he will rise again in the resurrection at the last day." She may have thought Jesus was simply consoling her because of his disappointing delay. His next words pointed to something different: "I am the resurrection and the life; he who believes in me, though he die, yet shall he live, and whoever lives and believes in me shall never die" (Jn 11:25-26).

These words contain the core of Jesus' message to Martha. The resurrection is not simply something that happens on the last day to all good Jews. I bring resurrection. I bring the only resurrection worth having, a resurrection to true life. I bring life. I am the one who can raise the dead and give life to whom I will (Jn 5:21). Even more, those who believe in me will here and now be given a life that will not be destroyed by normal human death but will last forever.

Jesus then went to the tomb. The body of Lazarus had already begun to putrefy, but he was undeterred. He had even delayed so that the death of his friend would be beyond doubt. Jesus cried out in a loud voice, "Lazarus, come out." And Lazarus came out.

It was for this that Jesus had come to Bethany. He did not come to keep himself safe, to save his own life. He knew that coming to Bethany was a step toward giving himself for the life of the world (Jn 6:51). Rather, he came to raise the dead. Moreover, he did not come only to raise them at some future point long after they had died. He came to give them new life on earth. He came so that they might have life and have it abundantly (Jn 10:10), even before they "go to heaven."

Paul described becoming a Christian as being "brought from death to life" (Rom 6:13). Of all the descriptions of the result of redemption, that is perhaps the most dramatic. Purchasing a slave or pardoning a criminal seems tame beside raising the dead. When Jesus called out to the putrefying Lazarus, "Come forth" and come forth he did, Jesus proclaimed by this sign the magnitude of the change he came to bring. It would be like raising the dead.

Moreover, giving life to those who believe in him would require the same kind of power as raising Lazarus. Christ would give them eternal life. By his power, human beings would be able to have a new kind of life on earth, one that could not be destroyed by their earthly deaths.

"As in Adam all die, so in Christ shall all be made alive" (1 Cor 15:22). Christ came to reverse what Adam did, to restore the life Adam lost, to bring human beings to the place where they could fulfill the purpose for which they were created. "If anyone is in Christ, he is a new creation; the old has passed away, behold, the new has come" (2 Cor 5:17).

We have considered what Christ did to make it possible for the human race to be redeemed. In the last chapter, we saw how Christ entered into the position where he could provide redemption for those who came to him. In this chapter, we will look at the way redemption is given to those who believe in Christ and join themselves to him.

IN AND BY THE SPIRIT

Passover and Pentecost were closely linked in the old covenant festal calendar, because Pentecost was the conclusion of the Passover season. The season began with "the Lord's Passover." The day after the sabbath of the seventh week, Pentecost was celebrated (Lv 23:15-16). As the fiftieth day of the season, the name is derived from the Greek word for "fifty." In New Testament times, the Jews celebrated Pentecost as the day of the giving of the Ten Commandments on Sinai, the day on which the people of Israel entered the covenantal relationship with God made possible by the Passover and Exodus.

The outpouring of the Holy Spirit did not happen on the day of Pentecost by accident. Just as the death and resurrection of Christ fulfilled "the Lord's Passover," the outpouring of the Holy Spirit fulfilled the feast of Pentecost. Through that gift of God, the disciples came into the fullness of the blessing of the new covenant, the new relationship with God made possible by Christ's redeeming work.

Such an understanding of the relationship between Sinai and Pentecost is probably behind a statement in Second Corinthians 3. Paul is defending himself from criticism by saying that the Christian community at Corinth is a letter of recommendation for him. Others can look at them and see that Paul is able to bring into existence a body of people who have the new life Christ came to bring. "You are a letter from Christ delivered by us, written not with ink but with the Spirit of the living God, not on tablets of stone but on tablets of human hearts" (2 Cor 3:3).

Paul is referring to the two stone "tablets" on which the ten commandments were written by God (Dt 5:22), and which Moses described as the covenant the Lord our God made with us (Dt 4:13). He is saying that in the new covenant, the Holy Spirit writes the commandments of God on the hearts of Christians so that the change in the way they live can be "known and read by all men" (2 Cor 3:2).

Paul then adds another statement. "God... has made us competent to be ministers of a new covenant, not in a written code but in the Spirit; for the written code kills, but the Spirit gives life" (2 Cor 3:5-6). The two statements go together. The new covenant relationship with God is not a matter of external instructions to be read and carried out, but a matter of a new life put into believers by the Holy Spirit. As a result, new covenant people will be enabled by the Spirit within to live the life of love of God and neighbor. Further on Paul adds, "We... are being changed into his image [RSV: likeness] from one degree of glory to another" (2 Cor 3:18). In other words, that new life is a restoration of the inner glory that Adam and Eve lost and that allowed them to live in the image and likeness of God.

The Holy Spirit is the life-giver, the one who gives life. Life is a kind of activity. A corpse cannot move by itself, nor is there any internal activity like the flow of blood or the process of digestion. Without this kind of activity, the complex organism built to sustain life will slowly crumble to dust, the dust from which the human race came. The presence of the Holy Spirit produces the opposite of death. He does not normally make corpses alive, but when he comes to people he makes a kind of activity possible for them that was not possible before—a life that fulfills the purpose for which human beings were made.

The Holy Spirit gives that life to Christians from the inside, "the heart." He "dwells in" the followers of Christ (Rom 8:7). He "fills" them. The Holy Spirit does not just "come upon" Christians from time to time as he did with old covenant people. He comes upon them and then abides or remains in them (Jn 1:32-33). Although present in the Christian as in a temple (Eph 2:22), the Holy Spirit is not there primarily to be worshiped. Rather, he is present to act inside of Christians so they can live in ways impossible without him.

Whenever the Scriptures speak about the Holy Spirit, they are normally describing some way in which God is acting in the world. He is the power of God at work or, as some have said, the executive of the Trinity. Christians are said to live or act "by" the Spirit or "in" the Spirit. "In" probably refers to his enabling agency. If we are walking along and come to a deep river, the water is an obstacle to our walking further. We cannot walk through the river to the other side. But if we go into the water and swim, we can move by means of the water to the other side. When the Holy Spirit dwells in Christians, his presence in them operates in a similar way. Like water, he operates as a kind of spiritual "medium" in relationship to God and the things of God. He enables us to have "access... to the Father" (Eph 2:18). He gives us a spiritual contact with God and knowledge of God that allows us to relate to God and spiritual realities in a way we could not otherwise.

The indwelling of the Spirit does even more than allow

Christians to act in ways they might want to but cannot. He changes the very way they want to live. The Letter to the Ephesians uses a vivid image in encouraging Christians to avoid carousing with pagans: "Do not get drunk with wine, for that is debauchery; but be filled with the Spirit, addressing one another in psalms and hymns and spiritual songs, singing and making melody to the Lord with all your heart, always and for everything giving thanks in the name of our Lord Jesus Christ to God the Father" (Eph 5:18-20).

This exhortation contrasts being "filled with wine" and being "filled with the Spirit." When people are filled with wine, others who have not even seen them drinking can recognize their condition by their drunken behavior. The word "filled" does not mean that the wine has simply taken up all the room inside. Rather, it means that the wine has entered into them in such a way that it affects or controls their behavior. They could be described as "under the influence." "Filled" here, as in other places in the Scriptures, means "ruled" or "directed."

Christians are encouraged to instead be filled with the Spirit. When people are filled with the Spirit, others can tell by their behavior. Being filled with the Spirit especially produces worship and thankfulness to God, as noted in the Ephesians passage. The change the Spirit produces, however, is not just restricted to worship.

A fuller description of the new life produced by the Holy Spirit is contained in the passage on the "fruit of the Spirit" in Galatians 5:13-26. Fruit is produced by life inside. Spiritual fruit is "love, joy, peace, patience, kindness, goodness, faithfulness, gentleness, self-control, and the like." These qualities form a way of living and acting, especially a way of treating others. Those, therefore, who "live by the Spirit," those who have the Spirit in them giving life, should "walk by the Spirit." They should act in a way which expresses the life they have been given (Eph 5:16, 25). Just as we expect to see a difference between the behavior of dogs and human beings, we should be able to see the difference between those who have spiritual life and those who do not.

The passage about the fruit of the Spirit also raises a crucial and somewhat subtle point in understanding the results of the redeeming work of Christ. In the course of discussing the fruit of the Spirit, Paul says Christians are not "under the law" (Gal 5:18). Another passage says they are "discharged from the law" (Rom 7:6).

Many understand "law" or "the law" in such passages to be referring to the law of the old covenant. They therefore understand Paul to be talking about freedom from old covenant regulations, especially those involving matters of ritual and purity and the rabbinic interpretations of those regulations. Others understand "the law" to refer to all law, including the moral law, and understand Paul to be talking about freedom from condemnation under the law because of what Christ has done. Still others understand Paul to be talking about freedom from any obligation to any moral law, although such a position seems clearly untenable.

Without going into the issues connected to freedom from the law, we can see that the Galatians passage makes clear that Christians should not act or behave in a way that violates the moral commandments of God. "Fornication, impurity, licentiousness" and the rest of the "works of the flesh" or actions that come from sinful human nature disqualify people from the kingdom of heaven (Gal 5:19-21). Such actions are so opposed to the life of Christ as to be intrinsically incompatible with it. Christians have to be "dead to sin and alive to God in Christ Jesus" (Rom 6:11).

The Galatians passage also makes clear that Christians have to choose or decide at times not to do such things, even to fight against them. They will not be able to passively let the Spirit produce all manner of good behavior in them, while they coast along. Christians are called to "walk" a certain way and not gratify certain desires (Gal 5:16). To use a stronger phrase from Romans, they need to "put to death" those desires (Rom 8:13). Since they experience conflicting desires (Gal 5:17), Christians must take an active role in deciding which ones will prevail.

Nonetheless, the Christian life is not supposed to be primarily a new summons to greater moral effort. Nor is it a matter of keeping the law, however necessary it may be to keep God's commandments (1 Cor 7:19). Christianity is a new life that comes from the indwelling presence of the Spirit. Fallen human beings cannot live in a way pleasing to God (Rom 8:7). Redeemed human beings not only can, but find within them a new life moving them to live in a new way.

The Holy Spirit is "power from on high" that allows redeemed human beings to live in the image and likeness of God. It is not the power of an alien being that controls and possesses them, but rather a divine presence that gives them a new capacity to live well by healing or restoring their human nature. The Holy Spirit within does not act like a drug which produces an abnormal or unnatural effect. Rather, he acts more like food or drink or healing medicine that strengthens human nature—taking away the wounds of sin, restoring appetite for goodness and truth, and stimulating an appetite for and delight in goodness and righteousness.

The Passover of Christ, then, results in new spiritual life. That life comes from a special gift, a new presence of God inside those who believe in Christ. The Holy Spirit acts within Christians to restore what was originally created within them so that they can live in a way they could not while under the slavery of sin. Redemption in Christians, then, is the restoration of the life-giving presence of God in human beings.

IN CHRIST

Two Adams. The Holy Spirit brings us the blessing or gift that comes to us as a result of the redeeming work of Christ. The Scriptures often use the phrase "through Christ" to speak about how the priestly service of Christ makes that life possible. For instance, Paul says in Romans, "We have peace with God through our Lord Jesus Christ. Through him, we have access to this grace in which we stand" (Rom 5:1-2). "Through Christ" here probably refers to the priestly, mediatorial activity of Christ that makes redemption possible.

A different phrase, used mainly in Pauline writings, also indicates how the new life comes to us: "in Christ." At times this phrase seems to be used fairly broadly as the equivalent of "Christian" (for instance, 1 Thes 1:1). In other passages, like the following, it seems to have a special meaning:

> Blessed be the God and Father of our Lord Jesus Christ, who has blessed us in Christ with every spiritual blessing in the heavenly places, even as he chose us in him before the foundation of the world, that we should be holy and blameless before him. He destined us in love to be his sons through Jesus Christ, according to the purpose of his will, to the praise of his glorious grace which he freely bestowed on us in the Beloved. In him we have redemption through his blood, the forgiveness of our trespasses, according to the riches of his grace which he lavished upon us.... In him you also, who have heard the word of truth, the gospel of your salvation, and have believed in him, were sealed with the promised Holy Spirit.... Eph 1:3-8, 13

We see in this prayer that it is "in Christ" that we receive blessing from God. It is in Christ, the High Priest, that we can be "holy and blameless before him," able to come into God's presence as priests ourselves. It is in Christ, the beloved or only Son of God, that we can be sons of God by adoption. It is in Christ that we receive the Holy Spirit.

The phrase "in Christ" indicates a personal union between Christ and the Christian. The truth is expressed throughout the New Testament that redemption and salvation come to people as a result of entering into a personal relationship with Christ. Paul puts a special emphasis on that relationship and develops it in important ways, especially with respect to the original creation, and he uses the phrase "in Christ" to refer to this special orientation.

Behind Paul's use of this phrase is probably the understanding of Christ as the New Adam. Paul does not necessarily have Adam explicitly in view every time, but his understanding of the way redemption comes to us is certainly connected to the way we were once "in Adam" and now have come to be "in Christ." "As in Adam all die, so also in Christ shall all be made alive" (1 Cor 15:22).

Christians receive the benefits of the death and resurrection of Christ by coming into a "personal relationship" with him. That term could mean a great variety of things, some not very substantial. Two people who simply walk past one another every day and nod in recognition could be said to have a personal relationship. The word "union" is a more traditional word and for the Christian's personal relationship with Christ. It is a better word to use in English because it indicates that there is some kind of ongoing bond that keeps two people together in an active relationship. We speak about a "marital union" to refer to the bond of shared life between husband and wife.

Redemption comes to us through a personal union with Christ which is both similar and dissimilar to the relationship we have with Adam. To be "in Adam" is simply to belong to the human race in its ordinary state. In many ways, the difference between one human being and another, or one family and another, is more important for determining how our life goes. But in certain respects, it is our humanity that counts, and our redemption is one of them.

We belong to a race that is not in a good relationship with God. In all its cultural variants our race has a way of life that in many respects is sinful. Moreover, we are born into that sinful way of life, which is rooted in weaknesses and tendencies inside of each one of us. As sons and daughters of Adam and Eve, we belong to a race with certain common unfortunate characteristics and a common spiritual predicament.

Human beings, however, now have the possibility of a new life. They can come into a relationship with the New Adam, the head of a new human race. They can join a body of people which belongs to him. When they do, they share the way of life of that body, which is derived from the head and reflects his character. They will be identified with him and treated differently. They will be persecuted by his enemies simply because they belong to him, but they also will be treated by God with special recognition simply because they belong to him.

Their relationship with the New Adam, however, differs in some important respects from that of the old Adam. They had an inherited relationship with Adam that comes from being born into a race with a common nature and way of life. Their relationship with the New Adam is immediate and contemporaneous. All human beings can have a direct personal union with Christ—indeed, must have in order to be a Christian. Their relationship with this New Adam is also spiritual. It comes through the presence and action of the Holy Spirit joining them to God in Christ, maintaining that union and giving them a new life.

New Life in Christ. Union with Christ brings restoration of the ability to fulfill the purpose for which we are made. In Christ the fall is overcome and the human race is recreated. The change this makes was described in the section on the work of the Holy Spirit. The new life that comes to us by means of the Holy Spirit is identical with the new life that comes to us in Christ. When we speak about new life coming to us "by the Holy Spirit," we are concerned with the way that life is produced by the abiding presence of God in us.

When we speak about new life coming to us in Christ, we are concerned with how our reception of that life depends upon the incarnation. It depends, in other words, on the way God joined himself to human nature through the Son of God becoming human, and then united other human beings to himself by way of a relationship with his incarnate Son.

Our relationship with God was originally intended to be one of sonship, as we saw in the creation of Adam. Redemption is based upon a restoration of that relationship with God. By being joined to the Son of God and sharing in his relationship with his Father, human beings can become sons and daughters of God—not by nature but by adoption.

This change is in part a matter of healing a bad or problematic relationship due to sin. It is also, however, a matter of restoring "closeness." In Christ human beings are "brought near" to God. As a result of being brought "into" Christ, redeemed beings can share his own relationship with God and relate to God "in his name," that is, in his person (Jn 16:23-27). They are given a share in Christ's own closeness to his Father.

They become like the children of a king. Thousands of people have a relationship with a king, although most of them may never see him or exchange greetings. The king's children, however, have a close relationship with him. They can come and go as they wish, ask his help when in need, even at times charge their bills to his account.

Along with a change of relationship comes a change inside of us. The Scriptures describe this change in a number of ways. Paul often says that God makes the dead alive in Christ. "You who were dead in trespasses and the uncircumcision of your flesh, God made alive together with him" (Col 2:13). He speaks about redeemed human beings having a new "nature" or more literally, becoming "a new human being" (Eph 4:24; Col 3:10). Other passages talk about Christians being "born anew" (Jn 3:3) or receiving "regeneration" (Ti 3:5).

When people become Christians, they are not literally dead, like Lazarus, and raised to life. Nor do they enter back into their mothers' womb to be reborn, as Nicodemus suggested. Nor do they receive a new nature like an angel, no longer human at all. Rather, they have been transformed from human beings who are so sinful that they normally live in a way displeasing to God, into human beings who can actually live in a way pleasing to God. The change is substantial enough to say that they have become a different kind of human being.

A helpful translation is "new human being," which indicates both that we remain human when we are redeemed, but also that we become capable of living in a genuinely new way. The change is similar to what happens when a caterpillar turns into a butterfly. We describe that change as a "metamorphosis." This is an anglicized form of the Greek word usually translated "transfiguration" when used to describe what happened to Christ on Mount Tabor. In the transfiguration and in the resurrection, Christ was metamorphosed into a new kind of human being. When we are redeemed, we are changed in a similar but less complete way into a new kind of human being.

When a caterpillar becomes a butterfly, the change is so striking that it is quite difficult to believe it is the same creature. Nonetheless, the similarities of structure and function are even greater than the changes. The butterfly remains the same species as the caterpillar. The change is not primarily a matter of adding or subtracting parts. Rather, the caterpillar is restructured and reshaped according to a new principle. As a result it becomes able to function very differently. In scriptural terms, we could say the butterfly has been "made new" or "raised to newness of life."

Redeemed human beings have also been reshaped or reformed by a new principle of life. Joined to Christ, they now receive a life that comes from him. They "bear the image of the man of heaven" (1 Cor 15:49), who in turn bears the image and likeness of God in a full way. The redeemed have been given the Holy Spirit, so that the way they live is no longer ruled by the principle of death and sinfulness, but by the principle of the Spirit of life in Christ Jesus (Rom 8:2).

Unlike butterflies who can no longer live like caterpillars, redeemed human beings can return to their previous mode of existence or slip back into it in various ways. However, that does not negate the fact that they have been given a new life. They now have a choice, an internal power to behave differently.

When Christians receive this new life, Christ shares with them what he himself is. Paul goes so far as to say, "It is no longer I who live, but Christ who lives in me" (Gal 2:20). Paul does not mean this in the sense of spirit-possession. Christ does not take away our freedom so that we become like puppets. He does not even mean it in the sense of an air controller directing a pilot. Christ does not continually tell us what to do: walk over here, say thanks to the nice lady, sit down and take a rest.

Rather, Paul is saying that the "I" of the old nature, the "sinful flesh," no longer determines how my life goes. It is now the life Christ himself lives, his attitudes and character, that shape how I live and act. His power and the internal change that comes to us from him make this possible.

Christ is the source of our new life, but not in a simply external way, the way human parents are. Once we receive life from them, our bodies can function on their own. Paul said "Christ... is our life" and "your life is hid with Christ in God" (Col 3:4, 3). Christ himself is not only the source of new life, but we can only keep that life as we stay united with him. We are like a kidney that cannot function outside the body. Or to use a more scriptural example, we are like a branch that will only die once separated from the vine (Jn 15:1-11).

In considering the redemption, we have focused largely on what Christ did for or instead of us, he paid a price instead of us. He underwent a punishment that was accepted for us, so we did not have to undergo it. He offered the sacrifice of himself so we did not have to die. Christ humbled himself and by his humility deserved something we could not deserve. But he also died, came back to life, and now lives a new kind of life. He does not live that life instead of us. Christ lives that life so that he can share it with us and make it possible for us to live it. He does that by letting us be joined to him and so live the way he does—in him.

The change in Christ when he died and came back to life was an integral part of our redemption. His glorification allowed him to share with us a life freed from the "weakness" of human fallenness. He gives us a human life transformed by the indwelling presence of God. When Christ died and rose, the divine nature and glory was present in his humanity and enabled his humanity to come back to life and live in a new way.

In a similar way, when he unites himself to us, the presence of his divine life in us through the gift of the Spirit gives us the power to overcome the fallenness of human life. We can grow into a godlike character. We have a life that will be able to last to all eternity. That divine life enters into and changes our spirits now. Someday it will transform our bodies as well.

The Eastern church commonly uses the term "divinization" (*theosis*) to describe the way Christ shares his own life with us. Western writers have tended to avoid the term since it seems to imply the claim that we can actually become the same as God. In Eastern Christian teaching, however, the word simply expresses the truth of Second Peter that Christ became human to allow us "to escape from corruption" or mortality and "become partakers of the divine nature" (2 Pt 1:4). It is another way to speak of newness of life, life raised to a new level by the presence of God in us. We do not receive a fully divine life. We receive a human life transformed by the divine presence working in us—or as some translations put it, energizing us.

This new divinized life comes to us through union with the humanity of Christ. His humanity is like a conduit that passes on the life he lives. He does not pass on human life. That we have already. Rather, he passes on the divine presence and power in the form that has shaped his own human nature and can shape ours.

To use a modern analogy, Christ's humanity is like an electric socket. When an electrical cord is plugged in, it does not receive an influx of more metal from the socket. It does not become thicker or longer by receiving more of the same sort of substance it already has. Rather, the wire in the socket makes steady contact with the wire in the cord and passes on the electricity. The cord thereby becomes able to function in the same way as the socket.

Furthermore, the wire in the cord cannot receive electricity from just any socket. Plugged into the wrong source, it could be burned out or receive nothing at all. By being joined to the right wire, properly adapted, the cord receives electricity in just the right form that allows it to become itself electrified and to transmit electricity. To use scriptural terms, we could say that the wire in the socket passes on its own "nature." It does so by transmitting a principle or source of new functioning that can transform the wire in the cord.

Christ has life in the form that is needed for us to live in a new way. He passes on to us a new life that is suited and adapted to humans. To be "in Christ" is to be in the sort of personal union with him that allows that life to be communicated to us. By being united with Christ, we can pass from death to life and live the way God intended.

TWELVE

Receiving Redemption

T HE TIME IS THE EVENING OF EASTER, somewhere toward the end of the second century A.D. The place is the city of Rome. Christians are gathering together from all over the city to celebrate the true Passover, the resurrection of the Lord. In the capital of the ruler of the known world, they gather to honor the true ruler of the universe and the passing away of "this world," the fallen state of the human race.

While the Christian community keeps the vigil that marks the passage of Christ from death to life, new converts gather to be initiated. They have come to believe in Christ; they have been instructed in what it means to live as a Christian; they have turned away from serious sin. Now they are ready to be baptized and to take their places as full members of the Christian people.

These new Christians come from all sections and all strata of Roman society. There are hundreds of them, men and women alike, because Rome is a great city. Together, their presence is a testimony to the hunger of the human race for redemption and to the reality of the new life witnessed to by Christians of all kinds.

One by one the new converts are brought into the place of baptism. They are separated by sex. As they enter, they put off their clothes as a symbol of putting off their old ways of life. They turn to the West, the place from which they have come, and renounce Satan. They then turn around and face East, the direction from which they believe Christ will come the second time and also the direction of the assembled Christian community, keeping vigil in faith in Christ. The new converts then profess their own faith in the one God, his only Son, and his Holy Spirit.

They are then led into the baptismal pool. As they are covered with water, they are baptized in the name of the Father, the Son, and the Holy Spirit. The baptismal waters pass over them, signifying the flood of judgment that destroys the old, fallen human being and signifying the death they die with Christ to the old life and the birth to the new. As they emerge from the pool, they are anointed with oil, signifying their consecration through the gift of the Spirit. They are given white garments to wear, a symbol of the new life they will live.

As the sunrise begins, itself a symbol of the risen Christ, the new converts enter the assembly of the Christian people. There they celebrate together the Eucharist or Lord's Supper in honor of his resurrection. When the new Christians take part in communion for the first time, they are also given a cup of milk and honey, symbol of their entry into the promised land of the new life in Christ.

This description of the baptismal service of the early Christian community is drawn from the *Apostolic Tradition* of Hippolytus. The ceremony itself vividly represents the transition of the convert from the old life to the new life in Christ. Because the baptismal ceremony occurs while the Christian community is celebrating the passage of Christ from death to life, it witnesses to the way the death and resurrection of Christ makes possible the transition of the convert to new life.

To help us understand this transition, we will use the imaginary example of one of those Roman converts who takes part. His name is Gaius, a veteran of the Roman army. He was a man of some strength of character and personal capacity. Over the years, he has not been very scrupulous about whether the disorderly people he killed really deserved death, nor whether the taxes he demanded were strictly due.

As a Roman soldier, Gaius had regularly sacrificed to idols to ensure personal protection and success in military operations. He had regularly engaged in what Christians consider adultery while away from his wife. As a veteran who had been honorably discharged at the end of his term of service, he was an eminently respectable man according to Roman custom. According to the old covenant law, however, he should have been a candidate for execution himself.

Gaius came into contact with Christians when he settled down after leaving the army. They were a conspicuous group, friendly and helpful but living lives that were disciplined in a way his was not. At the invitation of one of these believers, Gaius attended sessions conducted by a Christian teacher. He learned about the truly wise way to live, about the only true God, and about the Son of God who came to bestow immortality. Gaius believed what was said and presented himself to become a Christian.

Considering an example like Gaius allows us to focus on how an individual is redeemed without raising many ecumenical issues. He is an adult pagan with a record of seriously sinful actions that need to be forgiven and a way of life from which he needs to be freed. He is not an infant, a young person raised in a good Christian family, or a nominal Christian without many signs of spiritual life. All such cases would raise some ecumenical divergences.

We are also going to consider Gaius at the point when he leaves paganism and is joined to Christ—not at the last judgment or at a point when he might fall into serious sin and be restored. Such cases would also raise some ecumenical divergences. Finally, we are not going to raise questions about the roles of conversion and baptism in the transition from paganism to Christianity, because these will also raise some differences. We will simply look at the transition itself.

In this final chapter, then, we will consider the way redemption comes to those who turn to Christ. We will then raise the question of how fully Christ reverses the fall for those who believe in him now and how much we have to wait for. We are saved in hope (Rom 8:24). This chapter will not so much describe a further benefit of Christ's redeeming work, but complete the picture by looking at how forgiveness and new life come to those who turn to Christ.

THE TRANSITION

There are several ways in which the New Testament describes the transition Gaius underwent in order to become a Christian. They can all be related to a judicial understanding, a ceremonial understanding, and a personal transformational understanding. We will begin with the aspect of his transition that is described in Scripture and much of Christian teaching with judicial terms.

Gaius was released from all the penalty due to sin. He had deserved or merited the sentence of condemnation by his own actions. He was also subject to the penal consequences due to the state of the human race, the way anyone shares in the consequences of the actions of the group to which they belong. To some extent, he personally deserved those as well, partly by his role in furthering the sinful condition of the race, partly in simply not deserving anything better. Those penal consequences included both the kind of death he would undergo at the end of his life as well as the spiritual death he was in as a pagan.

Gaius needed to be freed from the consequences of his sinful state. This required his redemption from his "debt of punishment," that is, the way in which those consequences were due to him. Scripture, as we have seen, most commonly describes that freeing as forgiveness of or release from sins. It also describes it as "justification," a word primarily used by Paul or those associated with him and picked up by later Christian teachers.

There is some debate over the meaning of the word "justification" as used in Scripture. Some hold that the word includes in its meaning the idea of being made just or righteous in the sense of being changed in character. Others hold that the word includes the idea of giving new life. However, most Christian teachers today would agree that the scriptural meaning of "justification," when used to describe the process of becoming a Christian, means restoration to a good or right relationship with God by the removal of offense, and most even see that as the primary meaning. Since "to justify" means to acquit those who have been charged with wrongdoing, the use of the word is probably based upon the idea of a judge acquitting a defendant.

Since Gaius was not innocent when he became a Christian, God, the judge, did not say that his previous life was acceptable nor that he did not deserve punishment. Rather, God simply said that he was freed from punishment and from the debt of punishment. This process was like acquitting a defendant rather than condemning him. Gaius was granted life rather than condemned to death. Gaius was justified by the supreme Judge.

We would be more likely to use the word "pardon" for what happened to Gaius. Paul probably used the word that means acquittal to emphasize the fact that Gaius was freed because of what Christ did. In his sufferings and death, Christ underwent a punishment that God accepted instead of what Gaius deserved. To use the technical theological term, Christ made satisfaction for Gaius so that no penalty was due to him anymore. Consequently, once justified, Gaius was in a good or right relationship with God, treated by God as a just or innocent man.

The second understanding of the transition Gaius underwent in becoming a Christian is ceremonial. While the judicial understanding focuses on the release from the obstacle in the way of Gaius' new life, the ceremonial understanding includes the way Gaius was positively established in that new life as well. In both old and new covenant teaching sin is understood to be a kind of uncleanness or impurity that defiles sinners. Unclean people or things are unfit to be in God's presence and cause offense to God when allowed to be in his presence. Therefore, someone like Gaius had to be cleansed to be put into a condition where he could come into God's presence, that is, enter into a relationship with God that involved any closeness or direct access.

At the same time, the positive side of what happened to Gaius is also described in ceremonial terms. When he became a Christian, he was not only cleansed but also consecrated or sanctified or made holy, to use three different translations of the same word. Christians are made holy the way a sacrifice is, the way a temple is, and the way a priest is.

As sacrifices, they have been given to God or made over to God for his honor or glory (Rom 15:16). As temples, they are places in which God dwells and in which he is glorified (1 Cor 6:19-20). As priests, they have access to come into God's presence and worship him (Eph 2:18). Therefore, Christians are holy. As a result, they belong to God and are filled with his presence. Moreover, they are like God and have a similar character or holiness of life (1 Pt 1:14-16).

The third understanding of the transition Gaius underwent is the personal transformational one. He went from death to life, and in the process he was made a new kind of human being. The focus here is on the result, the new life, not on the release from sin that is the necessary precondition. But the New Testament presents this transition as closely tied up with freedom from sin. Gaius was dead because of sin, since sin itself is destructive of life and since it cuts people off from the source of true life, God himself.

A number of passages concerning the death of Christ also concern the transition of human beings from death to life by becoming a Christian. They assert in one way or another that Christians have died in or with Christ and that "death" has produced a new life in them. "We were buried therefore with him by baptism into death so that... we too might walk in newness of life" (Rom 6:4). "You were buried with him in baptism, in which you were also raised with him.... You, who were dead in trespasses and the uncircumcision of your flesh, God made alive together with him" (Col 2:12-13). There are many similar passages, almost all in Pauline writings.[1]

These passages can only be understood in light of what it means to be in Christ. Gaius can be said to have died "with Christ" because he was joined to him and left behind his old life. He can be said to have risen "with Christ" because he received new life in him. In other words, Gaius left behind the old kind of human existence and became a new kind of human being. To describe this as dying and rising is to emphasize the radical nature of the change.

The change is so great, in fact, that Paul understands it as giving Christians a new identity, at least in the eyes of God. The old Gaius has ceased to exist. As a consequence, he no longer has to live according to obligations contracted in his previous life (Rom 7:1-6). As a new person in Christ, he is freed from the past.

Moreover, because Gaius is now in Christ he can share in the results of Christ's death, resurrection, and ascension. To say that when he became a Christian Gaius died, rose, and ascended with Christ does not mean that Gaius went back in time and joined Christ on the cross. Nor does it mean that Christ died a second time (or a millionth time) at the point of Gaius' conversion or baptism so Gaius could die with him.

Rather, it means that Gaius became identified with Christ when he became a Christian. Because of this personal union, Christ's past became his own past and the benefits of what Christ did became his own inheritance. To say Gaius died, rose, and ascended with Christ means that he is incorporated into the one who died, rose, and ascended. Now he can be treated as one to whom those events happened and properly share in what those events produced.

These three descriptions—condemnation to justification,

---

1. For further passages which speak of one dying and coming to life with Christ, see page 303.

uncleanness to holiness, and death to life—all describe the same transition from a state of death, uncleanness, and condemnation due to sin to a life of holiness in a reconciled relationship with God. Each is an analogous description. Together they describe what happens when someone becomes a Christian.

Christian teachers have a variety of views about how these descriptions go together. These differences cannot be stated adequately without introducing considerations that go beyond the scope of this book. All would agree, however, that the transition to fully becoming a Christian involves a change expressed by the three understandings. Together they speak about a transition that involves both release from the debt of punishment or penalty due to sin and an internal change which gives people the power to live without sin. The two aspects of release and change are spoken about in different terms and related to one another in different ways, but all Christian traditions recognize them.

All orthodox Christians recognize that Gaius was helpless to save himself. He was spiritually dead, in slavery without any means to purchase his freedom, under a just condemnation. He did not deserve new life, but could only look to the mercy or grace of God. Gaius needed a Redeemer.

Christ paid the price, underwent the punishment, and offered the sacrifice that allowed the debt to be taken away and new life to be given. He also in his own person underwent the process of self-lowering and exaltation that gave Gaius a new kind of life, freed from the power of fallenness. For those who would come to Christ and seek redemption from him, he could give it. He could join them to himself, releasing them from the penalty due to sin and sharing his own life with them by pouring out upon them the Holy Spirit.

Gaius needed the grace or mercy of Christ. He did not deserve the new life, but deserved the opposite. He could not earn the new life, but had to turn to Christ to receive it.

He did so because he understood from the gospel that Christ was offering it. At the same time, to receive the new life Gaius did not have to do anything other than turn to Christ. To turn to Christ, he had to turn in faith to Christ as his Lord and Redeemer. He had to repent of his sins and his old way of life. He had to be baptized, being joined to the Christ who died and rose and being joined to his body, the church.

To consider everything involved in turning to Christ would take us beyond the topic of this book. Here we can simply say that Christ is the Redeemer, that Gaius could turn to Christ and be joined to him to receive redemption, and that once he did, he became a new person.

ALREADY... NOT YET

Two Comings and Redemption. In the Letter to the Colossians, Paul gives us an image of the completion of the redemption: "You, who were once estranged and hostile in mind, doing evil deeds, he has now reconciled in his body of flesh by his death, in order to present you holy and unblemished [RSV: blameless] and irreproachable before him" (Col 1:21-22).

Paul is probably speaking about Christ as a Priest because his reconciling work is described in the previous verse as "making peace by the blood of his cross." Christ is standing "before" God, before the throne of his Father in the heavenly temple and presenting an offering to him. His redeeming work has been completed and he can now make of the restored human race an offering that truly honors God. The surrounding angelic beings raise the song and blow the trumpets that accompany such an offering, a song both to honor and thank God for what he has done and to proclaim the victory he has won.

Paul calls us "holy and unblemished," words commonly used to describe something consecrated to God. Christ could be presenting us as a body of priests, people who will now be able to be in God's presence and worship him (1 Pt 2:5; Rv 5:10; Eph 1:4). More likely, he is presenting us as a sacrifice, a gift to God, acceptable to the Lord (Rom 15:16; 12:1; Phil 2:17). He could be doing both.

But in what state are we being offered? Is Christ offering the Christian people who, joined to him, are living holy and unblemished lives before their earthly deaths? Or is he offering the Christian people after his Second Coming when he presents the kingdom to the Father, when all his enemies are defeated, and when sin and death are completely gone?

In this passage from Colossians Christ is here pictured as presenting the members of his body at the end. The next verse indicates that offering will only happen "provided that you continue in the faith, stable and steadfast, not shifting from the hope of the gospel which you heard." Earthly endurance is necessary for the Christian people to achieve complete victory and fully become God's possession. But if that is so, what have we received by becoming Christians? Are we even redeemed now or do we have to wait for a future time?

Four major events demarcate human history. The first two occur at the beginning: the creation of the human race in the state God wanted and their fall away from that state. The second two events occur at the end. Both could be described as the coming of the Redeemer to raise up the human race from where it has fallen. The Redeemer comes twice. Christ came the first time "at the end of the age to put away sin." Some day he will come again "to save those who are eagerly waiting for him" (Heb 9:26-28). Each of his comings is a redemption, a freeing from bondage. Each of his comings is a raising up of the human race and a giving of life.

It can be difficult to tell whether particular Scripture passages are referring to the results of the first coming or the Second Coming. They are purposely described in much the same words. Scripture scholars at times use the phrase "already... not yet" to describe the relationship between the two. There is only one redemption which is given to us through the two comings of Christ, so that we already have it to some extent, but do not yet have it in its full extent.

What Christians are given after the first coming is the same reality that they will have after the Second Coming: justification, union with God, holiness, victory, and freedom. The pardon or freedom from condemnation we receive now is the same one we will have at the last day. We will be found "in him" with a righteousness or justification that comes through faith in him (Phil 3:9). The new life we have now is the same life we will have at the last day. "When Christ who is our life appears, then you also will appear with him in glory" (Col 3:4). "We know that when he appears, we shall be like him" (1 Jn 3:2).

We do not have to wait until the last day for redemption to come. We experience the life of the age to come now. Even now the presence of the Spirit in our hearts is a down payment or first installment (Eph 1:14; 2 Cor 5:5) of what is to come. The Spirit himself bears witness to our spirit that we are children of God (Rom 8:16). As some Christian teachers have put it, we have an assurance through faith that we have already received the relationship with God that will be ours in the age to come.

Yet there is certainly a difference between what we are experiencing now and what we will experience after the Second Coming. Although for Christians the age of this fallen world has already passed away so that they now live in the age of the new creation, the old has not yet completely passed away and Christians are not completely free of it. To experience the full results of the redemption, they will have to persevere until a further deliverance comes.

Redemption Now: A full discussion of the Second Coming, the final judgment, and the restoration of all things is beyond the scope of this book. But in order to look at the reality of redemption in this fallen world, we need to consider what redemption will be when fully manifest. That look will reveal a certain modesty to the benefits we now enjoy, but also a success whose importance could be underestimated.

To begin with the success, those who have received the risen Christ after his first coming have already been given new life fully enough to achieve the purpose of human beings. The reversal of the defeat and ruin of the human race as a whole has already occurred. It is now possible for human beings to be freed from sin and live in friendship with God. Those who "continue in the faith...not shifting from the hope of the gospel" will some day make up the human race as God originally intended it to be. At the end the redeemed race will be everything God planned it to be in the beginning.

The passage in Colossians states that the human race will be "holy and unblemished," blameless with the holiness of an offering that is truly acceptable to God. That means that the race will be in a good relationship with God, living the way God intended it to live. Paul implies that this description can also be true now when he exhorts the Philippians to be "blameless and innocent, children of God without blemish in the midst of a crooked and perverse generation, among whom you shine as lights in the world, holding fast the word of life, so that in the day of Christ I may be proud that I did not run in vain or labor in vain" (Phil 2:15-16). The very fact that he needs to exhort them indicates that they need to endure in living a life pleasing and acceptable to God, but it also implies that it is possible to do so. Ephesians even uses the Colossians phrase "holy and unblemished," but probably applies it to our life now as priests to God (Eph 1:4; 5:27), indicating that such a state is possible here on earth.

Christians, then, can live a life that is pleasing to God as the result of the redemption. They can not only be freed from the guilt of sin, but also from the power of sin. That means at the least that it is possible for Christians to live free from the kind of serious wrongdoing that would lead to their being ineligible to inherit the kingdom of God (1 Cor 6:9-10;

Gal 5:21). It does not mean, however, that they can be free from all defects in the way they live, much less completely free from their fallenness or "flesh." It also does not mean that they will necessarily be heroic or even outstanding in virtue.

The claim that Christians can live a life pleasing to God is a somewhat modest claim. It simply means that they need not murder people nor deliberately cause serious injury, that they need not steal, rob, or defraud people of significant financial or material possessions, and so on. Although some fail, many do live in such a way.

Freedom from such serious sin may not be a high standard. The claim, however, that Christians do live such lives is a claim of immense importance. It means that in Christ the human race can live in a way that achieves the purpose for which it was created—imperfectly perhaps, but truly. It also means that the human race is on the road to bringing all of creation to where God wants it to be.

The Two Stages. Because of the very way Christian redemption happens, the results of Christ's redeeming work will never be other than imperfect or incomplete until his Second Coming. Paul describes the current state of the redeemed in Romans 8:

I consider that the sufferings of this present time are not worth comparing with the glory that is to be revealed to us. For the creation waits with eager longing for the revealing of the sons of God; for the creation was subjected to futility, not of its own will, but by the will of him who subjected it in hope; because the creation itself will be set free from its bondage to decay and obtain the glorious liberty of the children of God. We know that the whole creation has been groaning in travail together until now; and not only the creation, but we ourselves, who have the first fruits of the Spirit, groan inwardly as we wait for adoption as sons, the redemption of our bodies. For in this hope we were saved. **Rom 8:18-24**

This passage is notable for the way in which it connects the fate of all material creation with what happens to the human race. When the human race fully becomes what God wishes it to be, all of creation will be changed in a way that we would not expect. Death will be banished for every creature and nothing will exist that will not attain the purpose for which it was created. Such a world is beyond what we can fully imagine.

For our purposes, the passage is more notable for the way it describes the two stages in the life of Christians. They now have the first fruits of the Spirit; they will some day receive the full harvest. They now have the spirit of adoption who makes their spirits know that they are sons of God; they will some day "come of age" and be able to fully live as sons of God. They now, in other words, have to some extent what they will some day receive fully. The change will happen in an event Paul here describes as "the redemption of our bodies."

Paul seems to be contrasting here what will happen to our bodies with what has happened to our spirits (Rom 8:16, 23). Elsewhere he speaks about what will happen to "the outer man" in contrast with what has happened to "the inner man" (2 Cor 4:16). In brief, the writings of Paul teach that through the first redemption, something changed inside of us. This change has liberated us so that we can live in a new way, be in a good relationship with God, and not be under the domination of sin. Only in the future will we be changed in such a way that we will be able to enjoy the fullness of the life God intends. Redemption has rescued the human spirit, in Paul's terms, the ultimately controlling element in how we act, but it has not yet liberated "the body."

We therefore now live in a "body" that is still part of the fallen world and consequently is still to some extent determined by it. We are subject to physical decay, disease, and death. Fallenness also affects us in non-physical ways. We still live "in the flesh," the fallen nature. We still experience what Western Christian teachers have often termed "concupiscence," the desires that come from the fallen human state. These desires are not just disordered physical desires; they are also disordered "desires... of mind" (Eph 2:3). They do not need to prevail since we are no longer enslaved to them (Rom 6:12-14). But such desires will not be gone until the physical body dies and is glorified, and consequently they affect our ability to live the life of Christ as well as we may desire.

The fallen world around us also affects the way our lives go. While Satan has truly been defeated, he has not yet lost all hold on most of the human race nor on most human events. Those who have not yet been redeemed in Christ are still "following the course of this world, following the prince of the power of the air, the spirit that is now at work in the sons of disobedience" (Eph 2:2). Satan's action makes the fallen world a place where God's rule is not acknowledged. Consequently, much of what happens to us here and now is more like Christ's path to the cross than like his glorious resurrection triumph.

In the crucifixion and resurrection Christ has won the victory over Satan, but the effects of the victory likewise come in two phases. At his first coming, those who believe in Christ are "delivered... from the dominion of darkness and transferred... to the kingdom of [God's] beloved Son, in whom we have redemption, the forgiveness of sins" (Col 1:13-14). At the end of his Second Coming, Christ will "put all his enemies under his feet" (1 Cor 15:25), and the devil, along with death and hades, will be "thrown into the lake of fire" (Rv 20:10, 14).

In between, much the same is true of the external source of sin, Satan and "the world," as of the internal source of sin, the "flesh" or our fallen desires. We are free from them "in the inner man," but subject to them "in the outer man." Satan can hinder us (1 Thes 2:18) and keep us from achieving what God wants us to achieve. He can harass us (2 Cor 12:7), cause us to fall sick, persecute us, and even put us to death.

We confront Satan in our weakness just as Christ did on the cross, with bodies that have not yet been glorified (2 Cor 12:9-10; 13:4). We live in a time of spiritual warfare. Like Christ, we have to be prepared for suffering, defeat, and death. Those "enemies" come our way simply as the result of the weakness of our fallen natures, but are also inflicted on us by the evil one, especially as we seek to free others from his dominion.

Yet our inner man has genuinely been delivered. We are free from Satan and the world. He cannot destroy our good relationship with God or make us sin—unless we, like Adam and Eve, give in to temptation and choose to follow him. "Provided we continue in the faith, stable and steadfast," we are safe from him. Even more, we are not just helpless in the face of Satan's attacks, but we can deal with them by the power of God because we live with Christ (2 Cor 13:4). Christ has taken up residence in us in the midst of this fallen world. His death on the cross has already won a great victory, only not yet all of it.

The correct balance in our understanding of the "already" and the "not yet" is difficult to achieve. Some Christians are so centered on the "not yet" that they seem not to have gotten much past the cross. They experience no genuine freedom from sin, no operation of resurrection power in healing and miracles, and little victory other than endurance. Life is simply a vale of tears, a way of the cross.

Some Christians, on the other hand, are so centered on the "already" that they believe the full transformation can be realized now, that they cannot sin, the sons of God can already be manifested, all diseases can be healed, and all satanic attacks can be ordered away. Such views are less common but in various combinations have been held throughout the centuries.

The truth does not lie somewhere in between the already and the not yet as a kind of compromise. It lies in seeing that both are true at the same time. We are already/not yet redeemed. The victory of Christ is already/not yet accomplished. In other words, we have resurrection life but live it in fallen bodies in a fallen world.

Even though the victory is incomplete, the most important part of it has already been won. The results of the second phase of redemption will surpass the first in regard to what most preoccupies fallen man. What has not yet happened— full immortality, freedom from pain, suffering, disease, and frustration—seems to fallen human beings more momentous. But in regard to what most preoccupies God, the first phase of redemption is much more important—release from sin, new life in Christ, and a good relationship with God.

The realities of the redeemed life are important in themselves, but they also make possible the benefits that come with the second phase of redemption.

Only those who have been joined to the Redeemer in this life will experience the full deliverance he will bring in the age to come. We are warned not to "be conformed to this world" but to be "transformed by the renewal of our minds." As we are, we will begin to see reality with the wisdom of God and so know what is truly good (Rom 12:2).

THE CONSUMMATION

The last pages of the Scriptures contain a vision of the end of human history. It is the end not simply in the sense of a conclusion but in the sense of a completion. As a mature tree brings to completion the process begun with planting the seed, this final vision presents the completion of what was planted in this world by Christ's victory.

An end can be the cause of what comes earlier. What an architect envisions as the final building produces and unifies the process of construction. In such a way, the vision of the new Jerusalem, the completed human race, is the motive force of history, because God uses it as he brings human history to its completion.

John is brought to a "great, high mountain" (Rv 21:10) by one of the angels who brought the seven last plagues. Because this mountain is the successor to Sinai, to Zion, to Eden, it is probably the highest mountain on earth (Is 2:2), next to this mountain, Everest is insignificant. This is the mountain of God.

As John looks, he sees the New Jerusalem, the city of God coming down out of heaven. It is not built up by human means, no tower of Babel reaching up to heaven. The holy city comes from heaven to earth. The New Jerusalem is grace from God, a dwelling place not claimed and established by human beings but given to them by God.

A jewel beautiful in substance and shape, pure gold, a perfect cube like the holy of holies, this new city is a reflection of the glory of God. Because sin has passed away, weakness, corruption, and defectiveness no longer keep creation from being a transposition of God's glory into a new medium. In a way we can now only dimly perceive in the created world around us, the beauty and goodness and truth of the New Jerusalem will be a clear reflection of God's own beauty and goodness and truth.

The New Jerusalem will have no temple. The holy city itself will be a temple, filled with the presence of God, the Lord God Almighty and the Lamb. The presence of God will not be found in a special place or building, but will be mediated to the whole city by the Lamb. He will be the lamp, the translucent being from which streams the glory of God. Like a good lamp, the light he provides will be brilliant without being blinding.

The Lord God Almighty and the Lamb are enthroned in the city. They are one in their reign, under which human history can finally fulfill its purpose. God's will is done on earth as in heaven. From that throne, the symbol of that reign, comes life. Simply to be united to God, to be under his reign, is to receive life. The Holy Spirit, the water of life, flows into this new creation from the Father through the Son. The city of God is paradise restored, the place where life is a delight. By the river of the water of life grows the tree of life, bringing healing and restoration for those who have been wounded by sin.

In the New Jerusalem, it is no longer the human race that is banished, but the curse that is banished.

The flaming sword of God's wrath is gone and paradise is now opened. The human race has returned home. There human beings see God the Father face to face, whom to see is happiness itself. In his presence, filled with his life, in his image and likeness, they reign over material creation and make it a temple to the glory of God.

This final vision of human life brought to its completion is not essentially different than what God had in mind when he first created the human race. Yet the New Jerusalem will not be the simple unfolding of a well-tended, protected seed to its complete development. The holy city of God had to be reached by a redemption that cost the blood of the Son of God himself. It is the Lamb who has been slain from whose face the glory of God streams and from whose throne the water of life flows.

Early Christian pictures depict the cross of Christ as a tree with its branches filling the city of God. These pictures make explicit what is implicit in the vision of the New Jerusalem. The tree of life was replanted in the midst of the human race when Christ was lifted up on the cross. By his death he made new life possible. In his resurrection, the cross sprouted into the tree of life, and its branches filled the whole earth. At the end of time, those who have eaten the fruit of that tree will be the citizens of the New Jerusalem.

The Redemption in Scripture

This section contains lists of passages in which the Scripture teaches about the meaning of the sufferings, death, and resurrection of Christ as the means of our redemption. The passages are grouped by topic and are intended to be useful for a follow-up study to the reading of this book. They also provide a summary of the scriptural basis for the presentation of Christ in the book.

Christ died for us: 1 Cor 15:3; Rom 5:6,8; 14:9,15; 1 Cor 8:11; 2 Cor 5:14-15; Gal 2:20-21; 1 Thes 5:10; 1 Pt 3:18; **and similarly** 1 Pt 2:21; 4:1.

Christ gave himself (up) or was given (up) for us: Mt 20:28; Mk 10:45; 1 Tm 2:6; Gal 1:4; 2:20; Eph 5:2,25; Ti 2:14; Jn 3:16; Rom 4:25; 8:32; **and possibly** Lk 22:19; Jn 6:51; cf. Is 53:6,12.

Christ's death as redemptive in the sense of buying a slave: 1 Pt 1:18-19; 1 Cor 6:20; 7:23; 2 Pt 2:1; Rv 5:9; 14:3,4; Gal 4:5; Acts 20:28; **and Christ's death as redemptive, possibly in the sense of buying a slave, possibly more broadly:** Eph 1:7; Col 1:14; Ti 2:14; Mk 10:45; Mt 20:28; 1 Tm 2:6; Rom 3:24; Col 2:13-15; Ti 2:14; Heb 9:12,15. **Becoming a Christian as freedom from the slavery of sin:** Jn 8:31-36; Rom 6:16-23; 8:12-16.

Christ's death as a punishment undergone: 1 Pt 2:21-25; 3:18; Gal 3:13-14; Is 52:13-53:12; Acts 5:30; 10:39; Heb 9:28; **and probably** Heb 2:9-10; Mk 10:45; Mk 20:28; 1 Tm 2:6.

Christ suffered when he died: Mt 16:21; 17:12; Mk 8:31; 9:12; Lk 9:22; 22:15; Acts 1:3; 2 Cor 1:5; Phil 3:16; Heb 2:9-10; 13:12; 1 Pt

1:11; 4:1,3; 5:1; **also it was the Messiah who suffered:** Lk 17:25; 24:26,46; Acts 3:15; 17:3; 26:23, **also the one who suffered or died was innocent:** Acts 3:13-14; 1 Pt 3:18; 2 Cor 15:21.

Christ's death as a means to reconciliation with God: Rom 5:9-11; 2 Cor 5:18-21; Eph 2:16; Col 1:19,21.

The word "blood" to indicate sacrificial death: Mt 26:28; **and parallels:** 1 Cor 11:25; 10:16; Acts 20:28; Rom 3:25; 5:9; Eph 1:17; 2:13; Col 1:20; Heb 9:12-14,25; 10:19,29; 12:24; 13:12,26; 1 Pt 1:12,18; 1 Jn 1:7; Rv 1:5; 5:9; 7:14; 12:11.

Christ gave himself (up) for us or was given (up) for us, probably indicating Christ's death to be a sacrificial offering: see above.

Further passages which speak about Christ's death as a sacrifice:

—**as a Passover sacrifice:** 1 Cor 5:7-8; 11:24-26 (Mt 26:24-28; Mk 14:22-24; Lk 22:14-20); Jn 19:36; **and probably** 1 Pt 1:18-19; Jn 1:9; Rv 7:1-8.

—**as a covenant sealing sacrifice:** 1 Cor 11:25 (Mt 26:28; Mk 14:24; Lk 22:20); Heb 9:10-22; 10:29; 13:20; **and probably** 1 Cor 10:16-17; 12:24.

—**as a fulfillment of the sacrifice in the Day of Atonement:** Heb 9:1-10:25; 6:19-20; **and possibly** Rom 3:24-26.

—**as a sin offering:** Heb 1:3; 5:1; 7:27; 9:26; 10:12,18; 13:11-13; Is 53:10; **and probably** Rom 8:3; 2 Cor 5:21.

—**in general:** Eph 5:2; Rv 5:6.

Other uses of sacrificial or ceremonial terminology in connection with the death of Christ:

—**atonement:** Heb 2:17; 1 Jn 2:2; 4:10; Rom 3:25; **and possibly** Jn 1:29; Heb 10:4; 1 Jn 3:5.

—**purification or cleansing:** Eph 5:26; Ti 2:14; Heb 1:3; 9:14; 22-23; 1 Jn 1:7; **and indirectly** Acts 10:15; 11:9; 1 Jn 1:9; 2 Pt 1:9; Mt 8:1-4 (Mk 1:40-44; Lk 5:12-14); Lk 17:11-19; Mt 9:18-26 (Mk 5:21-43; Lk 8:40-56); Jn 2:1-11, 3:22-30; 13:1-20; 15:1-3.

—**sprinkling with blood:** 1 Pt 1:2; Heb 9:13-14,19; 10:22; 12:24; **and possibly** Jn 19:34; 1 Jn 5:6-8.

—**access:** Eph 2:18; 3:12; Rom 5:2.

—**priesthood:** Heb 1:3; 2:10-18; 4:14-5:10, 6:9-10:25, 12:24; 1 Tm 2:5; Rv 1:12-13; **and possibly** Jn 19:23-4.

—**intercession:** Rom 8:34; Heb 7:25; 9:24; 10:21; 1 Jn 2:1.

—**unblemished: as a sacrificial offering:** 1 Pt 2:19, 22; Heb 9:14; **as a Priest** Heb 7:26.

Christ's death as an act of love: Jn 3:16; Rom 5:8; 8:31-39; 1 Jn 4:9-10; Jn 10:11-18; 13:1-17; 15:13; 1 Jn 3:16; 2 Cor 5:14-15; Mk 10:45; Mt 20:28.

Christ's death as an act of obedience: Mt 26:39 (Mk 14:36; Lk 22:44); Jn 10:17-18; 14:31; Rom 5:18-19; Phil 2:8; Heb 5:8; 10:5-9; 1 Pt 2:18-25; **and more broadly** Mt 4:1-11 (Mk 1:12-13; Lk 4:1-13; Heb 2:18; 4:15); Jn 4:34; 5:30; 6:38; 8:29; 8:55; 15:10; 17:17-19.

Christ's death as a moral example to be imitated: Mt 10:38-39 (Lk 14:27); Lk 16:24-27 (Mk 8:34-36; Lk 9:23-27); Mt 20:20-28 (Mk 10:35-45; Lk 22:24-27); Jn 10:17-18; 12:24-26; 13:1-17; 15:12-13; 1 Cor 11:1; 2 Cor 8:8-9; Eph 5:2; Phil 2:1-11; Heb 2:10; 12:1-13; 1 Pt 2:18-23; 3:17-18; 4:1-2; 1 Jn 3:16.

Our sharing in Christ's sufferings as a way of following him: Rom 8:17; 2 Cor 1:5; 4:8-12; Phil 3:10-11; Col 1:24; 1 Pt 4:3.

Christ's death as a combat with or victory over Satan and his kingdom: Jn 12:31; 14:30-32; 16:8-11; Col 2:15; Heb 2:14-15; Lk 22:53; 22:3; Jn 13:2; **and possibly** Lk 11:21-22 (Mt 12:29; Mk 3:27); 1 Cor 2:8; Rv 12:4; **and indirectly, the subjection of the kingdom of Satan after Christ's death and resurrection:** 1 Cor 15:24-25; Phil 2:10; Col 3:20; 1 Jn 3:8; Rv 19:11-20:3; Rom 8:38.

Our dying with Christ: Rom 6:2-14; 2 Cor 5:14-15; Gal 2:20; 5:24; 6:14; Eph 2:1-10; Col 1:20; 2:9-15; 2:20-3:4, 2 Tm 2:11.

Background and Ecumenical Differences on the Redemption

FOR AN ORTHODOX CHRISTIAN TEACHER or theologian, any presentation of the redeeming work of Christ is based upon New Testament texts which in turn draw upon Old Testament texts. These in turn are read in the light of the earliest Christian teachers, the Fathers of the Church, and the great Christian theologians of subsequent centuries. They are also read in the light of modern scholarship and modern thought. Since this was intended to be a book without extensive footnotes and bibliography, I am adding the following notes for a brief orientation to the bodies of material that I have drawn upon.

MODERN SCHOLARSHIP

Until the 18th century, and afterwards in large parts of the Christian world, the traditional orthodox theology of the redeeming work of Christ in the Western Christian world was similar in all the church traditions, Catholic and Protestant alike. The objective need for the suffering and death of Christ for human salvation was consistently taught, usually in a way that has been described as "Anselmian." The central concern was the need for divine justice to be satisfied, and Christ's obedience and sacrifice was seen as making that possible. The Western or Latin theological understanding was the background from which modern scholarship on Scripture and Christian doctrine developed.

With Enlightenment thought and the development of liberal

theology, some of the support for the traditional theological positions was undermined, often in favor of a theology which interpreted New Testament texts about the redeeming work of Christ in a reductive manner. What once seemed to Christian theologians to refer primarily to an objective interaction between Christ and God the Father was reduced, sometimes without remainder, to a description of a subjective effect on the redeemed. This was coupled with an interpretation of the person and work of Christ that left little room for an intervention of divine action in human history. It was also often linked with an interpretation of traditional Christian doctrine and theology that saw it largely to be the result of Hellenistic influences on the primitive Christian message.

Biblical scholarship in this century has increasingly altered the situation. Much of the change has come through the cumulative scholarship in biblical vocabulary, thought-forms, and social history. This has resulted in a richer understanding of the scriptural texts, words, and images used to develop traditional teaching on the redeeming work of Christ and has given greater support to many traditional positions. While the influence of liberal thought has continued in discussions of the redeeming work of Christ, as shown by the influence of a scholar like Dodd in the English-speaking world and beyond, the tendency to project such views back upon the biblical writers has been considerably reduced.

The topic of the atonement has especially benefited from studies in the Jewish background of the New Testament. The period after World War II saw the rise of a new appreciation of the Jewish roots of traditional Christian teaching about the redeeming work of Christ. Names like Jeremias, Davies, and Daube mark a move towards a new understanding that has persisted, even though the topic of the sufferings and death of Christ has received much less attention in scholarly discussion. A similar trend among Catholic scholars would be marked by names like De Vaux, Benoit, and Lyonnet.

While this development has been useful in a variety of ways, it has been most useful for seeing how considerations of penal justice in regard to Christ's death are rooted in Judaic thought and were only translated into a somewhat different vocabulary and judicial approach by later Latin writers. It is therefore possible to see Medieval Latin theology of the redeeming work of Christ as a development of one aspect of the biblical teaching on the topic rather than to see it as an aberrant development of its own.

Perhaps the most significant change, however, in the way the redeeming work of Christ has been approached in the English-speaking scholarly world would be the gradual obsolescence of the discussion on rival "theories of the atonement." Much theological writing in the nineteenth and early twentieth centuries on the redeeming work moved in terms of discussions on various theories of the atonement or redemption: the ransom theory, the realist theory, the physical theory, etc. Gustav Aulen's book *Christus Victor* re-oriented the discussion through his use of a threefold typology of the objective or Anselmian, the subjective and the "classical" theories. Some contemporary theological writings still use his conceptual framework. His typology of theories of the atonement has the advantage of being based upon some broad historical differences: the orientation that prevailed in Latin theological teaching (the objective), the development of liberal theology after the Enlightenment (the subjective), and the patristic, especially the Greek patristic carried on in the Eastern Orthodox theological traditions.

Probably the chief reason for the increasing disuse of the conceptual framework of "theories of the atonement" is the recognition that most Christian teachers on the redeeming work of Christ, especially those in the patristic period, have employed all the theories at one point or another in one form or another. They have usually juxtaposed them without any awareness that they were moving from one theory to another. In this they followed the scriptural texts themselves. Since World War II the trend has been toward a recognition that the scriptural and traditional teaching on the redeeming work of Christ has been made up of a mosaic of what is perhaps most commonly called metaphors of images.

Helpful as this trend is, the words "metaphor" and "image" have an ambiguity built into them. They are used for figurative speech as distinguished from literal speech as well as for analogical speech as distinguished from univocal speech. Because of the ambiguity, those who employ the terminology of metaphor and imagery often see traditional teaching on the redeeming work of Christ as figurative and sometimes move toward a traditional liberal position without apparently noticing it. For this reason I have adopted the term "analogical description." In this as in other areas of theology, a commonly understood terminology of semantic description is one of the greater needs in contemporary theological discussion.

ECUMENICAL DIFFERENCES

This book has been written for those who hold or are interested in what C.S. Lewis has called "mere Christianity." The positions held here should be acceptable to those from Oriental Orthodox, Eastern Orthodox, Roman Catholic, Anglican, Lutheran, Reformed, Methodist, and "Radical Reformation" ("Anabaptist") theological positions, unless they hold a strongly liberal version of those positions. That does not mean, of course, that the redeeming work of Christ is presented in the way teachers from all those traditions would normally present it.

The topic of the redeeming work of Christ is relatively free of ecumenical doctrinal incompatibilities. An ecumenical doctrinal incompatibility exists between two doctrinal statements which are contrary to one another, which are meant in the same sense and asserted of the same objects in the same respect, and which are both held by some church to be integral to their beliefs. Some churches are more clear than others about what is included in their doctrinal positions, but at least for the older churches official doctrinal definitions and confessions serve as a guide for what they view as integral.

The topic of the redeeming work of Christ proper contains no clearly established doctrinal incompatibilities between orthodox Christian churches. The same is not true, of course, in the area of the application of the redeeming work of Christ to the individual. That topic brings us to the heart of the Reformation controversies. The area, then, of clear ecumenical incompatibilities is restricted to the last two chapters of this book, and since these are only presented to show the personal implications of the redeeming work of Christ, treatment of the ecumenical differences has been avoided.

The topic of the state of unredeemed human beings likewise contains what seem to be ecumenical doctrinal incompatibilities. These for the most part seem functionally dependent on doctrine about the application of the redeeming work of Christ, because

Christian teaching about the unredeemed state arises as a way of asserting the need for redemption. However, the impact of questioning about the salvation of non-Christians, even among fairly conservative Christians, has made the doctrinal status of earlier understandings of the unredeemed state somewhat unclear. The lack of attention given to them in ecumenical dialogues is perhaps another indication that traditional differences in this area are not currently viewed with any firmness as doctrinal incompatibilities.

There are, of course, other ecumenical differences in Christian teaching, and these can be more of a source of inaccessibility and alienation than strict doctrinal incompatibilities. Vocabulary, thought-forms, structure of presentation can all be quite different. Moreover, since different church bodies have different histories, their teachers will take into account different authoritative interpretations, different controversies, and a different set of positions to uphold and to guard against.

The topic of the redeeming work of Christ has such differences to a marked degree. Those differences are not so strongly marked between earlier Catholic and Protestant teaching in the area, because both stemmed from the tradition of Latin Medieval theology. They exist in a more marked degree between Conservative Evangelical and Eastern Orthodox theology. Stott and Stavropoulos in the attached bibliography, would exemplify what seem like different worlds of thought on the same subject. The entry of Eastern Orthodox theologians into dialogue with Western Christians since World War I and their increasing influence since World War II has modified considerably Roman Catholic teaching in this area, as well as some Protestant teaching, in an Orthodox direction.

Although the traditional Latin and the Eastern Orthodox approaches are often presented in terms of strong contrasts, they seem rather to be complementary. They simply concentrate on different aspects of the redeeming work of Christ. The two approaches can be synthesized and doing so leads to an overall stronger understanding.

Both the Greek and Latin Fathers, the sources of the respective approaches, provide models for a teaching on the redeeming work of Christ that includes both sets of the features that we might associate with the Latin or Eastern Orthodox theological approaches. I have found Aquinas surprisingly helpful in theological synthesis in this area. Heir to the Augustinian and Anselmian traditions of doctrinal teaching, he lived at a point in time when Western Christians first found Greek theological thinking accessible again, and he sought to include the teaching of the Greek Fathers in his synthesis. His approach to theological synthesis is particularly helpful for an area that requires relating various strands of teaching to reach an ordered whole, but that resists a simply deductive or rigorously systematic approach.

Modern ecumenical dialogues have been only tangentially helpful because they rarely deal with the redeeming work of Christ as a topic itself. Those on justification have been the most helpful, but since they often do not address the topic of sanctification, they do not provide comprehensive help for how Reformation theology approached the consequences of the redeeming work of Christ.

CONCLUSION

We live in an age when the perennial Christian gospel needs to be restated to a world marked by a new mentality. There is a great deal that is helpful in modern scholarship and theological writing. In fact, however, the most helpful teaching on any area of Christian truth is found in the Fathers and great "Doctors" of the Christian tradition who have desired to present the unchanging gospel to their own contemporaries.

Select Bibliography

THE TOPIC OF THE REDEEMING WORK of Christ could lead to extensive footnotes and bibliography. It has been discussed for almost two thousand years and even now articles and books are appearing with regularity. Not only have there been many theological approaches to Christ's redeeming work, there is also much modern scholarly material that deals with exegetical and historical questions related to the scriptural texts about the redemption as well as much material about the history of the doctrine of the redemption. While the redeeming work of Christ has not been a major focus of theological concern in the past twenty-five years, the accumulated writing about it is substantial and discussion about it is still current.

The following bibliographical note is designed to provide help for pursuing the topic further and to provide background to the approach adopted in this book. Due to limitations of space, it does not touch on all the main issues and currents, but only those most relevant to the treatment in this book.

The following are books which are currently accessible to an English-speaking audience. They are selected primarily for the way they give an overview to a body of material. They are also selected because they treat bodies of scholarly or theological material in ways which substantiate or give background to the main lines of the approach taken in this book. Many of the individual points or interpretations in this book diverge from those found in the books in this bibliography, but as a whole they provide a helpful background.

Ancient Israel by Roland de Vaux (New York: McGraw-Hill, 1961) provides a good summary of the Old Testament sacrificial system in the light of modern research. De Vaux's book *Studies in Old Testament Sacrifice* (Cardiff: University of Wales Press, 1964) contains helpful supplementary material, as well as his views on the propitiation-expiation discussion, but it is not easily accessible.

The Atonement by Martin Hengel (London: SCM, 1981) contains a summary of contemporary New Testament scholarship related to Jesus' death understood as atoning, as well as Hengel's own approach to many of the current issues. *The Atonement* supports the main lines of the historical interpretations given by this book to the New Testament texts. The chapter in *Paul and Rabbinic Judaism* by W.D. Davies (New York: Harper, 1948) on "The Old and the New Obedience: The Death of Jesus" gives a good discussion of the relationship between Pauline theology and rabbinic thought about the atonement that supplements what is presented by Hengel.

Greek Word and Hebrew Meanings by David Hill (Cambridge: Cambridge University Press, 1967) is the most helpful overview of the semantic questions connected to the scriptural statements about Christ's redeeming work and is somewhat under-utilized by writers on the subject. His approach to the modern propitiation-expiation discussions coincides for the most part with the one followed in this book.

The Resurrection by F.X. Durrwell (New York: Sheed and Ward, 1960) is a helpful presentation of biblical theology covering the relationships between the incarnation, the sufferings and death, and the resurrection-ascension of Christ. It treats the different "theologies" of redemption in the New Testament, and how they can be synthesized. It brings to the fore the questions connected to the humanity of Christ and its transformation in the process of redemption.

"Christ Made Sin (2 Cor 5:21)" by Leopold Sabourin in *Sin, Redemption, and Sacrifice* (Rome: Biblical Institute Press, 1970) is an abridgement in English of his longer French work *Redemption Sacrificielle*. It centers on the exegesis of Second Corinthians 5:21, but in doing so gives an overview of the history of the theology of the redemption. The English abridgement is joined with word studies of the terminology of redemption by Stanislas Lyonnet that supplement the material in Hill.

Man and Woman in Christ by Stephen B. Clark (Ann Arbor: Servant, 1981) gives in chapters one and two a fuller treatment of certain questions and issues connected with the Book of Genesis, although the discussion is oriented to a different topic.

In order to present the redemption, there are many individual points of scriptural exegesis, historical background, and theoretical issues to consider. There is also, however, the need to put together all of what is said, that is, to synthesize it in a way that creates a unified presentation. The following are some modern treatments of the redemption which provide examples of how particular theological traditions can be restated in the light of modern scholarship.

The Cross of Christ by John Stott (Downers Grove: Inter Varsity Press, 1986) is the most comprehensive and useful presentation of the contemporary Evangelical Reformed position.

"Christ, Priest and Redeemer" by Martin D'Arcy in *The Teaching of the Catholic Church,* edited by George Smith (New York: Mac-Millan, 1949) is the best summary presentation I have found of a modern Catholic approach that reflects the special emphases of the Catholic theological tradition.

Partakers of Divine Nature by Christoforos Stavropoulos (Minneapolis: Light and Life, 1976) is a popular presentation of Eastern Orthodox teaching on the redemption. It can be supplemented by "New Life in Christ: Salvation in Orthodox Theology" by John Meyendorff in *Theological Studies* 50 (1989), which gives an overview of the theological approaches of modern Orthodox theologians.

Another Book of Interest
from Servant Publications

Prophecy Past and Present

An Exploration of the Prophetic Ministry
in the Bible and the Church Today
by Clifford Hill

As the third millennium approaches and tensions increase in the Middle East and Eastern Europe, Christians and non-believers alike are asking what biblical prophecy has to say about modern events—and even the end of the world. What are Christians to make of this sudden spotlight on prophecy?

In *Prophecy Past and Present*, Dr. Clifford Hill provides an invaluable overview of prophecy using the Bible as his standard—from the days of the Old Testament prophets to the practice of prophecy in modern-day Pentecostalism and the charismatic renewal.

Prophecy Past and Present gives concerned Christians, especially pastors and other church leaders, the tools they need to evaluate prophecy against the yardstick of the Bible. *$9.99*